I0477196

Alois Riegl

Collected Essays

Alois Riegl
Collected Essays

Translated by

Karl T. Johns

Ariadne Press
Riverside, CA

Alois Riegl
Collected Essays

© 1929 Filser Verlag

Studies in Austrian Literature, Culture and Thought, Translation Series
Translated and edited by Karl T. Johns

© 2023 Ariadne Press
Riverside, CA

Publisher's Cataloging-in-Publication data

Names: Riegl, Alois, 1858-1905, author. | Johns, Karl T., translator.
Title: Alois Riegl : collected essays / translated by Karl T. Johns
Description: Original title: Gesammelte Aufsätze. | Includes bibliographical
references. | Riverside, CA: Ariadne Press, 2023.
Identifiers: LCCN: 2023920287 |
ISBN: 978-1-57241-226-2 (hardcover) | 978-1-57241-227-9 (paperback) |
978-1-57241-228-6 (ebook)
Subjects: LCSH Art--History. | Art criticism. | BISAC ART / History /
General
Classification: LCC N7445.4 .R5315 2023 | DDC 701--dc23

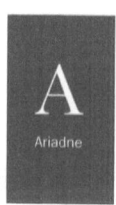

Dedicated to the memory of my father,
Donald C. Johns

CONTENTS

PREFACE BY THE EDITOR

The growing scholarly interest in Alois Riegl is due to recent new editions of his *Stilfragen, Die Entstehung der Barockkunst in Rom* and *Spätrömische Kunstindustrie*. The present and further volumes are intended to expand this new edition of Riegl's writings not previously available as separate books, to include the scattered essays, the study of the Dutch group portrait, unpublished manuscripts, his lectures about 17th-century Netherlandish painting and the book manuscript of *Historische Grammatik der bildenden Künste*.

The present volume realizes the unfulfilled plan originally devised by Max Dvořák and Johannes Wilde to collect the shorter writings by Riegl. They are an essential supplement to his main works that have until now been the exclusive source for understanding his ideas. Hans Sedlmayr has been the editor. He has also added an introduction on the theories of Riegl and a bibliography of Riegl's writings [expanded in the present edition]. Those first learning of Riegl from the present publication can best find further details about his personality, life and work in the obituary published by Max Dvořák, "Alois Riegl," *Mitteilungen der K K Zentral-Kommission für Erforschung und Erhaltung der Kunst- und historischen Denkmale*, ser. 3, vol. 4, no. 7-8, July-August 1905, [col. 255-276, reprinted in Dvořák, *Gesammelte Aufsätze zur Kunstgeschichte*, Munich: Piper, 1929, pp. 279-298].

Karl Maria Swoboda, Vienna, August 1928

INTRODUCTION

Republishing the writings of Riegl has a very different significance than providing a new edition of Winckelmann for instance. Although it might someday become the case, Riegl is not a classic from a past period of art-historical research to be presented to the scholarly public in a carefully mummified way. His work is actually the vehicle of ideas now affecting nearly all quarters of scholarship in art and beyond, and the conditions for their greatest influence are emerging only now. The content of Riegl's ideas, especially of problems as he posed them, is surprisingly topical. This is unexpected because they are hidden in a completely self-made terminology and weighed down by theories, such as a notion of perception, that have since been abandoned and were partially obsolete during Riegl's own lifetime. We would be doing no service to Riegl to leave this unmentioned. To judge his system of ideas (Ideengebäude) from the exterior is impossible, and its "interior" remains practically unknown. It is at once both simpler and more complicated than generally assumed. In this case, more complicated means more cavernous, voluminous and evocative; simpler, because it is less obscure and more clearly structured.

This clearly delineated the requirements for an introduction. It must prove the claim of an "internal" topicality of his ideas. It must show that to construct a didactic system of problems in an exclusively objective way, our current historical stage in art-scholarship would lead largely to the same conclusions as Riegl. It must show that Riegl's terminology can be abandoned without affecting the meaning of his thoughts, and also that the mistaken theories can be emended without disabling the edifice. To achieve all of this the introduction must lead into the interior of this theoretical "edifice" and grasp its structure and organization.

Such a task is clearly not to be accomplished in the space of twenty pages as circumstances force us to do it here. In spite of this, we must attempt to extract the quintessence of Riegl's teachings from his disparate writings. This is not a study of how his thoughts must be interpreted in order to reach a correct conclusion, but rather how Riegl intended them, even if they might be shown to have been wrong. In a separate essay in another place, we shall address the question arising at various points, of how the doctrines of Riegl relate to those of Heinrich Wölfflin.

The Quintessence of Riegl's Teachings[1]

There is a general consensus that the concept of "Kunstwollen" or "will to art" stands at the center of Riegl's thinking. How did this concept come about?

The point of departure for this was the verification of "styles" as it occurred during the 19th century (cf Gurlitt review GA p. 44). When arranged according to types and outward appearance, the manifold artworks fall of their own accord into various groups and

---

1 [SRKI refers to the pagination of Riegl, *Spätrömische Kunstindustrie* ed. 1927, GA to Riegl, *Gesammelte Aufsätze* ed. 1929.]

sub-groups of different sizes. These groups generally form fairly self-contained units in terms of chronology and geographical distribution. They array themselves around certain central examples embodying the "pure style." The style does not reveal itself with the same clarity in each work. We could also say: style is not a class, but rather an "idea" or an "ideal type." In each of these cases, "style" refers to something only to be grasped intuitively, something akin to the phenomenal colors in another field. Combinations of other concepts cannot explain what style is, but only provide an intuitive reference.

Strict rules exist for these sorts of indications, and history has experimented in this for our benefit. A given artistic "form," a "motif" such as the ornamental motif of the "spiral" or the architectonic form of the "basilica" is chosen, and the genetically subsequent forms then traced. This brings about genetic sequences where an identical genetic form, "motif," goes through metamorphoses of its artistic qualities, of its style.[2] A single "form" can play a part in more than one "style." It is also possible to observe correlations among the genetic sequences insofar as each of these occasionally experiences the same changes. In observing the stylistic peregrinations in the form of the "spiral" through a given

---

2 The discovery and pursuit of such genetic sequences and the construction of ideal models of such sequences is the basic subject of Riegl's first main work, *Stilfragen*, 1893 [*Questions of Style*, ed. 1992].) Classic illustrations for this method are plates 109-110, 167-167a and 192-192a in the 1893 [and 1992] publication. The establishment of such sequences yields an original new concept of "earlier" and later," completely unrelated to the parallel idea of chronology, but instead to the relative place within such sequences. Two forms might be chronologically later and genetically earlier or vice versa. Cf. Kurt Lewin, *Der Begriff der Genese in Physik, Biologie und Entwicklungsgeschichte*, Berlin: Springer, 1922, mutatis mutandis.

historical period, and then those of another ornamental "form" in the same way, changes can be directly observed which are identical in both cases. This situation is not limited to individual areas of art. Such correlations can be made between sequences within different fields. If we choose a relevant form, it can be shown intuitively (anschaulich) that the changes undergone by a given architectural form, let us say the "basilica," or a certain sculptural "motif," have been the same as those already observed in connection with the ornamental form. On the basis of a visual comprehension, the concept of style can be expanded in this way.

As it is grasped intuitively and then described by the collection of individual "stylistic characteristics," the conception of style is by nature shifting and uncertain. "The purely empirical representation of the styles according to their individual characteristics is not in the final analysis scholarly. It remains stuck in external descriptions." We can see that this can be overcome (in part three of our introduction below).

The phenomenon we observe is: "forms" change their "external character. Their style" changes (cf. GA p. 51; present ed., pp. 122-123). The simple question arises as to what is the force that causes them to change? What is it that actually changes when the "style" changes on the surface? The second question can be posed as follows: we are familiar with the dependent variable, the style of the artwork. What is the independent variable? These two questions are not quite equally important. For the moment we pose the second first.[3]

---

3 The first question leads to the problem of the origins of the "basic artistic forms or motifs" ("Urformen or "Urmotive") On this cf. Riegl, *Stilfragen*, passim.

This question has been answered in a variety of ways. One answer, or apparent answer to be more truthful, has been that of Gottfried Semper and his followers. Functions, materials and techniques change. These constitute the determining factors of style. Aside from this there is a secondary ideal factor, neglected since it is secondary, and therein lies the error. If we pursue the question as to what determines the three variables, and unless blind coincidence is the answer, we are left with the material culture as the independent variable – crass materialism! We need not take this to its logical conclusion. In this answer, "style" obviously means something completely different than in our question, and for this reason our question has only apparently been answered. If we trace a given functional form (Zweckform) such as the fibula through a variety of materials and techniques, that is to say study it in relevant historical cases, it becomes obvious. The qualities changing in these examples are very different than those we define as stylistic changes. Forms of varying materials and diverse techniques, made to perform all sorts of functions, can according to our concept of it be equivalent to style. And so, this answer is irrelevant to us. This proposal, and another that has since been abandoned, were thoroughly criticized by Riegl ("Works of Nature and Works of Art," pp. 54-60; present ed., 126-133).

Riegl himself gave the answer: the independent variable is "the direction of the artistic will (Kunstwollen)," the "goal of the artistic will," expressed succinctly if imprecisely "the artistic will." The functions, materials and techniques also undergo changes, but these are "negative" factors, "frictional coefficients" (Reibungskoeffizienten) necessarily "subtracted" in order to recognize the "direction of the artistic will," which presents the decisive positive element.[4] Furthermore, two of these are themselves derived from the "direction of the artistic will," and this contributes to the choice of material and technique.[5]

The concrete practice of scholarly research has led us to the concept and theory of the "artistic will." The concept was introduced to explain very concrete phenomena – surrounding the styles. The theory of "artistic will" constitutes a "new explanation of style."[6]

Its necessity can be seen in a far more general theoretical context: "All of the problems of art historical method arise from the question of arranging the art works, its primary material, according to the purpose of their origin, to the extent to which it has a specifically historical function. Viewed purely in its own terms, the work of art is a 'dead' product, deposited from a creative intellectual process. It presents but a single pole of an original unity of experience lacking its complementary pivot. It is precisely the other pole that would make all of the difference; for this is the origin of the art work, and if the history of art is to be objective or scholarly, it must explain the works of art in terms of their origin."[7] On the way to a metahistory of art, the "will to art" presents the last station that can still be passed within the limits of the positive study of art.

We should note outright that according to the conception

4 SRKI p. 9, GA p. 97 "Die Enstehung der altchristlichen Basilka"; present ed., pp. 175-176.
5 SRKI p. 83.
6 Anna L. Plehn, "Neue Stylerklärung," *Die Gegenwart: Zeitschrift für Literatur, Wissenschaftsleben und Kunst*, vol. 62, pp. 280-282 presents the earliest appreciation and interpretation of Riegl's theories and is still worth reading.
7 Ludwig Coellen, *Die Methode der Kunstgeschichte: Eine gechichtsphilosophische Untersuchung*, Darmstadt Traisa: Arkadenverlag, 1924.

of Riegl, the empirical history of art can no longer revert behind the "Kunstwollen" in the search for the "profounder reasons for the changes in style." For the history of art this is the absolute contingent, not possible to trace any further.[8] Beyond this, nothing other than metaphysical theories – meaning essentially hypothetical – might have an effect. Metaphysical conjectures beyond the purview of the art historian are all that are possible toward deciding what determines the aesthetic urge to reproduce the objects of nature in one or the other manner (*Works of Nature* p. 63; present ed., p. 137).[9]

II.

So far we have shown merely which phenomena are explained by the introduction of this concept. It might in fact turn out to be the case that the concept does not correspond to anything in reality, similar to the notion of "phlogiston" in earlier chemistry or "Seelenvermögen" to a certain period of psychology. There are those who consider the will to art, "Kunstwollen," to be one such word.

Is there an object to correspond to this concept? What is actually meant by the will to art, the "Kunstwollen"? A distinct body of secondary literature has arisen around this question.[10] If the so-called

---

8 On the concept of contingency which is also important for the humanities, Cf. Adolf Meyer, *Logik der Morphologie*, Berlin: Springer, 1926, pp. 156-169 and the further bibliographical references given there.

9 Of course this also applies to works of art with subjects other than natural objects.

10 Erwin Panofsky, "Die Theorie des Kunstwollens," *Zeitschrift für Ästhetik und allgemeine Kunstwissenschaft*, vol. 14, no. 4, 1920, pp. 321-339 ["The Concept of Artistic Volition," transl. Kenneth J. Northcott and Joel Snyder, *Critical Inquiry*, vol. 8, no. 1, Autumn 1981, pp. 17-33], Karl Mannheim,

"Vornahmeakt," the "entrance into a transaction" is considered as an action generated by the will, or more simply if "willing" is taken to be necessarily conscious, then it will never be possible to discover the subject denoted by Riegl.[11] Such an interpretation is already precluded by the fact that Riegl used the term "Kunstwollen" without distinction alongside such expressions as "aesthetic urge," desire, tendency or need. This has been overlooked by Erwin Panofsky when he distinguished desire and will in a way Riegl did not.

Panofsky began by listing a number of inadequate interpretations, chief among them being that of viewing the will to art, the "Kunstwollen" as a "synthesis of the artistic intentions of a period" which we make. As Panofsky has correctly noted, such a synthesis is an abstraction, and as a mere thought, an abstraction cannot be the cause for changes among things of the world, including ideal formations (Gebilde) such as works of art.

Panofsky has himself suggested a positive interpretation of the concept of "Kunstwollen" – he sees "Kunstwollen" as the immanent objective meaning of artistic phenomena. Yet his resolution is also not adequate. For one, the term "meaning" might even be more ambivalent than that of "Kunstwollen." Then also, it is simply impossible to replace

---

"Beiträge zur Theorie der Weltanschauungsinterpretation," *Jahrbuch für Kunstgeschichte*, vol. 1 (15) 1921-22, pp. 236-274, Edgar Wind, "Zur Systematik der künstlerischen Probleme," *Zeitschrift für Ästhetik und allgemeine Kunstwissenschaft*, vol. 18, no. 4, 1925, pp. 438-486 [English translation by Fiona Elliott, "On the Systematics of Artistic Problems," *Art in Translation*, vol. 1, no. 2, 2009, pp. 211-257, Italian "Per una sistematica dei problemi artistici," *Annali di critica d'arte*, vol. 4, 2008, pp. 7-71].

11 "Vornahmeakt" is a concept discussed by Kurt Lewin, *Vorsatz, Wille und Bedürfnis, Psychologische Forschung*, vol. 7, Berlin: Springer, 1926.

the term "Kunstwollen" as used by Riegl with that of "meaning," since we cannot speak of a "direction of meaning" or a "tendency of meaning" while a "direction of the artistic will" or "Kunstwollen" makes perfect sense. This would completely ignore the dynamic aspect inherent in the term. Ultimately, Panofsky falls into the same error as those who would see the artistic will as an abstraction. Something having an actual effect upon the artistic objects and changing them must naturally be something effective, concrete and real. As against Panofsky, this has been properly stressed by Wind when he stated: "In fact, Riegl saw the will to art as an actual force" [Wind "Systematik" 1925 p. 443].

In deciding what Riegl actually meant with the term "Kunstwollen," it is easier to reach conclusions by considering who actually are the possible vehicles of "Kunstwollen" – whatever it may be. Certain assumptions can be eliminated from the outset since the mass of artistic objects, when they are viewed in terms of their style, reveal a chronological and regional distribution, and that this distribution is precisely what requires explanation. Certain types that would be unlimited in time, psychic constitution or structure types cannot be vehicles of the artistic will. If style were a dependent variable of individual types of psychic constitution, then the art works of similar styles would necessarily be distributed differently than they actually are. In such a case, works of the same style would necessarily occur evenly throughout all periods and regions. The nations in a racial sense are equally impossible as the vehicle for the will to art. The distribution of styles and their borders do not correspond to those of the nationalities. It is also completely impossible to equate the

"Kunstwollen" with "the period" or "the spirit of the age." If we were to take these vague expressions literally, then all of the art produced in a given year or at the same time would necessarily exhibit the same style.[12] The protagonists of a given "Kunstwollen" always form a certain group of individuals varying greatly in size. This accounts for the necessary variability that explains the variety of styles coexisting in the same geographic area and the differing scope of their stylistic genres and subdivisions.

Such considerations are not even necessary any longer. Modern non-atomistic sociology has in the mean time established the doctrine of the "objective spirit," and along with this, the idea of "objective comprehensive will" which directly coincides with the concept introduced by Riegl.

"To a marvelous extent, the facts of human culture reveal the effects of a supra-individual spirit."[13] It manifests itself in a "will of a supra-individual sort, appearing to the individual as a normative force. This is referred to as an objective will, or specifically also an objective comprehensive will, referring to a force properly felt by the individual as an objective power." This would appear to be exactly what Riegl meant.

Just as the "objective spirit," so is the "supra-individual will" borne by a certain group of people. Although it is neither a "substance hovering mystically between individuals," nor something phenomenal,

---

12 The historical concept of style in Riegl, as alluded to above, can easily be distinguished from other uses of the term "style," and neutralize those highly dubious equivocations.

13 Albert Vierkandt, *Gesellschaftslehre: Hauptprobleme der philosophischen Soziologie*, Stuttgart: Enke, 1923, p. 343. On this, cf. also the entire paragraphs 38-40, especially 39/1, 5 and 6, as well as the 2nd edition of 1928.

something detectable in the conscious emotional lives of individuals such as individual "Vornahmehandlungen," the "entrance into transactions," it is a real factor like the "spirit" and an actual force.

III.

In spite of this, the attempt of Panofsky to uncover the question of "meaning" in the theories of Riegl contains a great element of truth. Nothing is achieved simply by introducing the concept of "Kunstwollen" in and of itself. Without overstepping, we can only say "the styles change because the will to art directs itself toward other styles." This is to observe that every change in style is anchored in a change of "spirit" among a group of people. We do not learn what actually constitutes such a change. This would add nothing in the manner. A number of admirers of Riegl have taken that route.

The positive significance of the new theory lies elsewhere, in the consolidation of the concept of style, in a more thorough comprehension of the phenomenon of "style." Riegl clearly considered the total outward appearance of the artwork to depend on the central structural principles according to which it was made. Works of art are configurations of meaning (Sinngebilde) and their parts are determined in their existence and particular meaning and placement by a structural principle of the whole.[14] "Style" is a dependent variable of the internal structural principles.

This accounts for the eminent importance of Riegl's theory and

---

14 Max Wertheimer, *Über Gestalttheorie I, Psychologiche Forschung* vol. 1, Erlangen: Verlag der philosophischen Akademie, 1921. It is here that the doctrines of Riegl sooner or later come into contact with "Gestalt Theory."

of his method: the manifold of stylistic qualities of an art work, which until then had only been registered descriptively, could now be derived from a limited number of central structural principles. Individual "stylistic characteristics" can be understood by one or more dominant structural principles, precisely those providing for this particular form. It can for instance be shown that the distribution of black, white and colors within a painting, or the grand "composition" and small details of a work of architecture, are determined by a single stylistic principle. A multiplicity of individual qualities could now be understood in terms of a few central characteristics.

Riegl himself distinguished "external stylistic character" (SRKI p. 267 note 1) from "stylistic principle" (SRKI p. 90) or more specifically also "compositional rule," and referred to the "new approach to art historical work which is able to penetrate behind the surface appearances" (*Spätrömisch oder orientalisch?* 1902 [ed. 1988, p. 186]). We now understand the term "rule." Of course this bears no relation to natural laws, but is precisely that structural principle which lends an "inner necessity" to the aspects and parts of the work of art (SRKI p. 22). This unprecedented and non-causal intrinsically meaningful concept of necessity, as opposed to historical necessity and causally determined, can only appear where the art works are recognized as configurations of meaning (Sinngebilde) in the above mentioned sense.

What is actually decisive for the new method is this step of deriving the individual stylistic characteristics from central structural principles. It is only in connection with this that the recourse to "Kunstwollen" (and ultimately also "Kulturwollen") becomes important. Changes of stylistic principles are in this way anchored in basic shifts in the intellectual structure of a group of people, in changes in the "ideals," reevaluations of the words, and with this the possible goals of the will in all of its applications.[15]

IV.

It would now be possible to pick out the structural principles as they determine the style of the historically given works of art. Previously, style had been nothing more than a quality discernible only during immediate autopsy, but now it became comprehensible in its individual characteristics, as the outward manifestation of a particular intrinsic organization of the artwork. This is the role of positive, comparative research in the meaningful configurations (Sinngebilde) of art.

Riegl took a decisive step further, and provided a basis for this doctrine of comparative structure in art with a theory of the essentially possible directions of the artistic will, a theoretical a priori discipline. This has been the most misunderstood aspect of his teachings and continues to be so today, although there are now similar attempts being made in other fields, and these should provide for a better understanding. (The difficulty is enhanced by the fact that this portion

---

15 In stressing, as has often been done, that the concept of "Kunstwollen" includes a rejection of the theory of "incapability" ("Nichtkönnen" – not that of "being obliged," or "Müssen," as Panofsky would have it), the implication s that every style harbors its own scale of good-bad, perfection-imperfection, beautiful-ugly. This is by the way often misunderstood to imply that Riegl's theory does not distinguish between levels of quality among individual works of art. It is true that it does not allow for differences of quality between individual "styles," that there are no "bad" styles and historically no periods of decline.

of Riegl's thought is encumbered by a theory of cognition, centered on individual perceptions recognized to be inadequate. This theory has no sustaining role in the system of Riegl's ideas.)

This attempt to assemble the essentially possible (wesensmögich) ultimate types of artistic will provides a direct parallel to that by Wilhelm Dilthey to determine the essentially possible types of philosophy. How is the list of these fundamental types made? There is a direct and an indirect way. The direct ascending mode proceeds from an insight into the "essential" qualities of the individual arts. The recognition that architecture creates "limited spaces" leads a priori, so to speak, to the possibility of accentuating either the "space" itself or its enclosure at the expense of the other (SRKI pp. 25-26). In realizing any of these essentially possible "goals of the artistic will" there are certain suitable means which then enter into the art work as its stylistic characteristics. A variety of formal possibilities also follow directly a priori from the nature of ornament as "pattern on a surface" (cf. SRKI p. 327). When these (four) basic possibilities of form in the various areas of the visual arts are seen together, certain correlations emerge among them. A given final basic type of architectonic form belongs to a certain ornamental type, and so forth. The results are ultimate types of "Kunstwollen."

The indirect descending mode makes use of a brilliantly discovered transition. To find the basic types of artistic form, we can use the types according to which the outside world is conceived. At one point Riegl wrote: "The decisive impulse to this change (in art) is apparent in the new mode of viewing nature."[16]

---

16 [Review of Julius Lessing] "Das Moderne in der Kunst" *Mittheilungen der*

This thought, which is based on a completely original and momentous insight into the relation of the "things" to the "phenomena" of the world, might be the most misunderstood of Riegl's ideas. How is our perception of the world outside related to the forms of art? Can this possibly be a hidden return to the "mechanistic" theories which Riegl had himself rejected?

Such an apprehension is understandable as long as perception is conceived as a mechanical and "blind" process. It is becoming increasingly clear that our perceptions are not completely determined by the stimuli (constellations of stimuli) from outside, but are affected by other internal factors. To mention only a single example, the same section of the outside world might be seen with an accent on the individual self contained things and the "intervening" space as empty, or the space might be seen as the primary fact transfusing and uniting all things (SRKI p. 231).[17] These led Riegl to say: "This double aspect of the objects of nature forms the basis for the development of the 'Kunstwollen'" (GA p. 60; present ed., pp. 133-134). There are other possibilities he did not mention.

As with the interior, the perception of the outside world also has latitude for historical change in terms of "ideals," "interests," "preferences" or "tendencies."[18] Since the historical changes among

---

Gesellschaft für vervielfältigende Kunst Beilage der "Graphischen Künste," 1899, no. 2, pp. 11-12.

17 It is possible to focus only n space to the extent that the objects are developed within it. This provides the basis for Riegl's distinction between corporeal space ("Körperraum") and open space ("Freiraum"). Cf SRKI ed. 1927, p. 262 and especially "Das holländische Gruppenporträt," ed. 1902, pp. 85-86 [ed. 1931 pp. 22-23, ed 1999, p. 82].

18 Regarding such preference, cf. E. Hollands, "Nature and Spirit," *Symposion:*

these "preferences" are interlinked with the entire intellectual structure of a group of people and its members, each of these ideal modes of perceiving the outside world is accompanied by a distinct type of artistic formal principle. The same preference for homogeneous open space, which in perceiving the outside world shifts the accent toward it from the "self enclosed objects" within it, leads to an emphasis of all factors in the artwork that would contribute to stressing "open space" rather than enclosed objects, and to suppress what might inhibit it. In the creative process of art, this would in Riegl's terms, lead to the will toward open space ("Wollen des Freiraumes").

Each of these intellectual "attitudes" is accompanied by preferred physical attitudes with the latter supplying the names for the former if it is so desired. For the conception of things as firm enclosed beings, the view from close range (nahsichtig) is preferable, this term suggests and to a degree supports that particular intellectual approach. This is the way we must understand Riegl's "categories" as they are well known and widely criticized. When he refers to the tendency to view at close quarters (nahsichtig) or from a distance (fernsichtig), he is always referring to those primarily intellectual attitudes. In principle, the same is true of the concepts "optic" and "haptic."

There are many other possible attitudes toward the outside world, including those we have mentioned as revolving around objects and space, and which can only be derived from an insight into the essence of perception.[19] It is possible to stress the more or less variable

---

Philosophische Zeitschrift für Forschung und Aussprache, vol. 1, no. 2, 1926, pp. 120 ff.
19 With Riegl these are usually polarities, conceptual pairs, but need not be bisections. On the tendency of that period to think in terms of antitheses,

qualities of objects (from the point of view of the subject): "subjective" or "objective" attitude.[20] It is possible to stress the lifeless or the vivid, the organic and living qualities, or equally well the inorganic and crystalline aspects and the organic-crystalline attitude. Each of these attitudes determines not merely how the outside world is viewed, but also which objects will be noticed or recorded "with preference." Each of these attitudes further determines a certain mode by which a world of art is given its form: here again both in terms of the how (style) and of the what (the choice of "motif").

However we might arrive at the possibilities for such formal qualities, there is one thing to be borne in mind: these possibilities are final and have been established not to empirically describe an individual trend of "Kunstwollen," but rather to discover the ultimate possible basic types within whose parameters all possible observable "Kunstwollen" moves.

The essential possibilities discovered in this manner also present the pure basic variants of all possible goals of the "Kunstwollen," and they relate to the verifiable forms of "Kunstwollen" much as the pure basic forms of crystallography for instance, where the empirical manifestations can be derived "a priori" from a knowledge of the structure of "crystal," although they can never completely attain the pure form.

---

see comments by Kurt Lewin, "Idee und Aufgabe der vergleichenden Wissenschaftslehre," *Symposion: Philosophische Zeitschrift für Forschung und Aussprache*, vol. 1, no. 1, 1925, pp. 61-93.

20 Cf. the important passage: Riegl, "Lovers of Art Ancient and Modern," ed. 1929 pp. 205-206, present ed., pp. 302-303 [2013 ed., pp. 8-9]. The preferred physical attitudes were "haptic" and "optic."

The common objection that these categories are far too crude to circumscribe the rich variety of particular empirical "Kunstwollen" (and with this the styles), arises from a simple misunderstanding of these categories. A completely different question is that as to whether we have discerned all possible basic forms of "Kunstwollen." This has certainly not been achieved. The other question, whether it is possible to arrive at a natural classification of the phenomena is also justified and must be answered in the negative.

V.

Many unprecedented insights emerge from completely new methods. If we are familiar with the sculpture of a given period for instance, we can extrapolate the accompanying style in painting or architecture from the formal principles, since they remain the same in all areas of art, and its goals correspond to given stylistic and technical means and materials. "I claim that a person who has properly observed a marble bust of Marcus Aurelius can imagine how contemporary" – or similar in their essence to be more precise – "painted portraits of the same subject must have appeared without ever having seen a single example of those encaustic portraits" (Riegl, *Spatrömisch oder orientalisch?* 1902 [ed. 1988, p. 186]).[21]

If the art of a given area is known, it is furthermore possible to reconstruct other aspects of the same culture, to then derive the essentially appurtenant religion, philosophy or sciences in their

---

21 Phenomena with similarities of essence in most cases appear contemporaneously, but not necessarily. Physical facts of history can cause suspensions or deferrals, a style of painting which relates to another in sculpture might have arisen later for instance. Cf. SRKI p. 369!

basic trends at least ("since the sciences, in spite of their apparent independence and objectivity, are ultimately also guided by the dominant trends" {"führende Neigungen"}). When we are familiar with these other areas of culture it becomes possible to understand the fact that they belong together and how this is the case. Earlier scholars could note that historically, the artistic trend to Impressionism occurred simultaneously with an interest in the art of earlier periods, but now it becomes possible to understand the "essential" relationship of these two phenomena.[22] By recognizing the "essence" of Impressionism in its fundamental "world view," a tendency to an amateur interest in art follows necessarily, independently of whether or not this trend was in fact realized in a given case or perhaps suppressed by other (concrete historical) factors in its expression. (Such an interest in art brings other specific phenomena of the material and social sphere along with it, such as an art market, forgeries or travel to study art.) Once we properly understand the nature of such an amateur interest in art, it will also reveal its necessary relation to Impressionism. "To demonstrate the relationship between the visual arts and the worldview would not be the calling of the art historian, but rather the actual future role of cultural historians. Yet the art historian cannot revoke their collaboration on this task, because their interest in its conclusion is too great to simply wait for others to accomplish it. All of the non-artistic cultural fields affect the history of art by providing the artwork with its content or subject matter (which never occurs without an external purpose). It is

---

22 Cf. Riegl, "Lovers of Art Ancient and Modern," as in note 20. Another example would be the phenomenon of the group portrait and the historical custom of "corporations". Cf. "Das holländische Gruppenporträt," 1902, pp. 72-74 [ed. 1932 p. 2-6, ed. 1999, pp. 62-65].

clear that the art historian will not be in a position to properly judge an individual work of art when they have recognized the identity of the will providing the impulse to a particular motif with the will that gave rise to unique choices of contour and color in the individual figure. In other words: the current trend to study the original place and date of individual art works, which along with iconography is being practiced so exclusively, will only become valuable to the history of art when it is recognized as congruent with the patent appearance of the artwork as form and color in surface and space – just as the determination of location and date of origin can only gain a true interest when we are able to recognize why this particular work could only have been created there and then."[23] It now becomes possible and challenges us to understand how the style of a work of art and its "motif" manifest an identical will.

In every regard, the "cult of individual facts and figures" is replaced by a consideration penetrating the core of things and discovering significant correlations along the way. In the transparent light of these theories, the opaque and leaden world of cultural history and particularly of art historical facts becomes translucent, and their inner structure (ihr innerer Bau) apparent.

---

23 Riegl, "Works of Nature and Works of Art," GA pp. 63-64; present ed., p. 137; SRKI ed. 1927, p. 229; present ed., pp. 132-134. Also the categorical call – particularly relevant today – for a careful distinction between iconography (in the sense intended by Riegl) and "Kunstwissenschaft," SRKI p. 394 note 2. Another application of the same thought can be seen in the essay about the Vaphio Cups, pp. 71-90, present ed., pp. 145-168, cf. also the passage dealing with ornament and symbol, *Stilfragen* p. 31 [ed. 1992, p. 39].

VI.

When we said "in every regard" we were anticipating something remaining to be seen. If this theory allows us to comprehend
which forms of art and world view, and which forms of art and science,
religion, law etc. belong together stylistically, and that a given sort of
coloration goes with a certain type of form or "composition" – then
there is still one thing we do not yet understand. This is the historical
sequence in the "directions of the Kunstwollen." Was it necessary for
the directions of "Kunstwollen" (the styles) to develop in the sequence
as they historically in fact did? Can a unified direction, an intrinsic
tendency or an internally meaningful necessity be distinguished from
the course of history?[24] Or did the direction of history result more
from a blind coincidence of components?

Such questions as these finally lead into those problems which
are art historical in the true sense – questions surrounding actual
events, yet they also lead beyond the traditional empirical practice
of the history of art. For this is limited to the actual development of
history, ascertaining the sequence of styles and can at best determine
a certain order or disposition among the actual facts. It is able to
distinguish whether in a certain area (such as the Mediterranean
for instance) during a given period (from the Egyptian-Babylonian
through the Greek, Roman, "medieval" and into the "modern" period)
the art called for viewing at a distance (fernsichtig) or in proximity
(nahsichtig). This very summary order of things and their internal
order can always be further corrected and refined, always on the basis
of empirical observations of the historical material. Riegl made various

---

24 This again leads to a connection with Gestalt Theory.

attempts at this, with the *Spätrömische Kunstindustrie* being the most refined.[25]

None of these assessments can be of service in leading us to an understanding of the verifiable order of this actual development. Is it necessary for a "haptic" style to yield to an "optic" style, or could the reverse process also take place? If a certain original situation is given, such as a "haptic" conception of art for instance, does this necessarily harbor a momentum of its own leading in one certain direction rather than another?

These are questions no longer limited to simple empirical verification, but address the doctrine of the essential and necessary movements of "Kunstwollen" as well as the "objective spirit," questions of the historical momentum of art, a theoretical discipline of history.[26]

Riegl believed that such developments did indeed occur by the nature of things in history. He spoke of the "intrinsic fate" ("inneres Schicksal"), by contrast to the external impulses which prompt the development of art of a given time in a certain direction. He recognized the "natural and inevitable expression (naturnotwendig) of a great and

---

25 Aside from this, Riegl also discovered other more self-enclosed developments (or "Entwicklungen"). He regarded the development of prehistoric art in southern France in this way. This "is apparently an isolated development, isolated from later Mediterranean art" (*Stilfragen* p. 18 [ed. 1992, p. 27]). He considered the development of American native art and that of the Polynesians to present similarly isolated developments. The early art of India and China would seem to belong with these before its exposure to Mediterranean Hellenism. I do not find references to this, but it would seem to follow from other passages in his work.

26 "Historical kinematics" would be more precise. This would leave the term "historical dynamics" free to apply to the "theory of the historical forces" – in accord with its literal meaning.

inexorable fate that had been immutably set for Greek art from its very beginnings" in the "lifeless" art of the later Roman Empire (SRKI p. 130). He also attempted to demonstrate that an optic conception of art must necessarily be preceded by a period governed by the haptic conception (*Stilfragen* p. 11 [ed. 1992, p. 22]). When he wrote in another spot that "every religious symbol is predestined to devolve into a merely decorative motif in the course of time if it contains the artistic appeal," this was exactly along the same lines – to discover the necessary directions of "Kunstwollen" (*Stilfragen* p. 43 [ed. 1992, p. 50]). There is nothing mystical about this predestination, but it is simply a tendency discernible with a knowledge of the nature of religious symbols and the structure of social and intellectual contexts where religious symbols are used. This alone can allow us to understand sentences such as: "Simply by observing the art of the early imperial period, it would be possible to construct a priori the character of the Constantinian-Theodosian period." (SRKI p. 126).[27]

Riegl never overlooked that individual phenomena exist which are not congruent with this theory of the development of history, and in this constructed and continual process do not occur in the spot

---

27 Other examples of such an internal momentum in art are: the optical conception being blunted by the disproportion resulting from the optical and diminishing the sense of proportion: the optical conception contains a tendency toward disharmonic proportions (SRKI pp. 126, 129) – the "emancipation" of open space and with it of spatial color creates a differentiation in coloration. – a less clear example: "A group portrait could not have been painted before an individual portrait existed" (Group Portrait, ed. 1902, p. 75, [ed. 1931, p. 7, ed. 1999, p. 67]). It makes no difference if these observations are factually correct (the latter is certainly not). The renunciation of mere empiricism and the progress to what some would today call "examination of essence" ("Wesensschau") can be seen even where it is untenable.

where their characteristics should place them. The cups from Vaphio, or the choir of the Franciscan church in Salzburg are examples of this, anticipating the "Kunstwollen" of far later dates (GA pp. 57 and 118; present ed., pp. 129-130 and 201-202). From an early moment onward, Riegl was preoccupied with the question of "anticipations" or "anachronisms" in the history of art, and produced a theory beside that which we have been outlining (GA, pp. 87-89; present ed., pp. 164-166, and "Zur spätrömischen Porträtskulptur" *Strena Helbigiana*, 1900, p. 255). Two "primeval" types of artistic will are inborn with humanity. One is "sculptural" and objective while the other is "optical" and subjective. In the Mediterranean cultures, the former was embodied in the culture from the "east" (Orientalen) and the later by the "Indo-Germanic" (Greek) cultures. At a later date, the Italic cultures assumed the position of the Greeks, and the "orientalized" Greeks that of the Near Eastern cultures. In the occidental development of art, the Romance nations expressed the "sculptural" and the Germanic nations the "optic" principle of art. "Each of these would become tedious and petrified on its own, but in a reciprocal interpenetration, often antagonistic, they have led to a development which has been fruitful into our own time" (GA, p. 59; present ed., pp. 131-132). Such reciprocal interpenetration often depends on real historical factors – movements of populations bearing given artistic properties like the "entrance of the Italic nations into the development"). This means that an element of coincidence enters into history which lends itself well to explaining the "anticipations," but negates the inner necessity of the development as it had apparently been demonstrated. While it had earlier seemed that an art based on "haptic" principles must yield to another of more "optic" character of its own accord, out of an opposition, internal tension and momentum of its own, we now read: "Greek art had developed not as a continuation of earlier Near Eastern examples but in an opposition to these which it exhibited from the very beginning" (GA p. 87; present ed., p. 164).[28] The "opposition," the driving factor is turned from the inside out (GA pp. 79-81; present ed. pp. 154-157).

Although this second conception clearly predominated in Riegl's later years, the former model still had its effect. The latent conflict of these two theories might have brought forth a third. However, there was not time for this.

VII.

As we have been rushing through along its main axis, the edifice of Riegl's ideas is far more voluminous than appears at a cursory glance. Aside from the brilliant publications in empirical comparative "Kunstwissenschaft" and history of art, culminating in a new theory of style and the history of style, it also includes at least the beginnings of the new, for his time, theoretical discipline of a typology of "Kunstwollen" and historical kinematics of art. To this were added a refined sociology of art and the beginnings of a philosophy of aesthetics. It is by far the grandest projection of a system of "Kunstwissenschaften" in existence.[29]

---

28 To the artist, such an internal opposition appeared as a "problem," cf. Wind loc. cit.

29 This sociology made its earliest appearance in "Volkskunst, Hausfleiß und Kunstindustrie" 1894, on which subject cf. SRKI p. 314. The most important relevant passages for his aesthetics are: "Stimmung als Inhalt" 1899 p. 31, SRKI p. 90, *Works of Nature*, 1901 passim. "Eine objektive Ästhetik" 1902

Finally there is the invisible foundation in the form of a theory of the visual arts and of the genres of art: fragments of a "general theory of art" ("allgemeine Kunstwissenschaft"). Riegl distinguished an "elevated art" from one that is merely decorative ("Mood as the Subject" GA p. 31; present ed., p. 100). He further distinguished four fields in the visual arts, aside from painting, architecture, sculpture, and "the decorative arts" as a fourth of equal value – which must seem paradoxical from the materialist point of view. The term "applied arts" ("Kunstgewerbe") is today too often considered to exist in opposition to "higher art," and best replaced by "ornamentation" ("Ornamentik") as Coellen uses the terms.[30] Riegl did not give a strict theory about the "essence" and the relationship of these four arts to one another, but he did provide a sort of hierarchy (SRKI p. 19, cf. also *Stilfragen* p. 3 [ed. 1992, pp. 14-15]). This is again based on an "essential analysis" ("Wesensbestimmung") of art as consisting of "its appearance as form and color on surfaces and in space," as the "actual artistic factor in the art work" (SRKI pp. 6, 229, 64 h.l.). It involves a circumscription of the "level" where the "artistic element" is to be found, and the recognition that works of art also include non-artistic levels, which become artistic only by being melded with the artistic layers. This is another of the precarious and misconstrued opinions of Riegl.

At this point we should add a reference to the "brilliant weaknesses" of Riegl's system (des Riegl'schen Gebäudes) because their

---

[transl. Karl Johns, *Journal of Art Historiography*, no. 11, December 2014, 6 pp.], *Der moderne Denkmalkultus*, 1903, passim; pp. 232-288 of the present volume.

30 Ludwig Coellen, *Der Stil in der bildenden Kunst: Allgemeine Stiltheorie und geschichtliche Studien dazu*, Traisa Darmstadt: Arkadenverlag, 1921, p. 177.

recognition will become the basis of its further construction. We are unable to do so presently, but this is not the result of a misunderstood piety, but simply due to lack of space.

* * *

Many of Riegl's basic views are by now widely held. Not a little of this is due to Oswald Spengler, who has popularized and vulgarized certain thoughts, only some in direct dependence, as Riegl proposed them approximately twenty years earlier. For this reason it is simple to overlook how much in the way of false conditions needed to be overcome in arriving at this position:

1. The idea that art was an epiphenomenon and not an autonomous, underivable expressive mode of the human spirit.

2. The view that only the individual is primal and real, and that groups constitute no more than a sum or embodiment of individuals, so that the intellectual aspects of the collective are merely abstract and not real.

3. Particularly the view that human nature and human reason are unified and immutable. For this is why it is completely mistaken to relate the work of Riegl with that of Kant. According to Kant, reason presents an unchanging constant – applied to the arts, this would imply a view which had become obsolete long before Riegl. According to Riegl, changes provide a transformation for the intellect or spirit, a modification in its constitution itself. Revisions in the direction of the "Kunstwollen," as art historians since Riegl have accepted them are a very different thing from the focus of a consistent "Kunstwollen" onto

various "purposes."[31] The ideas of Riegl relate to all of those organically congruent with Kantianism like fire to water. This is apparent from the failure of the excellent attempts at interpretations by Erwin Panofsky and Karl Mannheim. Any attempts to harmonize Riegl's views with the teachings of Heinrich Rickert-Wilhelm Windelband on the nature of history are particularly hopeless and alien to the spirit of Riegl's doctrines.

4. The view that the artist either embodies or "stylizes" a constant nature. This radically eliminates the opposition of art as either similar or distorting of nature (naturalism and idealism, the two roots of style according to Wölfflin).[32] This is a view at which Riegl only arrived relatively late (cf. "Die Pflanze in der Kunst," 1898, "Works of Nature," GA p. 61, present ed., pp. 132-133, and SRKI p. 394 note 2).

5. The thesis that the entire development of history is nothing more than a result of random individual forces, a net of individual causal threads. This is the historical variant of the erroneous view of the structure of society refuted above as number 2. It is replaced by the idea that truly complete historical wholes of action and meaningful autonomous movements of the spirit or intellect exist, that they are delayed, inhibited, sped up, distorted or broken by the practical occurrences and configurations of actual history (Realgeschichte), but

---

31 I here paraphrase sentences from Max Scheler, *Die Wissensformen und die Gesellschaft" Probleme einer Soziologie des Wissens*, Leipzig: Neuer Geist, 1926.

32 Panofsky op. cit., and especially the fine observations of Coellen, *Die Methode der Kunstgeschichte*, Traisa Darmstadt: Arkadenverlag, 1924, pp. 20-24.

which cannot be evoked or affected by it.[33]

The reversion from these views did not occur widely until relatively recently, since approximately 1918. The bold construction of Riegl, which originally hovered on just a few delicate, but as we now see firm supports, has since received substantial sustenance from the other sciences.[34] This caused him to lose the imaginary character which enshrouded him in the 1880's and 1890's – and Riegl became "natural."

This meant abandoning the fear of theory and the resulting "cult of individual facts and figures" as it had been so deeply rooted since about the mid-19th century. When Riegl began, the situation was similar to that described in 1819 by Goethe in relation to a different subject: "The slightest whiff of theory created a fear, since for more than a century they had fled away as if from a ghost, and then they finally embraced the most common of ideas on the basis of even the slightest experience." Since Hegel and Wilhelm von Humboldt, Riegl has been the first to emerge with the conviction that theory remains the highest ideal of scholarship in the historical sciences as well. After an interlude of untheoretical art history disoriented by the "philosophy of life" ("Lebensphilosophie"), this attitude is only now becoming widespread and fulfilling the first condition for an extensive influence of Riegl's teachings.

This new situation has led to the present edition of his most important essays.[35] Each one of these includes virtually the entire

---

33 cf. also Max Scheler op. cit.

34 It is to demonstrate this that we have been making our frequent references to publications from outside of the history of art.

35 This idea and the plan for these publications originated with Johannes Wilde in Vienna. The editors owe him a debt of gratitude in many ways.

complex of Riegl's thoughts.

This edition has been organized to reflect the development of Riegl's ideas. Almost all of them are already present from a very early date. In 1890, in the report on ornamentation from New Zealand [English transl. Karl Johns, *Journal of Art Historiography*, no. 12, June 2015, 7 pp.], the quintessence of the *Stilfragen* (Questions of Style 1893) and all of the later Riegl is present in a nutshell. Aside from a few minor ideas, and we can do more than allude to this, only the color of the more general theoretical and "ideological" substratum which embedded his ideas ever changed since that time. In the earliest period lasting until 1897, a sharp change both biographically (appointment as full professor at the university) and objectively, his basic approach was more or less that of the "historical school."[36] In the period from 1898-1900/1901, while he worked on his main work, *Spätrömische Kunstindustrie*, it was colored by "naturalism."[37] The main work of this second period is the grand, unpublished *Formengrammatik der bildenden Künste* (Grammar of Form in the Visual Arts 1898 [*Historische Grammatik der bildenden Künste*, 1966, *Historical Grammar of the Visual Arts*, 2004].

36 The most important dates in his biography: born 1858, first studied law, then philosophy and universal history, changes to the history of art and enrolled at the Institut für österreichische Geschichtsforschung. Worked as "Volontär" at the Österreichisches Museum für Kunst und Industrie in 1886. From 1887 to 1897 he was director of the department for textile arts, following Franz Wickhoff in this position. Since 1889, he was "Privatdozent" at the university of Vienna, "Extraordinarius" since 1895 and "Ordinarius" since 1897. He died 1905. Cf. the bibliography and obituary by Max Dvořák [cited in the preface above and bibliography below].
37 We use this term approximately in the sense used by Erich Rothacker, *Logik und Systematik der Geisteswissenschaften*, Munich: Oldenbourg, 1926.

In his final years since 1901, a new basic approach slowly emerged which might summarily be called "objective idealism."[38] This places Riegl in the historical progression of Goethe, Hegel – Humboldt, (Comte), Dilthey. Yet this "objective idealism" is still strongly colored by naturalism. Characteristically, he uses terms such as "natural law" or "cause" until the very end, when he is actually referring to "structural principles" and parts and wholes. For this reason, his ideas are often difficult to understand. Riegl proudly considered himself a "positivist" and, like Dilthey, rejected metaphysics.

These terms with their exaggerated connotation of classification and lack of clarity can only serve as indications for objective differences apparent in comparing essays such as "The History of Art and Universal History" ("Kunstgeschichte und Universalgeschichte" 1898) with "A New History of Art" ("Eine neue Kunstgeschichte" 1902) or "Mood as the Subject of Modern Art" ("Die Stimmung als Inhalt der modernen Kunst" 1899) with "The Modern Cult of Monuments" ("Der moderne Denkmalkultus" 1902), each of them treating similar questions.

Today the shorter publications from his earliest years only have historical interest and were therefore not included in the present collection. This refers to three essays from the second period 1898-1900, and nine from the years 1901-1904. During these years the theoretical level remained constant, and for this reason a strictly chronological order was neither possible nor meaningful. We have therefore arranged these closely knit studies according to their subjects.

Hans Sedlmayr Vienna, July 1927

---

38 For this term, cf. Rothacker op. cit.

BIBLIOGRAPHY

MIöG: *Mitteilungen des Instituts für österreichische Geschichtsforschung.*

MöM: *Mittheilungen des K. K. Österreichischen Museums für Kunst und Industrie Monatschrift für Kunstgewerbe.*

"Paul Müller, Das Riesenthor des St. Stephansdomes zu Wien, seine Beschreibung und Geschichte," *Zeitschrift für die österreichischen Gymnasien*, vol. 34, 1883, pp. 690–694.

"Alphons Nestlehner, Das Seitenstettener Evangeliarum des XII. Jahrhunderts," *Zeitschrift für die österreichischen Gymnasien*, vol. 34, 1883, pp. 849–852.

"Neue Erwerbungen für die Textilsammlung des Österreichischen Museums im Jahre 1885," *MöM*, 20th year, no. 243, December, 1885, pp. 546–550.

"Alfons Müllner, Die Krypta in St. Florian Ein Beitrag zur Baugeschichte der Stiftskirche St. Florian, Linz, 1883," *MIöG*, vol. 6, 1885, pp. 318–319.

"Josef Dernjač, Zur Geschichte von Schönbrunn," *MIöG*, vol. 6, 1885, pp. 661–663.

"Die Apokalypse in den Bilderhandschriften des Mittelalters. Eine kunstgeschichtliche Untersuchung von Th. Frimmel. Wien 1885, C. Gerold's Sohn. 8°," *MöM*, new ser., 1st year, no. 1 (244), January 1886, pp. 13–14.

"Le Meuble. Par A de Champeaux. Paris, Quantin. 2 Bde, 8°. 320 und 318 S.," *MöM*, new ser., 1st year, no. 1 (244), January 1886, p. 16.

"Histoire de la tapisserie depuis le moyen-âge jusqu'à nos jours. Par J. Guiffrey. Tours, Alfred Mame et fils, 1886. 8°. 533 S.," *MöM*, new ser., 1st year, no. 2 (245) February 1886, p. 39.

"Geschichte der Renaissance in Frankreich von Wilhelm Lübke. Zweite verbesserte und vermehrte Auflage. Mit 163 Illustrationen in Holzschnitt, Stuttgart, Ebner & Seubert (Paul Neff), 1885. 8°. 448 S.," *MöM*, new ser., 1st year, no. 3 (246) March 1886, p. 62.

"Zur Kenntnis und Würdigung der mittelalterlichen Altäre Deutschlands.

Ein Beitrag zur Geschichte der vaterländischen Kunst von E. F. A. Münzenberger, Stadtpfarrer. Frankfurt a. M., Fösser's Nachfolger, 1885. Fol.," *MöM*, new ser., 1st year, no. 3 (246) March 1886, pp. 63–64.

"Zur Geschichte des Möbels im 18. Jahrhundert. 1. Ein Schreibkästchen von Pierre Denizot," *MöM*, new ser., 1st year, no. 4 (247) April 1886, pp. 75–78.

"Kunstgeschichte des Mittelalters von Franz von Reber. Erste Hälfte. Leipzig, T. O. Weigel, 1885, Zweite Hälfte ibid. 1886, 8°. 652 S.," *MöM*, new ser., 1st year, no. 4 (247) April 1886, p. 83.

"Zur Geschichte des Möbels im 18. Jahrhundert (Schluss.)," *MöM*, new ser., 1st year, no. 5 (248) May 1886, pp. 98–100.

"Die Ausstellung weiblicher Handarbeiten im Österreichischen Museum (März, April, Mai 1886)," *MöM*, new ser., 1st year, no. 6 (249), June, 1886, pp. 115–119.

"Die Ausstellung weiblicher Handarbeiten im Österreichischen Museum (März, April, Mai 1886.)....(Schluss.)," *MöM*, new ser., 1st year, no. 7 (250), July, 1886, pp. 135–140.

"Needlework as art by Lady K. Alford. London, Sampson Low, Marston, Searle and Rivington, 1886. 8°. 422 S.)," *MöM*, new ser., 1st year, no. 8 (251) August 1886, pp. 163–164.

"Fifteenth century ornament chiefly taken from brocades and stuffs found in pictures in the National Gallery. London, by Sydney Vacher, architect, published by Bernard Quaritch. London, 1886, Fol. 30 Taf.," *MöM*, new ser., 1st year, no. 9 (252) September 1886, p. 185.

"Frühmittelalterliche Gewebe im Österreichischen Museum," *MöM*, new ser., 1st year, no. 11 (254), November 1886, pp. 213–218.

"Éléments d'archéologie chrétienne par le chanoine Reusens, 2me édition. Tome Ier, p. 576, grav. 608. Tome IIme, p. 622, grav, 578. Aix–la–Chapelle, R. Barth, 1884–1886, 8°.," *MöM*, new ser., 1st year, no. 11 (254) November 1886, pp. 229–230.

"Sammlung moderner Holzsculpturen aus der Preisbewerbung, veranstaltet im Juni 1886 vom Mitteldeutschen Kunstgewerbevereine in Frankfurt a M. Lichtdruck von Kühl & Co. Frankfurt a M., H. Keller. 25 Taf. 1 S. Text. Fol.," *MöM*, new ser., 2nd year, no. 13 (256) January 1887, p. 271.

"Ueber den decorativen Stil in der altchristlichen Kunst. Von Friedrich Portheim, Stuttgart, W. Spemann, 1886. 8°, 43 S.," *MöM*, new ser., 2nd year, no. 14 (257), February, 1887, pp. 288–289.

"Die Textilindustrie im nordöstlichen Böhmen, betrachtet von der Seite der kunstgewerblichen Production. Bericht über eine Studienreise im Juli 1886, erstattet von Dr. Alois Riegl.," *MöM*, new ser., 2nd year, no. 15 (258) March 1887, pp. 303–306.

"Die Textilindustrie im nordöstlichen Böhmen, betrachtet von der Seite der kunstgewerblichen Production. (Schluss.)," *MöM*, new ser., 2nd year, no. 16 (259) April 1887, pp. 325–327.

"Archäologische Beschreibung der Münster- oder Krönungskirche in Aachen, nebst einem Versuche über die Lage des Palastes Karl's d. Gr daselbst, von F. Nolten. Neuer, durch biographische und sachliche Zusätze vermehrter Abdruck, besorgt von Johannes Chorus. Aachen, Anton Creutzer, 1886. 8°. 80 S, 1 Taf.," *MöM*, new ser., 2nd year, no. 16 (259) April 1887, p. 331.

"Histoire du point d'Alençon, depuis son origine jusqu'à nos jours par Mme G. Despierres. Paris, Renouard, 1886. 8°. 276 S., 8 Tafeln, 7 Vignetten.," *MöM*, new ser., 2nd year, no. 19 (262) July 1887, pp. 392–393.

"Ein angiovinisches Gebetbuch in der Wiener Hofbibliothek," *MIöG*, vol. 8, 1887, pp. 431–454.

"Josef Neuwirth, Geschichte der Miniaturmalerei in Österreich," *MIöG*, vol. 8, 1887, pp. 662–663.

"Die Textilausstellung in Rom, 1887," *MöM*, new ser, 2nd year, no. 20 (263) August 1887, pp. 397–400.

"Bibliothèque internationale de l'art. "Histoire de l'art byzantine,", considerée principalement dans les miniatures par N. Kondakoff. Edition française originale, publiée par l'auteur sur la traduction de M. Trawinski, et precédé d'une preface de M. S. Springer. Tome premier. Librairie de l'Art. Paris, J. Rouam. Londres, Gilbert Wood et Comp., 1886. 4°. 202 p., 29 grav.," *MöM*, new ser., 2nd year, no. 21 (264) September 1887, pp. 433–434.

"Guide for drawing the acanthus, and every description of ornamental foliage, by J. Page. London, Bernard Quaritch, re–printed 1886. 8°. 245 S., über 200 Holzschnitte, 53 Radierungen.," *MöM*, new ser., 2nd year, no. 22 (265) October 1887, pp. 451–452.

"Wandgemälde und Maler des Brixener Kreuzganges. Eine Skizze von Hans Semper. Mit 15 Lichtdruckbildern. Innsbruck. Wagner, 1887. 8°. 89 S.," *MöM*, new ser., 2nd year, no. 22 (265) October 1887, pp. 452–453.

"Zur Geschichte des Möbels im 18. Jahrhundert 2. David Roentgen," *MöM*, new ser., 2nd Year, no. 23 (266) November 1887, pp. 467–470.

"Die Möbel. Ein Musterbuch stilvoller Möbel aus allen Landern in historischer Folge aufgenommen und herausgegeben von A. Lambert und E. Stahl. Stuttgart. J. Hoffmann. Fol. 1.–4. Liefg. A M 2–.," *MöM*, new ser., 2nd year, no. 23 (266) November 1887, p. 482.

"Zur Geschichte des Möbels im 18. Jahrhundert 2. David Roentgen (Schluss.)," *MöM*, new ser. 2nd year, no. 24 (267) December 1887, pp. 494–497.

"La tapisserie de la chaste Suzanne, notice historique et critique par Jules Guiffrey, avec une introduction par Paul Marmottan. Paris, 1887. 4°. 45 S.," *MöM*, new ser., 2nd year, no. 24 (267) December 1887, pp. 498–499.

"Die Holzkalender des Mittelalters und der Renaissance," *MIöG*, vol. 9, 1888, pp. 82–103.

"Die Holzschnitzerei und damit zusammenhängende Arbeiten. Handbuch für Bildschnitzer und Galanterieschreiner von J. Stockbauer. Mit 30 Abbild. Leipzig, Quandt & Handel, 1887. 8°. 136 S. M. 3.60.," *MöM*, new ser., 3rd year, no. 25 (268) January 1888, pp. 18–19.

"Donatello's Leben und Werke. Eine Festschrift zum 500jährigen Jubiläum seiner Geburt in Florenz. Von Hans Semper. Mit 8 Tafeln in Lichtdruck. Innsbruck, Wagner, 1887. 8°. 135 S. fl.,"

MöM, new ser., 3rd year, no. 26 (269) February 1888, p. 38.

"Mémoire sur anciens sacramentaires par M. Leopold Delisle. (Extrait des mémoires de l'académie des inscriptions et belles lettres, t. XXXII, 1er partie.) Paris, imprimerie nationale. 4°. 423 S., Atlas 11 Taf.," *MöM*, new ser., 3rd year, no. 26 (269) February 1888, p. 38.

"Josef Strzygowski, Cimabue und Rom Funde und Forschungen zur Kunstgeschichte und zur Topographie der Stadt Rom, Wien 1888," *Kunstchronik: Wochenschrift für Kunst und Kunstgewerbe*, vol. 23, no. 20, February 23, 1888, col. 317–318.

"Das arabische Papier, von J. Karabacek. — Die Faijûmer und Uschmûneiner Papiere, von J. Wiesner. [Mittheilungen aus der Sammlung der Papyrus Erzherzog Rainer, II u III. Bd. S. 87 ff. Wien, k k Hof- u. Stastsdruckerei, 1887. 4°.," *MöM*, new ser., 3rd year, no. 27 (270) March 1888, p. 59.]

"Der Beil und seine typischen Formen in vorhistorischer Zeit. Ein Beitrag zur Geschichte des Beiles von W. Osborne. Mit 19 Taf in Lithogr. Dresden 1887, Warnatz & Lehmann. 4°. 67 S. M. 10.," *MöM*, new ser., 3rd year, no. 27 (270) March 1888, p. 60.

"F. Engel-Dollfus, sein Leben und Wirken, dargestellt von X. Mossmann.

In deutscher Sprache herausgegeben vom niederöstrr. Gewerbeverein, übersetzt von Dr. E. Auspitzer. Wien, Hölder, 1888. 8°. 247 S. M. 3.20.," *MöM*, new ser., 3rd year, no. 29 (272) May 1888, pp. 115–116.

"Entwürfe zu praktisch verwendbaren Objecten der Holzbrandtechnik nebst einer Anleitung über die polychrome Ausführung derselben. Herausgegeben mit Unterstützung des k k Ministeriums für Cultus und Unterricht von J. Tapper. Wien, 1888, R v. Waldheim. Fol. 40 Taf und Vorwort fl. 20.," *MöM*, new ser., 3rd year, no. 30 (273) June 1888, p. 139.

"Broderie et dentelles, par E. Lefébure. (Bibliothèque de l'enseignement des beaux-arts.) Paris, Quantin, 1888. 8°. 320 S. M. 4.50.," *MöM*, new ser., 3rd year, no. 32 (275) August 1888, pp. 179–180.

"Vorbilder-Hefte aus dem kön. Kunstgewerbe-Museum. Herausgegeben von J. Lessing. Heft 1-4. Rahemen. Text von J. Lessing. Berlin, E. Wasmuth. 1888. 4 Hefte in Fol mit je 12 bis 13 Lichtdrucktafeln. M. 40.-.," *MöM*, new ser., 3rd year, no. 33 (276) September 1888, pp. 195–196.

"Textile Hausindustrie im Bregenzer Wald," *MöM*, new ser., 3rd year, no. 34 (277) October 1888, pp. 213–217.

"Stoffmuster des 16. bis 18. Jahrhunderts, herausg von Emil Kumsch. Serie I: Fünfzig Tafeln in photographischem Drucke, mit einem Vorworte von Hofrath Prof. C. Graff. Dresden, Stengel & Markert, 1888. Fol. M. 60.," *MöM*, new ser., 3rd year, no. 35 (278) November 1888, p. 241.

"Das Kunstgewerbe auf der Kaiser-Jubiläums-Ausstellung zu Brünn," *MöM*, new ser., 3rd year, no. 36 (279) December 1888, pp. 256–259.

"Die Kalenderbilder des Chronographen vom Jahre 354, herausgeg von Josef Strzygowski. (Jahrb des k deutschen archäol. Inst. Ergänzungsheft I.) Mit 30 Taf. Berlin, G. Reimer, 1888, 8°. 106 S.," *MöM*, new ser., 3rd year, no. 36 (279) December 1888, pp. 263–264.

"Adolf von Oechselhäuser, Die Miniaturen der Universitäts-Bibliothek zu Heidelberg," [part 1,] *MIöG*, vol. 9, 1888, pp. 521–522.

Die ägyptischen Textilfunde im K. K. Österreichischen Museum Allgemeine Charakteristik und Katalog von Alois Riegl, Vienna: Waldheim, 1889, 68 pp., xiii plates.

"Études iconographiques et archéologiques sur le moyen-âge par E. Müntz. I. série. (Petite bibliothèque d'art et d'archéologie.) Paris, E. Leroux, 1887.

12°. 173 S.," *MöM*, new ser., 4th year, no. 37 (280) January 1889, p. 281.

"Mustergültige Möbel des XI. bis XVII. Jahrhunderts, ausgewählt und herausgegeben von Ludw. Caspar, architect. Aufgen und in Lichtdruck ausgef von Nöhring in Lübeck. Frankurt a M. Verlag von H. Keller, 1888, 25 Taf. Ohne Text. M. 30.-.," *MöM*, new ser., 4th year, no. 37 (280) January 1889, p. 282.

"Alte kunstvolle Spitzen auf der Ausstellung zu Brüssel 1884, herausgeg. von Joseph Claesen. 30 Taf. Fol. Berlin, Chr. Claesen & Co.," *MöM*, new ser., 4th year, no. 38 (281) February 1889, p. 307.

"Documents relatifs à l'art de la decoration et au dessin industriel. I. série: Étoffes anciennes, nouveau choix des specimens des XVII°, XVIII° et XIX° siècles, reproduits par la phototypie et précédés d'une notice. 30 Taf. Paris, A. Calavas, 1888. Fol. M. 60.," *MöM*, new ser., 4th year, no. 38 (281) February 1889, 307–308.

"Sammlung von kunstgewerblichen Objecten, herausgeg unter Mitwirkung der Abtheilung für Kunstgewerbe des niederösterr. Gewerbevereines. Interieurs. Lief. I, Blatt 1–10. Fol. Wien, A. Schroll & Co., 1888.," *MöM*, new ser., 4th year, no. 40 (283) April 1889, p. 361.

"Les manufactures nationales: Les Gobelins, la Savonnerie, Sèvres, Beauvais.

Par H. Havard et M. Vauchon. Paris, Georges Decaux, 1889. 4°. 632 S. 75 Taf. M. 30.," *MöM*, new ser., 4th year, no. 41 (284) May 1889, pp. 384–385.

"Die mittelalterliche Kalenderillustration," *MIöG*, vol. 10, 1889, pp. 1–74. Reviewed by Eduard Chmelarz, *MöM*, new ser., 4th year, no. 42 (285) June 1889, pp. 401–402.

"Naborre Campanini: Ars siricea Regii; vicende dell'arte della seta in Reggio nell'Emilia dal secolo XVI al secolo XIX. Reggio nell'Emilia, stab tipo-litografico degli artigianelli 1888. 4°. 344 S. 7 Taf.," *MöM*, new ser., 4th year, no. 42 (285) June 1889, pp. 400–401.

"Textile Hausindustrie in Österreich Vortrag gehalten am 14. Februar 1888," *MöM*, new ser., 4th year, no. 43 (286) July 1889, pp. 411–419.

"Textile Hausindustrie in Österreich (Schluss.)," *MöM*, new ser., 4th year, no. 44 (287) August 1889, pp. 431–435.

"Ein Weltbild unserer kirchlichen Kunst, gezeichnet in der vaticanischen Ausstellung von Heinrich Swoboda. Mit sechs Kunstbeilagen, Paderborn, Ferd. Schöningh, 1889, 8°. 48 S. M. 1.80," *MöM*, new ser., 4th year, no. 44 (287) August 1889, p. 439.

"Die Geschenke aus der Sammlung Figdor," *MöM*, new ser., 4th year, no. 46 (289) October 1889, pp. 465–467.

"Eugène Müntz, Études iconographiques et archéologiques sur le moyen-âge, 1st ser., Paris 1887," *MIöG*, vol. 10, 1889, pp. 162–163

"Mustergiltige Holzintarsien der deutschen Renaissance aus dem 16. und 17. Jahrhundert. Gezeichnet und herausg von Karl Lacher. Graz, F. Pechel, 1889. Gr. Fol. 30 Taf fl. 10," *MöM*, new ser., 4th year, no. 47 (290) November 1889, pp. 507–508.

"Hessische Bauernstühle," *MöM*, new ser., 5th year, no. 49 (292), January 1890, pp. 11–15.

"Beitrag zur Geschichte der Taptenindustrie von Friedrich Fischbach. Darmstadt 1889, A. Koch. 8°. 43 S.," *MöM*, new ser., 5th year, no. 49 (292), January 1890, p. 19.

"Eine Bildwirkerei mit der Kreuzabnahme nach Raffael," *MöM*, new ser., 5th year, no. 50 (293), February 1890, pp. 25–35.

"Die Gobelins–Ausstellung im Oesterr. Museum," *MöM*, new ser., 5th year, no. 51 (294), March 1890, pp. 49–58.

"Gamle norske Taepper (altnorwegische Teppichmuster), herausg von der Direction des Kunstindustrie-Museums zu Christiania. Text (4 S.) von H. Grosch, Conservator. Berlin, A. Asher & Co., 1889. Fol. 9 Taf in Farbendruck. M. 24.," *MöM*, new ser., 5th year, no. 51 (294)

March 1890, pp. 62–63.

"Die Gobelins–Ausstellung im Oesterr. Museum," *MöM*, new ser., 5th year, no. 52 (295), April, 1890, pp. 81–85.

"Vorbilder–Hefte aus dem königl. Kunstgewerbe–Museum zu Berlin, Heft 5 u 6. Stühle. Text von Jul. Lessing. Berlin, E. Wasmuth, 1889. Fol. Je 15 Tafeln a Heft M. 10.," *MöM*, new ser., 5th year, no. 52 (295) April 1890, p. 92.

"Preisgekrönte und andere decorative Holzarbeiten aus der Concurrenz–Ausstellung des Württemberg'schen Kunstgewerbe–Vereines in Stuttgart, herausgeg von Wilh. Kick. In 15 Liefergn zu 4 Tafeln. Stuttgart, A. Zimmer. Fol a Lief. M. 2.," *MöM*, new ser., 5th year, no. 53 (296) May 1890, p. 110.

"Sammlung von kunstgewerblichen Objecten, herausgeg unter Mitwirkung der Abtheilung für Kunstgewerbe des Niederöster. Gewerbevereines. Möbel, erste Serie. Wien, A. Schroll & Co., 1889. Fol. M. 12.," *MöM*, new ser., 5th year, no. 54 (297) June 1890, p. 133.

"Die Trierer Ada-Handschrift, bearbeitet und herausg von K. Menzel, P. Corssen, H. Janitschek, A. Schnütgen, F. Hettner, K. Lamprecht. Mit 38 Taf. Leipzig, A. Dürr, 1889. Fol. 120 S. M. 80.," *MöM*, new ser., 5th year, no. 55 (298) July 1890, p. 154.

"Wandtäfelungen und Holzdecken,

eine Mustersammlung kunsthand-
werklicher Schöpfungen alter und
neuer Zeit, mit einer kunstgeschichtlichen Abhandlung herausgeg von
Hans Issel. Leipzig, Scholtze. 40 Tafeln,
47 S. Text. M. 18.," *MöM*, new ser., 5th
year, no. 55 (298) July 1890, p. 155.

"Die Ausstellung weiblicher Handarbeiten in Florenz," *MöM*, new ser., 5th
year, no. 57 (300) September 1890, pp.
181–184.

"Lübecker Malerei und Plastik bis 1530.
Von Adolph Goldschmidt. Mit 43 Licht-
drucktaf. Lübeck, Nöhring, 1889. Fol.
39 S. M. 25.," *MöM*, new ser., 5th year,
no. 57 (300) September 1890, p. 196.

"Die Beziehungen der orientalischen
Teppichfabrikation zum europäischen
Abendlande Unter Benützung eines
am 14. October 1889 im Oesterr. Museum gehaltenen Vortrages über 'Orientalische Teppiche'," *MöM*, new ser.,
5th year, no. 58 (301) October 1890, pp.
210–216.

"The Viking age, by Paul B. du Chail-
lu, with 1366 illustrations and map.
London, J. Murray. 8°. I. Bd. 591 S., II.
Bd. 562 S. M. 50.40.," *MöM*, new ser.,
5th year, no. 58 (301) October 1890,
pp. 217–218.

"*Kunsthistorischer Atlas*, herausg von
der k k Central-Commission zur Erforschung und Erhaltung der Kunst- und

historischen Denkmale. I. Abtheil. Sammlung von Abbildungen vorgeschicht-
licher und frühgeschichtlicher Funde
aus den Ländern der österreichisch-
ungarischen Monarchie. 100 Tafeln
und zahlreiche Abbildungen im Texte. Wien, Kubasta & Voigt, 1889. Fol.
Fl. 12.," *MöM*, new ser., 5th year, no. 58
(301) October 1890, p. 219.

"Die Beziehungen der orientalischen
Teppichfabrikation zum europäischen
Abendlande (Schluss.)," *MöM*, new ser.,
5th year, no. 59 (302) November 1890,
pp. 234–241.

"Die Reiterstatue Karl's des Großen aus
der Kathedrale zu Metz von Dr. Georg
Wolfram. Mit 2 Taf. Strassburg, Trüb-
ner, 1890. 8°. 26 S. M. 2," *MöM*, new ser.,
5th year, no. 59 (302) November 1890, p.
244.

"Neuseeländische Ornamentik," *Mitteilungen der anthropologischen Gesellschaft in Wien*, vol. 20, new ser, vol, 10,
1890, pp. 84–87. English transl. Karl
Johns, "Alois Riegl and the Maori,"
Journal of Art Historiography, no. 12,
June 2015, 7 pp.

"Julius von Schlosser, Die abend-
ländische Klosteranlage des früheren
Mittelalters, Wien 1889," *MIöG*, vol. 11,
1890, pp. 328–330.

"David Ritter von Schönherr, Alexan-
der Colin und seine Werke, 1562–1612,

Heidelberg 1889," *MIöG*, vol. 11, 1890, pp. 143–144.

"Karl Menzel et alii, Die Trierer Ada-Handschrift, Leipzig, 1889," *MIöG*, vol. 11, 1890, pp. 460–462.

"Die Wirkerei und der textile Hausfleiß," *Kunstgewerbeblatt*, new ser., vol. 1, no. 3, 1890, pp. 21–23.

"Zur spätrömischen Ikonographie der Monate," *Archäologisch-epigraphische Mitteilungen aus Österreich-Ungarn*, vol. 13, no. 1, 1890, pp. 8–11.

Altorientalische Teppiche, Leipzig: T. O. Weigel (C. H. Tauchnitz), 1891, 214 pp., 36 figs. Reprinted with a bibliographical introduction by Ulrike Besch, Mittenwald: Mäander, 1979, xxi, xii, 214 pp. Italian translation: *Antichi tapeti orientali*, translated by Alberto Manai with Sergio Bettini, "Poetica del tappeto orientale," *Quaderni Quodlibet 4*, Macerata: Quodlibet, 1998, 247 pp. 16 plates.

"Zur Geschichte des orientalischen Teppichs," Artur von Scala ed., *Ausstellung orientalischer Teppiche im K K Österreichischen Handelsmuseum*, Vienna: Österreichisches Handelsmuseum, 1891, pp. 11–23.

"Die Porträtdarstellungen Karls des Großen. Von Paul Clemen. Mit 17 Abbild. Aachen, C. Cazin, 1890. 8°. 233 S. M. 6." *MöM*, new ser., 6th year, no. 62

(305) February 1891, p. 312.

"Les tapisseries coptes. Par M. Gerspach. Paris, Quantin, 1890. 4°. M. 8." *MöM*, new ser., 6th year, no. 62 (305) February 1891, p. 313.

"Orientalische Teppiche. Ein Vorlagenwerk zum Studium von Farbe und Ornament, nach Originalen aufgen von W. Fröhlich. 14 Farbentafeln. Berlin, Ch. Claesen & Co. M. 36." *MöM*, new ser., 6th year, no. 62 (305) February 1891, pp. 313–314.

"Tapisseries, broderies et dentalles. Recueil de modèles anciens et modernes, precédé d'une introduction par E. Müntz. (Bibliothèque international de l'art.) 150 Grav., 43 S. Text. 4°. Paris, librairie de l'art. M. 20." *MöM*, new ser., 6th year, no. 63 (306) March 1891, p. 333.

"Ulm's Baumwollweberei im Mittelalter. Urkunden und Darstellung. Von Eugen Nuebling. Leipzig, Duncker & Humblot, 1890. 8°. 207 S. M. 5." *MöM*, new ser., 6th year, no. 63 (306) March 1891, pp. 333–334.

"Monumenti storici ed artistici degli Abruzzi. Studi di Vincenzo Bindi, con prefazione di Ferdinando Gregorovius. Napoli, F. Giannini e figli, 1889. 4°. 966 S." *MöM*, new ser., 6th year, no. 65 (308) May 1891, pp. 373–374.

"Die Ausstellung orientalischer Teppiche im K. K. Österreichischen Handelsmuseum," *MöM*, new ser., 6th year, no. 66 (309), June 1891, pp. 383–391.

"La broderie du XIe siècle jusqu'à nos jours d'après des specimens authentiques et les anciens inventaires par M. Louis de Farcy. 1 fasc. Paris, E. Leroux, 1890. Fol. M. 80," *MöM*, new ser., 6th year, no. 66 (309), June 1891, pp. 397–398.

"Die Ausstellung orientalischer Teppiche im K. K. Österreichischen Handelsmuseum (Schluss.)," *MöM*, new ser., 6th year, no. 67 (310) July 1891, pp. 405–414.

"Histoire de la dentelle, par Mme. Bury Palliser. Traduction française. Ouvrage illustrée de 161 grav sur bois et de 16 planches en couleur. Paris, Firmin Didot et Co., 1890. 4°. 340 S. M. 5.80," *MöM*, new ser., 6th year, no. 68 (311) August 1891, p. 445.

"Leinen–Damastmuster des XVII. und XVIII. Jahrhunderts. Von königl. Kunstgewerbemuseum zu Dresden hersugeg durch Emil Kumsch. 25 Taf mit 148 Mustern in photograph Drucke. 1 Blatt Text. Fol. Dresden, Stengel & Markert. M. 40," *MöM*, new ser., 6th year, no. 71 (314) November 1891, p. 511.

"Ein kärntnerischer Bauernkalender," *Carinthia I: Mittheilungen des Geschichtsvereins für Kärnten*, vol. 61, 1891, pp. 13–23.

"Wilhelm Effmann, Heiligkreuz und Pfälzel: Beiträge zur Baugeschichte Triers, Freiburg 1890–1891," *MIöG*, vol. 12, 1891, pp. 527–528.

"Adolf von Oechselhäuser, Der Bilderkreis zum wälschen Gaste des Thomassin von Zerclaere," *MIöG*, vol. 12, 1891, pp. 664–665.

"Georg Buschau, Über prähistorische Gewebe und Gespinste, 1891," *Mitteilungen der anthropologischen Gesellschaft in Wien*, vol. 21, pp. 82–83.

"Spätantike Stickereien," *Kunstgewerbeblatt*, new ser., vol. 2, 1891, pp. 127–131.

"Die Heimat des orientalischen Knüpfteppichs," *Österreichische Monatschrift für den Orient*, 18th year, no. 1, January 1892, pp. 9–12. Reprinted, *Bayerische Gewerbezeitung*, 1893, p. 487.

"Beschreibung der abgebildeten Teppiche," *Orientalische Teppiche*, Vienna: Österreichisches Handelsmuseum, 1892–1896. Reviewed by Jakob von Falke, *MöM*, new ser., 7th year, no. 78 (321) June, 1892, pp. 116–117.

"Ältere orientalische Teppiche aus dem Besitze des Allerhöchsten Kaiserhauses," *Jahrbuch der Kunsthistorischen Sammlungen des Allerhöchsten Kaiserhauses*, vol. 13, 1892, pp. 267–331.

"Lessings Orientalische Teppiche," *MöM*, new ser., 7th year, no. 76 (319) April 1892, pp. 62–68.

"Die Brixener Malerschulen des 15. und 16. Jahrhunderts und ihr Verhältnis zu Michael Pacher, von Hans Semper. Mit 15 Abbildungen (Zinkographie). Innsbruck, Wagner'sche Universitäts–Buchhandlung, 1891. 8°. 138 S fl 1'40," *MöM*, new ser., 7th year, no. 76 (319) April 1892, p. 77.

"Geschichte der Wandteppichfabriken des Wittelsbachischen Fürstenhauses in Bayern, mit einer Geschichte der Wandteppichverfertigung als Einleitung von Dr. Manfred Mayer. Mit 21 Taf in Lichtdr. München und Leipzig, G. Hirth's Kunstverlag, 1892. 4°. 139 S. M. 15," *MöM*, new ser., 7th year, no. 76 (319) April 1892, pp. 77-78.

"Ruthenische Teppiche," *MöM*, new ser., 7th year, no. 77 (320) May 1892, pp. 85–94.

"Königliches Kunstgewerbemuseum zu Dresden und Kunstgewerbemuseum zu Leipzig. Posamente des 16.–19. Jahrhunderts, herausgegeben von Prof. E. Kumsch. 25 Tafeln in photogr. Drucke mit 515 Abbild. Dresden, Stengel & Markert, 1892. Fol., ein Blatt Text. M. 50.," *MöM*, new ser., 7th year, no. 77 (320) May 1892, p. 98.

"Ruthenische Teppiche (Schluss.)," *MöM*, new ser., 7th year, no. 78 (321) June 1892, pp. 109–113.

"Textiler Hausfleiß in der Bukowina Bericht über die Ausstellung orientalischer Teppiche und bukowinischer Hausfleißarbeiten in Czernowitz," *MöM*, new ser., 7th year, no. 79 (322), July 1892, pp. 134–139.

"The grammar of the lotus, a new history of classic ornament as a development of sun worship, by Wm. G. Goodyear, with numerous illustrations. London, Sampson Low, Marston & Co., 1891, 4°. 408 S.," *MöM*, new ser., 7th year, no. 79 (322) July 1892, pp. 140–141.

"Wood carvings from the South Kensington–Museum, edited by Eleonore Rowe. London, Sutton Drowley & Co. Fünf Lieferungen von je 18 Taf in Lichtdruck. Fol fl. 40." *MöM*, new ser., 7th year, no. 79 (322) July 1892, p. 142.

"Textiler Hausfleiß in der Bukowina Bericht über die Ausstellung orientalischer Teppiche und bukowinischer Hausfleißarbeiten in Czernowitz (Schluss.)," *MöM*, new ser., 7th year, no. 80 (323) August 1892, pp. 154–160.

"Zur Geschichte des Posamentiergewerbes, mit besonderer Rücksichtnahme auf die erzgebirgische Posamentenindustrie. Nach zahlreichen gedruckten und handschriftlichen Quellen bearbeitet von Eduin Siegel, Lehrer an der Bürger– und Posamentierschule zu Geyer. Mit 18 Abb. Annaberg, Herm. Graser's

Verlag, 1892. 8°. 126 S. M. 2.50," *MöM*, new ser., 7th year, no. 80 (323) August 1892, pp. 162–163.

"Motive. Sammlung von Einzelheiten aller Techniken des Kunstgewerbes als Vorbilder und Studienmaterial. Herausgeg. von Max Keiden, Verwalter der Stoffsammlung des königl. Kunstgewerbemuseums zu Berlin. 30 Doppelhefte von je 10 Blatt. Preis der Doppel h. 2 Mark. Leipzig, Arthur Seemann, 1890 ff.," *MöM*, new ser., 7th year, no. 81 (324) September 1892, pp. 182–183.

"Die Ausstellung der K. K. Stickerei-Fachschule zu Dornbirn," *MöM*, new ser., 7th year, no. 83 (326), November 1892, pp. 211–217.

"Die Kilim–Teppichweberei in Galizien und die Weberschule in Okno," *Zentralblatt für das gewerbliche Unterrichtswesen in Österreich*, vol. 11, 1892, supplement, pp. 1–7.

"H. William Goodyear, The Grammar of the Lotus A New History of Classic Ornament as a Development of Sun Worship, London 1891," *Mittheilungen der anthropologischen Gesellschaft in Wien*, vol. 22, (new ser., vol. 12) 1892, p. 121.

"Alois Raimund Hein, Mäander, Kreuze, Hakenkreuz und urmotivische Wirbelornamente in Amerika, Wien 1891," *Mittheilungen der anthropologischen Gesellschaft in Wien*, vol. 22, 1892, pp. 120–121.

"Spanische Aufnäharbeiten," *Zeitschrift des Bayerischen Kunstgewerbevereines in München*, vol. 32, no. 11–12, December 1892, pp. 65–73.

Stilfragen Grundlegungen zu einer Geschichte der Ornamentik, Berlin: Georg Siemens, 1893, xix, 346 pp. Reprinted: Hildesheim: Olms, 1975. Karl Maria Swoboda and Otto Pächt ed., Berlin: Richard Carl Schmidt, 1923, xix, 346 pp. Mittenwald: Mäander–Kunstverlag, 1977, 1985, XIX, 346 pp., 197 Illustrations. Italian translation by Mario Pecor, ed. Arturo Carlo Quintavalle, *Problemi di stile. Fondamenti di una storia dell'arte ornamentale*, Biblioteca scientifica Feltrinelli 10, Milan: Feltrinelli, 1963, XXV, 336 pp. English translation by Evelyn Kain with annotations, glossary and introduction by David Castriota, *Problems of Style. Foundations for a History of Ornament*, Princeton NJ: Princeton University Press, 1992, XXXIII, 406 pp. French translation: *Questions de style: Fondements d'une histoire de l'ornementation*, "Collection 35/37," Paris: Hazan, 2002, XXI, 289 pp. Reviewed: Ms (Karl Masner), *MöM*, new ser., 9th year, no. 98 (341), February 1894, pp. 49–51.

"XVI. Textilkunst," Bruno Bucher ed., *Geschichte der technischen Künste*, vol. 3, Stuttgart: Spemann, 1893, pp. 333–400.

"Zur Frage des Nachlebens der altägyptischen Kunst in der späten Antike," *Eranos Vindobonensis, Festschrift zur 42. Versammlung deutscher Philologen und Schulmänner in Wien, dargebracht von der Philologisch-archäologischen Gesellschaft in Wien*, Vienna: Hölder, 1893, pp. 191–197.

"Der antike Webstuhl," *MöM*, new ser., 7th year, no. 86 (329), February, 1893, pp. 290–303.

"Die Pariser Ausstellung weiblicher Kunstarbeiten," *MöM*, new ser., 7th year, no. 87 (330), March 1893, pp. 317–328.

"Kirchenmöbel des Mittelalters und der Neuzeit. Chorgestühle, Kanzeln, Lettner und andere Gegenstände kirchlicher Einrichtung. Herausgeg von Arthur Pabst. 30 Tafeln in Lichtdruck. Frankurt a M., H. Keller, 1893. Fol. M. 30.," *MöM*, new ser., 7th year, no. 87 (330) March 1893, pp. 340–341.

"Methodik der Bindungslehre, Decomposition und Calculation für Schaftweberei. Bearbeitet für k k Fachschulen und zum Selbstunterricht von Franz Donat, Lehrer an der k k Fachschule für Weberei zu Warnsdorf in Böhmen. Mit 57 Taf. Wien, Pest, Leipzig, A. Hartle-ben. 8°. 112 S. M. 6.," *MöM*, new ser., 7th year, no. 91 (334) July 1893, pp. 419–420.

"Die Wandstickereien des Königs René in der Kathedrale zu Angers, Darstellungen aus der Apokalypse. 72 Photographien. Leipzig, Karl W. Hiersemann. Fol. M. 133.50.," *MöM*, new ser., 7th year, no. 92 (335) August 1893, pp. 436–437.

"Stickereimuster. Neue Entwürfe in verschiedenen Stilarten für allerlei Nadelarbeit von Hermine Steffahny. Leipzig, Verlag der Arbeitsstube (Eug. Twietmayer). Serie I. Lief. I, M. 1.," *MöM*, new ser., 7th year, no. 92 (335) August 1893, p. 437.

"Koptische Kunst, A. Gayet, Les monuments coptes du musée de Boulay, 1889, Al. Gayet, 'La sculpture copte,'" *Gazette des Beaux-Arts*, 1892, G. Ebers, *Die koptische Kunst*, Leipzig: Engelmann, 1893," *Byzantinische Zeitschrift*, vol. 2, 1893, pp. 112–121.

"Die Schmuckformen der Denkmalbauten aus allen Stilepochen seit der griechischen Anitke. Von Gustav Ebe, Architekt. I und II. Theil: Antike und altchristliche Zeit. Mit 33 Abbild im Text, 3 Lichtdruck- und 1 Farbentafel. Berlin, Georg Siemens, 1893, 4°.," *MöM*, new ser., 7th year, no. 95 (338) November 1893 pp. 511–512.

"Königliches Kunstgewerbe-Museum

zu Dresden. Muster orientalischer Gewebe und Druckstoffe. Herausgegeben von Professor Dr. E. Kumsch. 40 Tafeln in unveränderlichem photographischen Drucke. Mit 212 Mustern. Dresden, Stegel & Markert, 1893. Fol. M. 70.," *MöM*, new ser., 7th year, no. 96 (339) December 1893, p. 540.

"Les tapisseries de Tournai. Les tapissiers et les hautelisseurs de cette ville. Recherches et documents sur l'histoire. La fabrication et les produits des ateliers de Tournai par Eugène Soil. Tournai, Vasseu-Delmée; Lille, L. Quarré. 8°. 460 S. M. 12.," *MöM*, new ser., 7th year, no. 96 (339) December 1983, pp. 540–541.

Volkskunst, Hausfleiß und Hausindustrie, Berlin: Georg Siemens, 1894, 82 pp. Reprinted, "Kunstwissenschaftliche Studientexte, 6," Mittenwald: Mäander, 1978, 87 pp.

"Les artistes célèbres. Les Boulle, par Henry Havard. 40 gravures. Paris, Allison & Co. 8°. 90 S. M. 4.," *MöM*, new ser., 7th year, no. 97 (340) January 1894, pp. 24–25.

"Geschichte der karolingischen Malerei, ihr Bilderkreis und seine Quellen. Von Franz Friedrich Leitschuh. Mit 59 Abbild. Berlin, G. Siemens, 1894. 8°. 471 S. M. 4.," *MöM*, new ser., 7th year, no. 99 (342) March 1894, p. 79.

"Die Kilimweberei und die Kilimweberschule des Wladyslaw R. v. Fedorowicz in Okno. Von Dr. Clemens v. Hankiewicz, Wien, C. Gerold's Sohn, 1894. 8°. 107 S. M. 2.," *MöM*, new ser., 7th year, no. 99 (342) March 1894, p. 80.

"Lehrgänge für Weißstickerei und Knüpfarbeit. Von Louise Schinnerer. Deutsche Verlags-Anstalt, 1893. 8°. 152 S.," *MöM*, new ser., 7th year, no. 99 (342) March 1894, p. 81.

"Spitzen des 16. bis 19. Jahrhunderts aus den Sammlungen des Kunstgewerbe-Museums zu Leipzig, ausgewählt von Prof. Melchior zur Strassen. Leipzig, Karl W. Hiersemann, 1894. M. 60.," *MöM*, new ser., 7th year, no. 99 (342) March 1894, p. 81.

"Vittorio Stringher: L'industria dei merletti nelle campagne. Roma, G. Bertero, 1893. 8°. 75 S. M. 3.," *MöM*, new ser., 7th year, no. 99 (342) March 1894, p. 81.

"Alfonso Ceccarelli und seine Fälschungen von Kaiserurkunden," *MIöG*, vol. 15, 1894, pp. 193–236.

"Dr. A. Riegl hält einen Vortrag über Die Volkskunst vom wirtschaftsgeschichtlichen Standpunkt [Monatsversammlung am 13. Februar 1894]," *Mitteilungen der anthropologischen Gesellschaft in Wien*, vol. 24 (new ser., vol. 14), no. 1–2, January–February 1894, pp. 2–3.

"Geschichte der karolingischen Malerei, ihr Bilderkreis und seine Quellen. Von Franz Friedrich Leischuh. Mit 59 Abbild. Berlin, G. Siemens, 1894, 8°. 471 S. M. 4.," *MöM*, new ser., 9th year, no. 99 (342), March 1894, p. 79.

"Die Kilimweberei und die Kilimweberschule des Wladyslaw R v. Fedorowicz in Okno. Von Dr. Clemens v. Hankiewicz. Wien, C. Gerold's Sohn, 1894. 8°. 107 S. M. 2.," *MöM*, new ser., 9th year, no. 99 (342), March 1894, p. 80.

"Das Rankenornament. Vortrag gehalten im K. K. Österreichisches Museum am 14. Dezember 1893," *MöM*, new ser., 9th year, no. 101 (344), May, 1894, pp. 122–130.

"Das Rankenornament (Schluss.)," *MöM*, new ser., 9th year, no. 102 (345), June, 1894, pp. 149–155.

"Die Wirk- und Webekunst, inbegriffen die Flechterei, Näherei, Stickerei, Spinnerei, Knüpferei und Strickerei etc. Von August Demmin. Mit 126 Abbild. Wiesbaden, Bechtold & Co.. 8°. M. 6.," *MöM*, new ser., 9th year, no. 102 (345) June 1894, pp. 157–158.

"Zur Frage der 'Polenteppiche,'" *Österreichische Monatsschrift für den Orient*, vol. 20, no. 8–9, August–September 1894, pp. 118–120. Reprinted *MöM*, new ser., 9th year

vol. 5, October 1894, pp. 225–230.

"Polen–Teppiche," *Illustrierte Frauen-Zeitung*, "Unterhaltungsblatt Beiblatt zur *Illustrierten Frauen–Zeitung*," 21st year, no. 20, October 14, 1894, pp. 158–159.

"Das Kreuz von St. Trudpert, eine alemannische Nielloarbeit aus spätromanischer Zeit. Von Marc Rosenberg. Freiburg i Br., Herder'sche Verlagsbuchhandlung. 4°. 34 S.," *MöM*, new ser., 9th year, no. 109 (352) January 1895, p. 305.

"Die Fischer von Erlach, Mit Förderung des k k Ministeriums für Cultus und Unterricht herausgegeben von Albert Ilg. I. Leben und Werke Johann Bernhard Fischer's von Erlach, des Vaters. Wien, C. Konegen, 1895, 8°. 819 S. fl. 10.," *MöM*, new ser., 10th year, no. 110 (353) February 1895, pp. 329–330.

Luise Schinnerer, *Antike Handarbeiten, mit einer historischen Einleitung von Alois Riegl*, Vienna: Waldheim, 1895, 25 pp. Reviewed: Ms (Karl Masner), *MöM*, new ser., 10th year, no. 114 (357) June 1895, pp. 419–420.

Ein orientalischer Teppich vom Jahre 1202 n. Chr. und die ältesten orientalischen Teppiche, Berlin: Georg Siemens, 1895, 33 pp. Reviewed by Karl Masner: *MöM*, new ser., 11th year, no. 121 (364) January 1896, pp. 19–20.

"Kunsthandwerk und kunstgewerbliche Massenproduktion," *Zeitschrift des Bayerischen Kunstgewerbevereines in München*, vol. 45, no. 1, 1895, pp. 1–8.

"Über Renaissance in der Kunst Vortrag, gehalten im K. K. Österreichisches Museum am 6. und 13, Dezember 1894," *MöM*, new ser., 10th year, no. 111 (354), March, 1895, pp. 342–348.

"Handbuch der Spitzenkunde. Von Tina Frauberger. (Seemann's Kunsthandbücher XI.) Mit 183 Illust. Leipzig, E. A. Seemann, 1894. 272 S. M 4.80.," *MöM*, new ser., 10th year, no. 111 (354) March 1895, p. 351.

"Über Renaissance der Kunst (Fortsetzung.)," *MöM*, new ser., 10th year, no. 112, April 1895, pp. 363–371.

"Über Renaissance der Kunst (Schluss.)," *MöM*, new ser., 10th year, no. 113 (356), May 1895, pp. 381–393.

"Die Zeugdrucke der byzantinischen, romanischen, gothischen und späteren Kunstepochen. Von R. Forrer. 57 Tafeln, 132 Abbildungen in Farben- und Lichtdruck, nebst Cliché-Abbildungen im Text, Straßburg 1894. Selbstverlag. 4°. 39 S.," *MöM*, new ser., 10th year, no. 115 (358) July 1895, p. 437

"Die Schatzkammer des Allerhöchsten Kaiserhauses," *MöM*, new ser.,

10th year, no. 116 (359), August, 1895, pp. 445–447.

"Das Monument von Adamklissi Tropaeum Trajani. Unter Mitwirkung von Otto Benndorf und Georg Niemann herausg von Gr. G. Tocilescu. Mit 3 Taf und 34 Abbild im Texte. Wien, Alfr. Holder, 1985," *MöM*, new ser., 11th year, no. 121 (364) January 1896, pp. 17–19.

"Die Wiener–Kongress–Ausstellung," *Wiener Zeitung*, no. 38, February 15, 1896, pp. 3–4, no. 61, March 13, 1896, pp. 2–4, no. 76, April 1, 1896, pp. 3–5.

"Die Fürstlich Liechtenstein'sche Galerie in Wien. Mit Text von Dr. Wilhelm Bode. Wien, Gesellschaft für vervielfältigende Kunst, 1896 (Gross 4, 138 Seiten.)," *Mitteilungen der Gesellschaft für vervielfältigende Kunst Beilage der 'graphischen Künste,'* 1896, no. 4, pp. 19–20.

"Literatur: Daniel Chodowiecki. Ein Berliner Künstlerleben im XVIII. Jahrhundert. Von Wolfgang von Oettingen. Mit Tafeln und Illustrationen im Text nach Originalen des Meisters. Berlin. G. Grote'sche Verlagsbuchhandlung 1895," *Mitteilungen der Gesellschaft für vervielfältigende Kunst Beilage der 'graphischen Künste,'* 1896, no. 4, p. 23.

"Literatur: Die königliche Gemäldegalerie in Dresden. Text von Hermann Lücke. München. Franz Hanfstaengl. 10

Lief. à 10 Mark," *Mitteilungen der Gesell-schaft für vervielfältigende Kunst Beilage der 'graphischen Künste,'* 1896, no. 5, pp. 31–32.

"Catalogue sommaire des monuments exposés dans le musée national de l'art arabe, par Max Herz, architecte en chef du comité de conservation des monuments de l'art arabe. Le Caire, G. Lekegian & Co., 1895, 8°. LXV und 187 S., 20 Taf. in Lichtdruck," *MöM*, new ser., 11th year, no. 132 (375) December 1896, pp. 254–255.

"Die Barockdecoration und die moderne Kunst. Vortrag, gehalten im K. K. Österreichisches Museum am 3. Januar 1897," *MöM*, new ser., 12th year, no. 133 (376), January, 1897, pp. 261–266.

"Die Kunst der Weißstickerei. Von Louise Schinnerer, Lehrerin an der k k Fachschule für Kunststickerei in Wien. Wien, Leipzig, Berlin, Stuttgart, Verlag der "Wiener Mode". 4°. 69 S.," *MöM*, new ser., 12th year, no. 133 (376) January 1897, p. 282.

"Die Kunst der Goldstickerei, nebst einer Anleitung zur Verwendung der Goldstickerei in Verbindung mit Application von Amalie von Saint-George, Lehrerin an der k k Fachschule für Kunststickerei in Wien. II. Auflage. Mit 6 Tafeln und 136 Textillustr. Wien, Leipzig, Berlin, Stuttgart, Verlag der 'Wiener Mode'. 4°.

54 S.," *MöM*, new ser., 12th year, no. 133 (376) January 1897, p. 282.

"Die Barockdecoration und die moderne Kunst. Vortrag, gehalten im K. K. Österreichisches Museum am 3. January 1897 von Alois Riegl. (Schluss.)," *MöM*, new ser., 12th year, no. 134 (377), February 1897, pp. 295–302.

"Thüren aus Turkestan. Fünf Tafeln nebst Text von F. R. Martin. Stockholm, königl. Buchdruckerei, 1897. 4°. 13 S.," *MöM*, new ser., 12th year, no. 138 (381) June 1897, p. 404.

"Die nordische Ausstellung und F. R. Martins Sammlung zu Stockholm," *Kunst und Handwerk: Zeitschrift für Kunstgewerbe und Kunsthandwerk seit 1851*, vol. 47, no. 6, 1897–1898, pp. 197–202.

"Kunstgeschichte und Universalgeschichte," *Festgabe zu Ehren Max Büdinger's von seinen Freunden und Schülern*, Innsbruck: Wagner, 1898, pp. 449–457. Reprinted *Belvedere Kunst und Kultur der Vergangenheit Zeitschrift für Sammler und Kunstfreunde*, vol. 7, no. 31, January 1925, pp. 1–6. Reprinted *Alois Riegl, Gesammelte Aufsätze*, ed. Karl Maria Swoboda, Augsburg: Filser, 1929, pp. 3–9; pp. 68–76 of the present volume.

"Möbel und Innendekoration," *Der Wiener Kongress Culturgeschichte Die bildenden Künste und das Kunstge-*

werbe Theater – Musik in der Zeit von 1800 bis 1825, Eduard Leisching ed., Vienna: Artaria, 1898, pp. 185–206. Reprinted *Alois Riegl, Gesammelte Aufsätze*, ed. Karl Maria Swoboda, Augsburg: Filser, 1929, pp. 10–27; pp. 77–96 of the present volume.

"Die Pflanze in der Kunst," *Allgemeine Zeitung Beilage*, [Munich] vol. 89, no. 5, January 8, 1898, pp. 4–6.

"Das Moderne in der Kunst: Vortrag, gehalten in der volkswirtschaftlichen Gesellschaft zu Berlin von Prof. Dr. Julius Lessing, erchienen im Verlage von Leonh. Simion zu Berlin als Heft 157 der 'Volkswirtschaftlichen Zeitfragen,'" *Mitteilungen der Gesellschaft für vervielfältigende Kunst Beilage der 'graphischen Kunste,'* 1899, no. 2, pp. 9–12.

"Die Baukunst als Steinbau, von Adolf Mauke. Basel, Benno Schwabe 1897. 4°, 230 S., 138 Tafeln mit 936 Abbildungen. Preis geb. Mk. 28; Frcs. 35.," *Mitteilungen der Gesellschaft für vervielfältigende Kunst Beilage der 'graphischen Künste,'* 1899, no. 2, p. 20.

"Adolf Oechselhäuser, Die Miniaturen der Universitäts–Bibliothek zu Heidelberg, [part 2,] Heidelberg 1895," *MIöG*, vol. 20, 1899, pp. 353–355.

"Die Stimmung als Inhalt der modernen Kunst," *Die graphischen Künste*, vol. 22, 1899, pp. 47–56. Reprinted

Alois Riegl, Gesammelte Aufsätze, ed. Karl Maria Swoboda, Augsburg: Filser, 1929, pp. 28–39; pp. 97–110 of the present volume.

"Zur spätrömischen Porträtskulptur," *Strena Helbigiana sexagenario obtulerunt amici*, Leipzig: Teubner, 1900, pp. 250–256.

"Studien und Forschungen: Cornelius Gurlitt, Die deutsche Kunst des neunzehnten Jahrhunderts, Berlin 1899," *Mitteilungen der Gesellschaft für vervielfältigende Kunst Beilage der 'Graphischen Künste,'* vol. 23, no. 1, pp. 1–4.

Die spätrömische Kunstindustrie nach den Funden in Österreich–Ungarn im Zusammenhange mit der Gesamtentwicklung der Bildenden Künste bei den Mittelmeervölkern, Vienna: Österreichische Staatsdruckerei, 1901, vi, 222 pp., xxiii plates. Reprinted as *Spätrömische Kunstindustrie*, Vienna: Österreichische Staatsdruckeri, 1927, xviii, 420 pp. Darmstadt: Wissenschaftliche Buchgesellschaft, 1973, 1987, xix, 420 pp., xxiii plates. Facsimile of 1927 ed., with an afterword by Wolfgang Kemp, Berlin: Gebrüder Mann, 2000. Italian translation by Bruna Forlati Tamaro and Maria Teresa Ronga Leoni with an introduction by Sergio Bettini, *Industria artistica tardo-*

romana, *Contributi alla storia della Civiltà europea*, Florence: Sansoni, 1953, lxii, 419 pp., xxiii plates, reprinted Milan: Ghibli, 2013. English translation by Rolf Winkes, *Late Roman Art Industry*, Rome: Brettschneider, 1985. English translation by Christopher S. Wood of selection 1927 ed., pp. 389– 405, Christopher S. Wood ed., *The Vienna School Reader: Politics and Art Historical Method in the 1930's*, New York: Zone, 2000, pp. 87–103. French translation by Marielène Weber, Augustine Terence and Sophie Yersin Legrand, *L'industrie d'art romaine tardive*, Paris: Macula 2014, 470 pp.

"Lorenzo Bernini," *Wiener Abendpost*, "Wiener Zeitung Supplement," No. 283, Monday, December 9, 1901, pp. 7–8.

"Naturwerk und Kunstwerk I," *Beilage zur Allgemeinen Zeitung* (München), no. 13, Wednesday, January 16, 1901, pp. 1–5; pp 122–138 of the present volume.

"Naturwerk und Kunstwerk II." *Beilage zur Allgemeinen Zeitung* (München), no. 48, Wednesday, February 27, 1901, pp. 1–3. Reprinted together, *Alois Riegl, Gesammelte Aufsätze*, ed. Karl Maria Swoboda, Augsburg: Filser, 1929, pp. 51–64, 65–70; pp. 138–144 of the present volume.

"Bericht über die Wandmalereien in der Kirche zu Lorch," *Mitteilungen der K. K. Central-Commission für Erfor-schung und Erhaltung der Kunst- und Historischen Denkmale*, 3rd ser., vol. 1, no. 8–9, 1902, pp. 256–258.

"Funde aus der Völkerwanderungszeit in der Bukowina," *Mitteilungen der K. K. Central-Commission für Erforschung und Erhaltung der Kunst- und Historischen Denkmale*, 3rd ser., vol. 1, no. 12, pp. 407–408.

"Das holländische Gruppenporträt," *Jahrbuch der Kunsthistorischen Sammlungen des Allerhöchsten Kaiserhauses*, vol. 23, 1902, pp. 71–278. Reprinted in 2 vols., ed. Karl Maria Swoboda, Vienna: Staatsdruckerei, 1931, viii, 301 and viii pp., 88 plates. Vienna: Wiener Universitäts–Verlag, 1997, xx, 417 pp. Excerpts in English translation by Benjamin Binstock, "The Dutch Group Portrait," *October*, no. 74, 1995, pp. 3–35. English translation by Evelyn M. Kain and David Britt with an introduction by Wolfgang Kemp, *The Group Portraiture of Holland*, Los Angeles: Getty, 1999, 412 pp. French translation by Aurélie Duthoo and Etienne Jollet, *Le Portrait de Groupe hollandaise*, Paris: Hazan, 2008, 539 pp.

"Jakob van Ruysdael," *Die graphischen Künste*, vol. 25, 1902, pp. 11–20. Reprinted *Alois Riegl, Gesammelte Aufsätze*, ed. Karl Maria Swoboda, Augsburg: Filser, 1929, pp. 133–143; pp. 219–231 of the present volume. English transl. Christopher Heuer, "Jacob van Ruisdael," *Art in Translation*, vol. 4, no. 2, 2012, pp. 149–161.

"Bildende Kunst: Eine neue Kunstgeschichte," [Gurlitt, *Geschichte der Kunst*, Stuttgart: Bergsträsser, 1902, vol. 1–2.] *Wiener Abendpost*, "Wiener Zeitung Supplement," no. 15, Monday, January 20, 1902, pp. 7–8. Reprinted *Alois Riegl, Gesammelte Aufsätze*, ed. Karl Maria Swoboda, Augsburg: Filser, 1929, pp. 43–50; pp. 113–121 of the present volume.

"Objective Ästhetik," [Jean Richer, Introduction à l'étude de la figure humaine] *Neue Freie Presse*, No. 13608, Morning Edition, Sunday, July 13, 1902, "Literatur–Blatt," pp. 34–35. English transl. Karl Johns, *Journal of Art Historiography*, No. 11, December 2014, 6 pp.

"Das Riesentor zu St. Stephan," *Neue Freie Presse*, Morning Issue, No. 14338, Saturday, February 1, 1902, pp. 1–4 Reprinted Ernst Bacher ed., *Kunstwerk oder Denkmal? Alois Riegls Schriften zur Denkmalpflege*, "Studien zu Denkmalschutz und Denkmalpflege 15," Vienna: Böhlau, 1995, pp. 145–156.

"Römische durchbrochene Bronzebeschläge," *Mitteilungen der K. K. Central-Commission für Erforschung und Erhaltung der Kunst- und Historischen Denkmale*, 3rd ser., vol. 1, no. 10, 1902, pp. 310–311.

"Spätrömisch oder orientalisch?" *Beilage zur Allgemeinen Zeitung* (München), Wednesday, April 23, 1902, no. 93, pp. 153–156.

"Spätrömisch oder orientalisch? (Schluß.)" *Beilage zur Allgemeinen Zeitung* (München), no. 94, Thursday, April 24, 1902, no. 94, pp. 162–165 English translation of both by Peter Wortsman, "Late Roman or Oriental?" *German Essays on Art History*, ed. Gert Schiff, New York: Continuum, 1988, pp. 173–190. French translation of both by Marielène Weber and Augustine Terence, *L'industrie d'art romaine tardive*, Paris: Macula, 2014, pp. 429–443.

Der moderne Denkmalkultus Sein Wesen und seine Entstehung, Vienna: Braumüller, 1903, 65 pp. Reprinted *Alois Riegl, Gesammelte Aufsätze*, ed. Karl Maria Swoboda, Augsburg: Filser, 1929, pp. 144–193. Reprinted within the full text, Ernst Bacher ed., *Kunstwerk oder Denkmal? Alois Riegls Schriften zur Denkmalpflege*, "Studien zu Denkmalschutz und Denkmalpflege 15," Vienna: Böhlau, pp. 49–144. Italian translation by Renate Trost and Sandro Scarrrocchia, "Il culto moderno dei monumenti Il suo carattere e i suoi inizi di Alois Riegl 1903," *Chiesa, Città, Campagna Rapporto della Soprintendenza per i Beni Artistici e Storici per le Province di Bologna, Ferrara,*

Forlì e Ravenna, Bologna: Nuova Alfa, 1981, pp. 132–185. Reprinted, Bologna: *Nuova Alfa*, 1981, 1985, 1990, 76 pp. English translation by Kurt W. Forster and Diane Y. Ghirardo, "The Modern Cult of Monuments, its Character and its Origin," *Oppositions*, no. 25, New York, 1982, pp. 21–51. French translation by Daniel Wieczorek with an introduction by Françoise Choay, *Le culte moderne des monuments Son essence et sa genèse*, Paris: Seuil, 1984, 2013, 168 pp.; pp. 232–288 of the present volume.

Entwurf einer gesetzlichen Organisation der Denkmalpflege in Österreich, Vienna: Verlag der K K Zentral-Kommission für Erforschung und Erhaltung der Kunst- und Historischen Denkmale, 1903, v, 132 pp. Reprinted within the full text, Ernst Bacher ed., *Kunstwerk oder Denkmal? Alois Riegls Schriften zur Denkmalpflege*, "Studien zu Denkmalschutz und Denkmalpflege 15," Vienna: Böhlau, 1995, pp. 49–144.

"Oströmische Beiträge," *Kunstgeschichtliche Beiträge Franz Wickhoff gewidmet von einem Kreise von Freunden und Schülern*, Vienna: Schroll, 1903, pp. 1–11.

"Bericht über eine im Auftrag des Präsidiums der K. K. Zentral-Kommission zur Wahrung der Interessen der mittelalterlichen und neuzeitlichen Denkmale innerhalb des Diokletianischen Palastes in Spalato durchgeführte Untersuchung," *Mitteilungen der K. K. Zentral-Kommission für Erforschung und Erhaltung der Kunst- und historischen Denkmale*, 3rd ser., vol. 2, 1903, col. 333–341. Reprinted, Ernst Bacher ed. *Kunstwerk oder Denkmal? Alois Riegls Schriften zur Denkmalpflege*, "Studien zu Denkmalschutz und Denkmalpflege 15," Vienna: Böhlau, 1995, pp. 173–181.

"Die Krainburger Funde," *Jahrbuch der K. K. Central-Commission für Erforschung und Erhaltung der Kunst- und historischen Denkmale*, new ser., vol. 1, 1903, col. 217–250.

"Pferdeschmuck aus Westungarn," *Jahrbuch der K. K. Central-Commission für Erforschung und Erhaltung der Kunst- und historischen Denkmale*, new ser., vol. 1, 1903, pp. 273–288.

"Besprechungen neuer Erscheinungen: Carl Neumann, Rembrandt," *Mitteilungen der Gesellschaft für vervielfältigende Kunst Beilage der 'Graphischen Künste,'* vol. 26, 1903, pp. 51–53.

"Völkerwanderungszeitliche Funde aus Eppan," *Mitteilungen der K. K. Central-Commission für Erforschung und Erhaltung der Kunst- und Historischen Denkmale*, 3rd ser., vol. 2, no. 4, 1903, pp. 120–123.

"Zur Entstehung der altchristlichen Basilika," *Jahrbuch der K. K. Central-Commission für Erforschung und Erhaltung der Kunst- und Historischen Denkmale,* new ser., vol. 1, 1903, pp. 91–110. Reprinted Alois Riegl, *Gesammelte Aufsätze,* ed. Karl Maria Swoboda, Augsburg: Filser, 1929, pp. 93–110; pp. 169–191 of the present volume.

"Zur Frage der Restaurierung von Wandmalereien," *Mitteilungen der K. K. Central-Commission für Erforschung und Erhaltung der Kunst- und Historischen Denkmale,* 3rd ser., vol. 2, 1903, no. 1–2, pp. 14–31. Reprinted, Ernst Bacher ed. *Kunstwerk oder Denkmal? Alois Riegls Schriften zur Denkmalpflege,* "Studien zu Denkmalschutz und Denkmalpflege 15," Vienna: Böhlau, 1995, pp. 157–172.

"Die Entwicklungsgeschichte der Textilkunst," [Moriz Dreger, Künstlerische Entwicklung der Weberei und Stickerei] *Wiener Abendpost,* "Wiener Zeitung Supplement," No. 247, Thursday, October 27, 1904, pp. 7–8.

"Die Restaurierung der Wandmalereien in der Heiligkreuzkapelle des Domes auf dem Wawel zu Krakau," *Mitteilungen der K. K. Central-Commission für Erforschung und Erhaltung der Kunst- und Historischen Denkmale,* 3rd ser., vol. 2, 1904, pp. 72–92. Reprinted, Ernst Bacher ed. *Kunstwerk*

oder Denkmal? Alois Riegls Schriften zur Denkmalpflege, "Studien zu Denkmalschutz und Denkmalpflege 15," Vienna: Böhlau, 1995, pp. 183–200.

"Salzburgs Stellung in der Kunstgeschichte. Vortrag," *Mitteilungen der Gesellschaft für Salzburger Landeskunde,* vol, 45, no. 1, 1905, pp. 1–22. Reprinted as *Salzburgs Stellung in der Kunstgeschichte, Österreichische Kunstbücher,* vol. 18, Vienna: Hölzel, 1921, 26 pp., 10 plates. Reprinted *Alois Riegl, Gesammelte Aufsätze,* ed. Karl Maria Swoboda, Augsburg: Filser, 1929, pp. 111–132; pp. 192–218 of the present volume.

"Das Denkmalschutzgesetz," *Neue Freie Presse,* no. 14553, Monday, February 27, 1905, pp. 6–8. Reprinted, Ernst Bacher ed. *Kunstwerk oder Denkmal? Alois Riegls Schriften zur Denkmalpflege, Studien zu Denkmalschutz und Denkmalpflege 15,* Vienna: Böhlau, 1995, pp. 201–215.

"Hundert Jahre Hof- und Staatsdruckerei," *Wiener Zeitung,* no. 12, Sunday, January 15, 1905, pp. 3–6.

"Neue Strömungen in der Denkmalpflege," *Mitteilungen der K. K. Central-Commission für Erforschung und Erhaltung der Kunst- und Historischen Denkmale,* 3rd ser., vol. 34, no. 1, 1905, pp. 85–104. Reprinted, Ernst Bacher ed. *Kunstwerk oder Denkmal? Alois Riegls Schriften zur Denkmalpflege,* "Studien zu Denkmalschutz und Denkmalpflege 15," Vienna: Böhlau, 1995, pp. 217–233.

"Bernhard Salin, Die altgermanische Thierornamentik," *Göttingische Gelehrte Anzeigen*, vol. 167, no. 3, January 1, 1905, pp. 228–236.

"Otto von Falke and Heinrich Frauberger, Deutsche Schmelzarbeiten des Mittelalters, Frankfurt am Main 1904," *Kunst und Kunsthandwerk Monatszeitschrift*, vol. 8, no. 1, 1905, pp. 8–24.

"Zur kunstgeschichtlichen Stellung der Becher von Vafio," *Jahreshefte des Österreichischen archäologischen Instituts in Wien*, vol. 9, 1906, pp. 1–19. Reprinted *Alois Riegl, Gesammelte Aufsätze*, ed. Karl Maria Swoboda, Augsburg: Filser, 1929, pp. 71–90. English transl. Tawney Becker as "The Place of the Vapheio Cups in the History of Art (1900)," Christopher S. Wood ed., *The Vienna School Reader Politics and Art Historical Method in the 1930's*, New York: Zone, 2000, pp. 105–129; pp. 145–168 of the present volume.

"Über antike und moderne Kunstfreunde, Vortrag gehalten in der Gesellschaft der Wiener Kunstfreunde," *Mitteilungen der K. K. Central-Commission für Erforschung und Erhaltung der Kunst- und Historischen Denkmale*, Beiblatt 1, 1910, pp. 1–14. Reprinted *Alois Riegl, Gesammelte Aufsätze*, ed. Karl Maria Swoboda, Augsburg: Filser,

1929, pp. 194–206. English transl. Karl Johns, *Journal of Art Historiography*, no. 9, December 2013. 10 pp.; pp. 289–303 of the present volume.

Die Entstehung der Barockkunst in Rom, ed. Arthur Burda and Max Dvořák, Vienna: Schroll, 1908, viii, 214 pp., 2nd ed, 1923, viii, 200 pp. Reprinted Mittenwald: Mäander, 1977, viii, 214 pp. French translation by Sibylle Muller with a preface by Paul Philippot, *L'origine de l'art baroque à Rome*, "L'esprit et les formes," Paris: Klincksieck, 1993, 2005, 210 pp. English translation by Andrew Hopkins and Arnold Witte, *The Origins of Baroque Art in Rome*, Los Angeles: Getty, 2010, x, 279 pp.

Filippo Baldinuccis Vita des Gio Lorenzo Bernini, ed. *Arthur Burda and Oskar Pollak*, Vienna: Schroll, 1912, iv, 284 pp.

Kunstgewerbe des frühen Mittelalters, Die spätrömische Kunstindustrie, ed. Ernst Heinrich Zimmermann, Vienna: Österreichische Staatsdruckerei, 1923, 111, XLVIII pp.

Alois Riegl, Gesammelte Aufsätze, ed. Karl Maria Swoboda with an introduction by Hans Sedlmayr, Augsburg: Benno Filser, 1929, xxxix, 206 pp. Reviewed by Hans Jantzen, *Kritische Berichte zur kunstgeschichtlichen Literatur, Jahrgang III und IV, 1930–1931 und 1931–1932*, pp. 65–74.

Reprinted with an introduction by Wolfgang Kemp and a bibliography of Riegl's writings, pp. xxxv–xxxix, Berlin: Gebrüder Mann, 1995, XXXIX, 222 pp., and as "Klassische Texte der Wiener Schule der Kunstgeschichte, Abteilung 1, Alois Riegl, 5," Vienna: Wiener Universitätsverlag, 1996, XLIII, 196 pp.

Historische Grammatik der bildenden Künste, ed. Karl Maria Swoboda and Otto Pächt, Vienna: Böhlau, 1966, 317 pp. Reviewed by Carlo L. Ragghianti, "Ritorno del Riegl," *Critica d'arte*, no. 79, 1966, pp. 3–8. French translation by Éliane Kaufholz, preface by Otto Pächt, *Grammaire historique des arts plastiques: Volonté artistique et vision du monde*, Paris: Klincksieck, 1978, xxxiv, 210 pp. English translation by Jacqueline Jung, foreword by Benjamin Binstock, *Historical Grammar of the Visual Arts*, New York: Zone, 2004, 495 pp. Reviewed by Larry Silver, *Sixteenth Century Journal*, vol. 37, 2006, pp. 856–857, Isabelle Frank, *Journal of the Decorative Arts*, vol. 13, no. 2, 2006, pp. 126–128.

Max Dvořák, "Alois Riegl," *Mitteilungen der K. K. Central-Commission für Erforschung und Erhaltung der Kunst- und Historischen Denkmale*, vol. 4, 1905, pp. 155–276, reprinted in Dvořák, *Gesammelte Aufsätze zur Kunstgeschichte*, Munich: Piper, 1929, pp. 279–298.

Moriz Dreger, "Alois Riegl†," *Kunst und Kunsthandwerk Monatszeitschrift*, vol. 8, no. 7–8, 1905, pp. 396–404.

Gustav Glück, "Nekrologe: † Alois Riegl," *Mitteilungen der Gesellschaft für vervielfältigende Kunst Beilage der 'Graphischen Künste,'* 1906, no. 1, pp. 16–17.

Hans Tietze, "Alois Riegl," *Neue österreichische Biographie*, vol. 8, 1935, pp. 142–150. Selma Krasa-Florian, in *Österreichisches biographisches Lexikon 1815–1950*, vol. 9, no. 42, 1985, p. 152 listing other obituaries and appraisals.

Essays from 1898-1899

The History of Art and Universal History[39]

My personal physician belongs to that minority within his profession who is not exclusively consumed by his practice, but entertains an unflagging interest in the theoretical questions of natural science. Such purely scientific passions among physicians can at times be detrimental to their work in caring for patients. I hope that it might be excused with sympathy if I stress that I have had nothing but the best to report regarding his professional work. By contrast, he is less pleased with me – or at least was until recently. He was not happy with my profession. It struck him as the fruitless and dry attempt to describe the indescribable, nothing beyond a faded copy of something that originated in a surge of the greatest excitement and for this reason must also be appreciated in the same way. He could not understand that anybody might profit from a chronological and extrinsic list of artistic creations, and to enlighten himself on this point, he decided to enroll in an art historical seminar for one semester. This chanced to have Dutch painting as its subject. He did not miss a single one of the forty hours. In retrospect, he naturally considered many of them to have

39 Originally published as; "Kunstgeschichte und Universalgeschichte," *Festgabe zu Ehren Max Büdinger's von seinen Freunden und Schülern*, Innsbruck: Wagner, 1898, pp. 449-457, reprinted in: *Belvedere: Kunst und Kultur der Vergangenheit Zeitschrift für Sammler und Kunstfreunde*, vol. 7, no. 31, January 1925, pp. 1-6.

been wasted, but others aroused his greatest interest. It was remarkable to learn specifically which of the subjects he considered interesting and which not. There was a discussion of the private life of Rembrandt for instance, as it was already being obscured by malicious authors quite early on, and has polarized in our own day into conflicting views. The main master of Dutch painting has also aroused the personal interest of those who studied his artistic development to such a degree that it has been considered worthwhile to seek clarity among the contradictory information circulating about his biographical circumstances. It is even considered to be among the more "interesting" subjects since it involves bankruptcy and concubinage. For this reason, it is always considered a good subject even for the entertainment of sleepy listeners on humid summer afternoons. Its effect on my physician was the precise opposite: the entire discourse did not strike him as any more valuable than a simple anecdote, more apt for reading material while traveling than for three quarters of an hour delivered from the heights of an academic rostrum. It was a different matter when the great subjects arose such as the balance of light and shadow in painting, when the portraits of Rembrandt were compared to those of the Roman imperial period, when the pedantic preoccupation with sources receded into the background and the horizon of observation expanded into immeasurable dimensions with the most remote conceivable subjects introduced for comparison. It was then that he was most interested and frustrated by the sound of the bell announcing the end of these fascinating questions, and that the history of art appeared to him in a more favorable light.

Of course, my personal physician is a layman in questions of the visual arts, and his opinion is generally not of great interest. I do however consider it worth recounting since it is typical of the most recent developments. Consider: this is a student of natural science, one who is reflective, dissatisfied with the cautious inductive method deriving its name from his own native discipline, examining the individual phenomenon, and making the following step toward the connection of cause and effect only with the greatest care. A natural scientist who seeks to connect the most remote entities does not regard the overwhelming gulfs in between, and nonetheless hopes to establish the truth! When the daily activities of natural scientists permit such lines of thought to arise – how much more obvious would this be in other fields such as the history of art, which face the imagination as something not completely alien! What my physician believes about the history of art is an opinion not merely shared by most laymen, in fact it is also that of most art historians.

As a discipline, the history of art is less than a century old, and has already undergone two fundamental changes. Those who founded it, such as J. B. G. S. d'Agincourt, Carl Rumohr and many others, conceived of the entire field of the arts as one broad unity. They were not specialists, either in the sources or in practical connoisseurship. Every form taken by the visual arts was considered of equal value and interest, and in fact, they surveyed the entire motley world from the pyramids to the Nazarene brotherhood, and viewed them all as part of a single coherent development. This caused them to recognize the common qualities, without overlooking the marked differences that separate the arts of individual nations and periods. Those pioneers who deserve to be better remembered than they were about the middle of the [19th] century discerned the great stylistic periods which provide the basis for any of our present day surveys of the visual arts. The history of art could not remain at this state of over-generalization if it desired to become an objective academic disciple. Those early "art experts" were familiar with an enormous number of monuments. This overwhelming quantity itself did not allow them to progress beyond a more superficial knowledge of the details. They also immediately recognized the value of the written and reprinted sources, and began to study them assiduously. Since they had neither the time, opportunity, or critical schooling, in most cases they accepted the traditions uncritically. Two things became necessary. The first was a closer study of individual monuments or in any case of groups of related monuments, and the second a critical study of the sources. A group of scholars from Franz Theodor Kugler and Karl Schnaase to Moriz Thausing and Wilhelm Bode found their way to dealing with these questions, and effectuated the first great shift in art historical research. Specialized studies replaced the earlier general surveys, and professional historians replaced the dilettantes. Since that time, it has been considered the greatest conceivable triumph for the history of art to associate the name of an artist with an individual painting, or to discover the date when a particular monument was made, and the joy was exalted if a mistake could be corrected among the early biographies. The monograph was considered the most dignified and successful form of study. The more general surveys were relegated to the authors of handbooks, and these were even viewed condescendingly when they advertised the findings of their own colleagues among the specialists. It was therefore only natural for the philological and historical method to gain in prestige.

While at the beginning of this second period, these disciples of art historical research naturally harbored a certain emotional interest in the visual arts, the increasing significance of source work then brought characters into these circles who had little or no knowledge whatsoever of the monuments themselves. The achievements of this sort of study should not be underestimated, and least of all is it incumbent upon the artists of the last decade to make fun of the "learned art historian," as this frequently occurred. While this was so, they themselves were ignorant of history and often delighted to learn of some information worthy of imitation about earlier manners, practices or the like from an art historian. Such art historians who lacked connoisseurship revealed an internal contradiction, and the signs became obvious that another shift was soon to occur in the discipline for the simple reason that it had become necessary.

Today we can see this second change in full swing. It is tending in the direction in which the history of art had operated in its earliest days. The inclination of the last thirty to forty years toward specialization seems again to be yielding to a more universal history. Scholars of the previous generation conceived every art historical phenomenon as individual, as caused by unique circumstances, and effecting consequences peculiar to itself. They endeavored solely to learn as much as possible about a given individual phenomenon and to discover its sources and influences for the limited purpose of placing it within the chronological chain of monuments. The most "modern" of the art historians now declare themselves to no longer be satisfied with such a chronological determination of a monument within a given sequence of development. They claim that the identification of immediate sources and influences cannot adequately explain the essential character of an individual monument or the conditions of its creation. They point out that artistic phenomena are not merely divided by individual characteristics, but also united by common ones. If the representatives of the philological-historical method overemphasized the significance of the distinguishing characteristics, the moderns believe they should call attention to the unifying and generalizing qualities. This has led them to point out the surprising similarities, which can be seen between the portrait paintings of the second century AD and those of the 17th century. There can be no doubt that the circumstances in which the Roman imperial painters worked were completely different from those surrounding Frans Hals and Velázquez. Since both of these phenomena are human creations, we are gradually led to the irrefutably powerful conclusion that the Roman, the Dutchman and the Spaniard were in both in their individual epochs following the same higher rules. Such a rule must have expressed itself in the direct causes of both phenomena, but this expression could only be recognized as veiled and sullied by the coincidental circumstances. To understand this in its purity, it is necessary to put aside the random additions of either, while the goal can only be reached by comparing the immediate sources of both. This can justify a comparison between two artistic periods as remote from one another as the 2nd and the 17th centuries. Indeed, such a universal historical mode of viewing might be viewed as the actual climax of art historical research.

Nobody will overlook the fact that the warrant to recognize such uppermost and invisible rules is only then given when it becomes possible to establish the immediate causes with complete certainty.

The more certain the results of specialized research, so much more unmistakable will be the results of universal historical reflection. It would be completely misguided to ask which of the two methods has greater merit. Both are necessary and rely on one another. It is desirable that they progress in tandem. This would be the ideal relationship, but it probably cannot be achieved. Just as the crest of a wave is followed by its depth, so did the present one-sided interest in universal history naturally follow the overemphasis on the specialized study of yesterday. For decades now, the specialist researchers have accumulated mountains of material, and this has inevitably inspired a move beyond the narrowness of individual phenomena and into the liberating height of a comprehensive overview. The original reason to concentrate on such detail had been to create a secure foundation for a more elevated standpoint. The earliest protagonists of the second generation, including Schnaase and even Anton Springer, never allowed their vision across the great distance to be sacrificed. For this reason, their narratives of the history of art most closely approach the ideal postulates. Eventually, the goal was lost sight of by an overemphasis on the means. Specialized research became an end in itself, and the individual monument was viewed as a worthy and satisfying subject for attention. In this, the study of the history of art reflects the history of painting. Painting also had its periods which we denote as naturalist, and those when any object from the world around us was considered worthy of inclusion and of being presented in art for contemplation and approval. With a mathematical regularity, such periods have been replaced by those described as idealist, where the decisive characteristics of art in relation to nature are described according to our individual sensibilities as stylization, beautification, or arrangement of nature – all resulting from technique, materials or individual imagination of the artist, and centering on the work of art as definitive. Painting was always as one-sided as were the art historians. Either they would be pursuing the unique goal of reproducing natural appearances of objects with no attention to any other factor, or they expected the entire effect to emerge from the aspects of stylization, and did not consider for a moment to alter nature in those instances where it did not of its own accord conform to the stylistic intentions of the artist.

Between the crest and the depth of the wave, there is a dead point in which the extremes meet. If the creative impulses propelling research are fresh, then it will get beyond this point quickly. This point nevertheless exists, and there will always be those who feel the necessity to stop there. That is what has occurred this time, and we could mention names. In the art historical literature, they are the ones who play the role equivalent to the skeptics in philosophy or the anarchists in social politics. Since the previous path strikes them as having been wrong, they despair that the terrain could ever be traversed. We have travailed for forty years to demonstrate an uninterrupted chain of development naturally leading from the simple and the primitive to the complicated and the perfect. Now we begin to recognize phenomena seeming to contradict all of our images of development. For instance, how could the same nation which in the Roman imperial period was able to reproduce the individual human face as a totally naturalistic illusion just a few centuries later be content with the stiff puppets of Byzantine art? Other closer parallels can be found in Italian and Dutch painting.

The skeptics among the art historians conclude very simply that there is no progress in the development of human art. This conception would appear to be no more than a transitional phenomenon comparable to skepticism and anarchy. After a short moment of reflection, these scholars will also joyfully resume their Sisyphean task in hoping the universal historical vision of the history of art will aid in resolving the great puzzle of the world of art. Such resolution, after all, is the goal of all the human disciplines.

Furniture and Interior Decoration of the Empire Period[40]

In none of the earlier styles are interior decoration and furniture related as closely and intimately, with the latter so decisively influenced by the former. Taken in the broadest sense, interior decoration presents itself as a totality in this period, with the furniture forming an essential and dependent part. This provides us with the sequence in which they must be treated: interior decoration as the general aspect and furniture as the particular.

We must say something in advance. By comparison to the others, this chapter is not as easily limited to the materials included in the exhibition, presenting "The Congress of Vienna," with its best examples present in this publication. The reason for this lay in the insuperable difficulties facing the committee who were commissioned with organizing the Congress of Vienna exhibition from the very beginning. During the period of the Congress of Vienna, interior decoration and furniture design were indisputably dominated by French art. To fulfill the ideal goals of the exhibition, it would have been necessary to reconstruct a sumptuous interior space from France in the galleries of the K. K. Österreichisches Museum [Museum für

40 Originally published as: "Möbel und Innendekoration des Empire," in Eduard Leisching ed., *Der Wiener Kongreß: Culturgeschichte Die bildenden Künste und das Kunstgewerbe, Theater, Musik in der Zeit von 1800 bis 1825,* Vienna: Artaria, 1898, pp. 185-206.

angewandte Kunst]. Since French participation was obviously not possible, and since the transportation and installation of such a space in the K. K. Österreichisches Museum would have provided obstacles, this undeniable omission has its practical reason, and might serve to attract attention to the successes of this exhibition as they stand in spite of this.

The same reasons must be given for the possible impression that the selection of furniture might appear incomplete. A clear example of the unique design of beds of the Empire period is lacking from the outset. The organizers of the exhibition have made an effort in this regard, and were able to borrow some examples of Empire bed designs. It is also obvious that typical examples of the cloth that gave the typical French Empire bed its character have only survived in very small numbers and could also not be included. The bed of Marshal Berthier, which we are able to reproduce with a woodcut, at least conveys the essentials.

Our illustrations give an idea of the development of French Empire furniture design outside of France, particularly in Austria and southern Germany, while typical and precious French examples are by no means absent. From derivations and secondary sources, it is impossible to give an account of the specific character of interior decoration and of Empire furniture, but this must come from the original source, and that is French applied art. For this reason, the following remarks will be devoted primarily to the French Empire style. We will in the second place consider its adaptations particularly in Germany and England. As we shall see, these changes occurred under the influence of other non-classical styles: in Germany this was primarily under the influence of the baroque style, in England under that of the Gothic.

The classicist element is generally believed to constitute the actual character of the Empire style. In fact it is true, if we examine the ornamental details in the fillings and moldings, on the supports and the main body of the furniture, we see motifs from classical and specifically Roman antiquity everywhere. Even the forms of the furniture themselves are many of them faithfully reproduced from those of antiquity. In discerning the main governing principle of interior design in the Empire style, it also seems at first glance to be no less derived from classical antiquity. In examining things more closely, certain details are striking which the French of the Napoleonic period could not possibly have derived from ancient examples, because those sources did not include them. In considering how previous periods conceived the rule of interior design, we are forced to conclude that the most intimate principles of interior decoration of the Empire style were not essentially taken over from another style, but actually constitute the logical end result of a development which had been progressing for centuries already and chose ancient classical forms for no other reason than that they fulfilled its goals most suitably and efficaciously. What is the main guiding principle of interior design in the Empire style?

To understand this with complete clarity it seems necessary to take a few steps backward into past phases of the development. It is sufficient to return to the medieval Gothic, a period in which the cultural development of our country is easily discernible. Material and practical needs were satisfied during the medieval period with the relatively copious inclusion of spiritual and artistic considerations. The latter are only then sacrificed in cases where a conflict arises between the practical necessities and the artistic rules. This is the relationship governing all exterior and interior decoration throughout the entire medieval period. It explains the fact that on the exterior of many medieval structures, the windows are often arranged asymmetrically or that a richly ornate alcove might suddenly protrude at an unexpected spot from a wall with no relation to the remainder of the building. This does not mean that medieval architects lacked a sense of symmetry as fundamental principle of their art: symmetry was used when and where it did not conflict with a practical requirement. Wherever practical functions made themselves felt, symmetry was immediately sacrificed as the lesser of the two. The interior decorations of these houses were not treated any differently than their facades. The largest bed was placed in the most comfortable spot, the oven where it would best heat the space and the closet where it was most convenient. Each of these articles of furniture presented a sort of architectonic object unto itself; none was related to that beside or facing it, and no aesthetic principle determined the whole.

A change gradually arose in this relationship. It began in late medieval Italy, grew increasingly stronger during the renaissance, and we find it complete in the baroque style. Individual architectural sections are no longer randomly added to one another, but instead the whole is designed from a unified plan. It became preferable to tear down an entire structure rather than place a smaller one un-harmonically beside it. Facades begin to be divided into central sections and wings, violations of symmetry become fundamentally inconceivable, and reductions in the comforts of quotidian life more acceptable than the violation of an artistic rule on the outwardly visible portion of architecture. This decisive change in subjecting the material function to artistic rules occurred only in terms of outward architectural decoration. During the heyday of the baroque style, interior decoration continued essentially in the traditional manner, placing individual pieces of furniture into individual rooms. Spaces are lined with paneling or tapestries, with cabinets and such things protruding much as the medieval alcove sprang out of an exterior wall. Artistically speaking, these baroque interior spaces were essentially pictorial and not architectonic.

It was left to the Empire style to complete this final change. The dominance of a fundamental harmonic artistic rule as the baroque had introduced it to the architectural exterior became the governing basic principle for interior decoration.

This fundamental harmonic rule of interior decoration in the Empire style expressed itself primarily in the creation of a dominant center in relation to two equivalent wings: in other words strict symmetry. Of course this could not be realized in each and every case. Particularly where older spaces were involved or certain practical considerations were simply unavoidable, the postulate of absolutely symmetrical unity could not be maintained without compromise. Where it could be done, especially in structures being built completely freshly, this principle was applied as thoroughly as possible. Unavoidable large pieces of furniture were placed centrally in one of the sides so as to reduce its projection over the wall space as far as possible. A large bed might have been moved to the center of one of the narrow walls with cloth at the head and foot to separate it from the remainder of the room, making it seem to stand in a niche. The mantle piece became a favorite element of interior decoration – it could after all be built into the wall and with its entire framing would protrude only slightly. In places such as Germany, where wood burning stoves were in use instead, these were placed in a separate semicircular niche at the center of the wall or in the worst instance placed in a corner, where its effect of breaking up the wall would be minimized.

While material needs had been the essential factor in the naïve medieval cultural period, it was subordinated to the dictatorship of aesthetic rules in the Empire style. Subordination was not even the end of it. There was a trend to completely suppress any evidence of the material functions, which after all provide the very purpose of interior furniture. It is as if the spectator were to be reminded of material needs such as the creation of living spaces and furniture as little as possible. The society of the Empire appeared to itself almost like a race of gods with no other requirements than to pursue beauty. Everything meeting the eye is intended to awaken an agreeable sensation in the spirit, while anything recalling a practical function and the attendant needs is banished or at the very least masked or camouflaged. In some cases even the doors by which one entered were felt to require draperies to cover them. This led to the disappearance of the monstrous armoires of the renaissance and baroque period from the stylistically pure examples of Empire palaces. There was no diminution in the size or function of the wardrobe, and a safe place for the storage of the clothing continued as a requirement; it came to be hidden in opened areas within the walls or in those separated spaces to either side of the bed, carefully concealed from the viewer with curtains. As they had been traditionally used to ostentatiously display the tableware belonging to the woman of the house, large pantries or credenzas would also have been felt to be annoying. Crockery was generally seen as inappropriate for decoration, and that necessary for use was stored in graceful small sideboards frequently with outlandish forms shrewdly concealing their function. The sideboard might also find its place in a niche within a wall facing a stove or fireplace. It only serves to further underscore the pervasiveness of this fundamental principle when all Empire furniture has the playful and dallying quality of display pieces all too often lacking any indication of the serious or practical function. Even swelling commodes and practical tables were replaced with coquette small cabinets with decorative pilasters, small console tables, stands with three legs and the like.

The center of attention for each interior are the walls because they define the space, completely creating it together with the ceiling. For this reason, the treatment of the walls plays the most decisive role in a style insisting on the absolute homogeneity in the overall impression. Two types of artistic treatment existed for walls in the Empire style, an architectonic and a textile type. They seem to follow two mutually exclusive principles, but as soon as we recognize the third principle they categorically exclude, it becomes clear how the two principles could be conceived from a single cohesive point of view.

The architectonic treatment of walls conceives of them as a series of supporting elements with a ceiling extending between them held by beams. The intervals between the supporting elements are neutral fillers each comprising a unity unto itself but unambiguously revealing their subordination to the whole in their relationships and often also in the ornamental motif. Usually, a series of pilasters run along the wall with the beam above and the ceiling over that. The filling spaces between the pilasters are not covered with a wall paper-like unending pattern, but rather divided into numerous smaller fields corresponding to the proportions of the whole, usually including concentric decorations. They were usually done as paintings, guided stucco or carved. There is generally a frieze above the beam itself divided into proportional compartments no differently than the ceiling. Concentric decorations and the subordination of flanks to a center are everywhere predominant. Perspective narrative paintings, the "grandes machines" of the baroque seeming to hover in the sky autonomously above the space have all now disappeared. The unity is evoked not merely by proportions and emphasis on the amalgamating central points, but also by the content of the decoration. To the extent that they include figures, there is a distinct idea pervading its motifs. These are primarily allegorical allusions. Emblems related to the function of the space, the character of those living there and similar subjects. The living quarters of an artist or a military man would each appear very different. The latter was particularly common in the warlike period of Napoleonic imperialism. For this reason, the Parisian decorative artists created a specific "style militaire" they were able to apply to every detail of an interior and its furniture.

This architectonic treatment of walls obviously had its model in classical antiquity. It was only taken up however because it seemed to correspond most completely to the fundamental principle of interior decoration that emerged in the Empire period. We can therefore believe Charles Percier and P. F. L. Fontaine, the editors of the *Recueil des decorations intérieures* when they assure their readers that they did not adhere to antiquity because it happened to be in style, but because this ancient form of decoration corresponded best to nature, meaning reason. For the aesthetic contemplation of the eye, it struck them as rational to have the ceiling carried by wall piers with the filler spaces strictly measured and distributed. We can see how independent their thinking was from the fact that there are nearly no playful Pompeian decorations that must have seemed like an obvious possibility.

Architectonic treatment of pilasters and filler spaces seems to have been the most noble and costly way of decorating a wall. A textile décor satisfied patrons with fewer pretensions. Its basic idea was clearly that the ceiling was here also supported by piers and the like, but this architecture of the wall is covered by curtains attached to the beams and reaching the floor. The entire surface of the wall is dressed with cloth hangings, but as folded draperies rather than wall paper either taut or pasted on. The oil paintings hung on the walls or suspended with bands from the ceiling beam form a contrast to these draperies of a single color or including a border hem at most. It was simpler and less expensive still to paint the draperies on the wall or do without them entirely and have the whitewashed wall seem like a spanned curtain without pleats. As far as this might have led from the strictest conception of interior decoration in the Empire style, there was one principle always being observed, and this was an avoidance of any patterns with an unending motif, the use of a single color and the wall either whitewashed or spanned with cloth.

This touches on a point that might be one of the most distinctive of the entire Empire style. It never found any justification for the unending pattern, the dense and even designs infinite and multipliable, cut out to fill any surface according to need, those we consider to be the oriental decorative principle. On this point, the art of the Empire style and the art of Islam can be seen as two opposing poles. This also explains the fact, certainly noticed by others as well, that the Empire style rejected oriental carpets, those carpets that were so highly valued in the medieval and renaissance periods throughout Europe and proven to have persisted by so many 17th and 18th century paintings. Indeed, these eastern carpets with their large and expressive stylized flowers and deep, saturated red and blue tones would have been at odds with the decoration of the Empire boudoir with its blurry overall tone of delicate, gauzy light gray. Instead, the French manufactories produced their light colored floor carpets with concentric patterns and antique details to excellently harmonize with decoration of the walls and ceilings.

Let us spend a moment on the decisive role of textiles in the interior decoration of the Empire style. Textiles could either be suspended as curtains or stretched tautly on a surface. We have just seen how draperies were used to decorate walls. An artistic effect was limited to the folds, even in the rare cases where the muslin or silk exceptionally included small, symbolic strewn patterns such as the Napoleonic bees and such things. Draperies of this kind were also widely used otherwise for the canopy of a bed, curtains at a window, occasionally even in front of doors or lambrequins over parts of furniture. It was considered to be an aesthetic necessity to drape festooned trimming, the so-called "Wolken" between the legs of a sofa or even chairs so as to conceal the yawning space from view. Draperies of this sort were also not infrequently suspended along the upper contours and over the back rests of the same furniture. In these cases, the festoon-like folds were considered aesthetically decisive. Decoration is usually limited to a narrow border strip or fray trim, the latter almost never absent from French furniture. Even in the filler spaces of chests behind protective glass panes, richly folded cloth is also not rare.

Drapery folds were partially inspired by ancient models with the layering often even imitating archaizing examples. In France, the symmetrical composition of folds was generally not taken too far. The light and airy material presumably seemed aesthetically not to tolerate too stiff a layering, so that the model books of French decorative artists of the Empire period instead suggest picturesque and animated draperies, particularly on the canopies of beds, but also even on curtains at windows.

Textiles were not used as extensively in the actual work of upholsterers where they occur drawn tautly over furniture. This is primarily with sofas and various types of chairs. The cloth used for this is usually smooth and without a pattern except for the strip along a border used in sofas to transversely distinguish the seating spots intended for two, three or more. Patterns were rare on the seat and rest surfaces, and then not composed from a larger scheme, that is a tapestry-like treatment from an unending pattern, but instead composed concentrically as we have seen in the filler spaces on the walls. Of course, such fabrics with precisely fitting patterns needed to be made to order so as to harmonize not only in color with the entire ornamentation of the interior they were intended for. This naturally increased the price substantially and explains why such patterned chairs are relatively rare. In Germany it was never done so fastidiously, and our examples include strip- and strewn patterns on covers.

As we have already noted, at least in the center of the filler spaces, decorations were required to evoke a more or less sophisticated intellectual association with the owner, the function of the space or some such topic. Framing elements could on the other hand be left completely decorative. At least among the French, the style not merely of the borders and corner fillers, but also the leitmotifs with figures, genius, personifications and the like was that from antiquity, particularly Roman antiquity. All of the model books by French decorative artists of the time, Percier and Fontaine, Beauvallet, Santi and the rest are filled with reproductions of ancient sculpture. Even as a half-figure or grotesque, the human form plays a leading role along with the plantlike acanthus. By contrast and quite distinctly, the geometric element is less important. As far as unclarity was being avoided, even the individual square, circular or polygonal segments of the walls are bordered by garlands, lines of fruit and the like rather than geometrical frames.

Only after recognizing how the Empire style eschewed the geometric element do we understand how it could occur that no other period spent so much time speaking about "nature" as that of the Empire style. They considered themselves happy to have curtailed the sphere of non-nature, to have rejected baroque gardens with trees trimmed architectonically and returned to the open nature of the English park. This was certainly true since nobody then was aware of how our sense of things today views the English park itself as bogus. We ask ourselves then how could a period so devoted to rhapsodizing nature adopt models for architecture and the applied arts that we consider to be so stylized? Does classical antiquity not strike us today as a style endorsing a pure and sincere idealism and the strongest possible contrast to the naturalist style?

The explanation can be none other than that the Empire period saw classical antiquity as nothing other than a vehicle of unadulterated nature. Architecture and the applied arts do not deal in imitation of natural objects in the way of sculpture and painting, but rather in using dead materials for human uses. Nature itself provided no examples for such things. What they called "nature" in this context was the raison d'être, the most rational composition of the objects. This was believed to be best found in the surviving monuments of antiquity, and not merely as the forms are concerned, but for ornament as well. We cannot hold it against the Empire artists for considering the acanthus tendril far more "natural" than a rococo curlicue, in spite of the fact that it also does not occur in nature.

One thing was unavoidable from this point onward and is important to note regarding subsequent developments down to our own time. Differences of opinion arose and with them the discussion about which sort of interior decoration and furniture can be considered rational and natural. This began the creation of a grammar of decorative art. If we read the remarks which the French decorative artists usually accompanied their publications, it is not difficult to recognize the predecessors to the handbooks of empirical aesthetics in our own time. When we read directives that furniture posts may only terminate in a head at the top and a foot at the bottom or that it is improper to embroider narrative scenes on the seats or rests of chairs

– something even the French did not consistently follow, it is almost as if we were reading principles expressed by Gottfried Semper or Jacob von Falke.[41]

Only in France did the details derived from antiquity rule absolutely. When even they occasionally used a Gothic pointed arch to frame a curtain for instance, it was only an isolated exception. The French were also alone in the pure and sincere application of the grand rules of Empire interior decoration as we have been describing them. This does not mean that they went furthest in consistently exploiting and interpreting these rules. The logical Germans did so while the French, as usual, maintained their innate Romanic sense of measure. French examples include draperies arranged the most picturesquely. Even in this period, the French did not in principle avoid large mirrors as the German purists did among decorative artists. Since they multiply the space optically, it is true that walls of mirrors often destroy the unified impression of a space to which the Empire style aspired. The apparent enlargement and multiplication of the spaces by artistic means is a more typical characteristic of the baroque style. Even under the rules of the Empire style, the French were able to reconcile a wall of mirrors with their approach to art, at the end of a narrow gallery flanked by columns so that the columns are multiplied to render a marvelous perspective vista.

Among the Germans and English, the conceptual changes in the

---

41 Gottfried Semper, *Der Stil in den technischen und tektonischen Künsten, oder praktische Ästhetik*, Frankfurt, Verlag für Kunst und Wissenschaft, 1860. Jakob von Falke, *Die Kunst im Hause: Geschichtliche und kritisch-ästhetische Studien über die Decoration und Ausstattung der Wohnung*, Vienna: Gerold, 1871.

Empire style bore less on interior decoration than the forms of details in furniture and are best discussed in that section further down. Pure and typical examples of French Empire interior decoration must have been very rare in Germany and Austria. The illustrations of such interiors in the present publication are valuable precisely for showing how the French rules of art were usually interpreted everywhere east of the Rhine. With the minimal exception of one spot above a door, the study of Emperor Francis of Austria excludes both drapery and painting from the wall and ceiling decoration. However the smooth un-patterned surface still reflects the Empire style no less clearly than the relatively narrow overhang of the wall cabinets, the "natural" and "rational" correctness of the furniture in general and the western quality of the carpets on the floor. Quite similar observations could be made of the study of King Friedrich Wilhelm III of Prussia in the Berlin city palace and that of Prince Metternich in the Ballhausplatz in Vienna.

In moving from the general toward the particular, we can consider the treatment of individual pieces of furniture in the Empire style. It is usually said that an essential characteristic of Neo-Classicism lay in returning furniture from the curving and swelling baroque and rococo forms to the straight contours and right angles. This is certainly true to some extent. Compared to the curved 18th century precedents, commodes in the Empire style have silhouettes like parallelograms with straight sides. If we on the other hand look at certain chairs from the Empire period, we might not find a single completely flat surface. This compellingly leads to the conclusion that the Empire style was not in principle devoted to straight lines and walls. If we note that it even avoids sharp corners with right angles to replace them with semicircular beveling, we soon conclude that the curve was the actual line of beauty for the Empire style as well. It was a curve always led in a soft and measured way with a particular predilection for cornice profiles while fundamentally banishing curlicues, capricious elements and a forceful succession of curves.

Another thoroughgoing characteristic at least of French Empire furniture has already been suitably discussed in connection with interior decoration. We refer to the conscious suppression and elimination of everything recalling functional needs and the compulsions of technical processes. Seams between the individual parts are carefully masked by decorative molding or ornament. After having been the pride of a piece of baroque furniture with pewter and etched ornament, the mounting of locks also now disappears and the lock itself is rendered invisible by ornamented bolts.

Empire furniture also assumes an original place in its relation to the materials. This distinguishes it fundamentally from baroque furniture. Since time immemorial, wood has been the natural material in making furniture. It accounted not merely for the frame and texture of the furniture, but also for its embellishment. The decoration of medieval, renaissance and even baroque furniture was carved and engraved. Painted décor was soon added to this and then later gilding, but even figure painting on furniture is no more than a colored covering like varnish on the wood. Intarsia is also an age-old decorative technique for furniture. Until the 17th century it was done predominantly in wood and even the Boulle technique of marquetry subordinated its metal, tortoise shell and mother of pearl inserts to the wood. David Roentgen, the great furniture maker working for King Louis XVI created the European reputation for Neuwied wood intarsia. Aside from Boulle furniture, when metal appeared on furniture along with the wood, it only occurred to fulfill functions that wood was not suitable to, such as making clasps, buckles, handles and the like.

By contrast to this, the Empire style distinguished the basic material from the decoration. Wood remained the basic material although occasionally such things as chairs were made of steel. Exceptions like that and others such as a silver table had already occurred in the baroque. In the Empire style however, the material for decorating furniture was fundamentally not wood. This was a development already prepared in the style of Louis XVI, but the Empire style was ultimately the applique style. Gilded bronze was the most common material. Porcelain inserts as used particularly in Sèvres for tables, or stone inlay as it became a specialty in Russia with its rich marble deposits, were by contrast still completely done on the basis of traditional intarsia. It was more important that the filled parts of the cabinets and other furniture are often completely absent and replaced by glass panes with folded cloth behind them. As we have already said though, the typical applique of Empire furniture was gilded bronze.

Such choices of taste only permitted the traditional middle class wood types such as nut wood and oak to appear bare for subordinate functions. Exotic veneer woods with delicate fibers and colors dominated the outward impression, such as mahogany with its reddish to black tones that would create a proper effect within the bright overall color of the interior. It was absolutely necessary for them to be shown smooth and shiny with polish. This was not done simply for the polished wood surfaces, much like the atlas silks in the realm of textiles, to combine most effectively with the golden sheen of the applique, but also because of another tendency which was the goal of purity. A polished or lacquered surface completely repels dust or any other uncleanliness that would stick to the pores of wood types left in their natural state or only treated.

Beside the French furniture of the Empire period, the English production has the greatest claim to independence. The frequent Gothic elements tend to be singled out as the most prominent characteristic of English Empire furniture. These Gothic features appear not merely as purely decorative additions applied to the body of the furniture, but to some degree they also condition its basic form. The small columns on commodes and cabinets are not used in the ancient sense of load carrying as the Empire style demands, but as primarily decorative motifs like the slender bundled columns of Gothic architecture decorated with rings. This is also the sense of the many cornice elements in English Empire furniture. Of course they are also not without elements alluding to antiquity that would go without saying in a country that produced an artist such as John Flaxman. However, the fundamental character of English Empire furniture is not so much the artistic raison d'être as its practical use. English Empire furniture is less striking by its style than French examples, but has more variety and inventiveness fulfilling the demands of comfort and practical use. We find chairs and tables with paws at the end of the legs, regularly with small wheels attached to allow them to be pushed and moved more easily while a small wheel beneath an animal paw would definitely have violated the French taste.

Ornamental detail of the English Empire furniture is striking for including far less plant motifs which alongside the figural element, had played a main role in French interior decoration. Acanthus leaves also occur in English examples but comparatively rarely and nearly always applied on a small scale and not developed independently. On the other hand, the geometric factor is more prominent in England than any other artistically productive country of the time, possibly due to the persistent inclination toward Gothic constructions. Surfaces often include fluting and parallel lines generally recalling the perpendicular style. There are also characteristic breaks particularly with seat rests in geometric mullions, zigzag, circle motifs and the like. There are as few curves in the English as there are in the French furniture of the time, but they are not as finely made, the volutes for example usually rolled in an oval instead of a pure circular form.

In spite of this, it is impossible to overlook many relations between the English interiors and the fundamental French stylistic rules of the time. It expresses itself in the greatest possible variety in phenomena such as the abundant use of draperies only slightly baggier and heavier than the French or the goal of unifying the interiors by evoking a single idea in the decorations all geared to one and the same side. England also had its own military style with the difference that its symbols were not Roman imperial, but naval in character, including Nelson chairs with anchors and towlines, dolphins, tridents and the like.

To characterize the German attitude to the Empire style, nothing is more apt than to compare its relation at that time to the Gothic style, as we have just seen among the English. In England there was no shying away whatsoever from combining Gothic constructive elements with decorative motifs from antiquity. From the outset, the Germans sought to keep the two as separate as possible. It is usually felt that the Germans did not imitate the Gothic style until approximately the 1820's in connection with the romantic cultural movement. This opinion seems completely mistaken if we look into Friedrich August Leo ed., *Magazin für Freunde des guten Geschmackes*, and find among other things the illustration of a Gothic cabinet published already in 1799 explicitly to serve as a model for the needs of the time. The editor naturally suggests expressly that cabinets like this should be used in rooms with less decoration, particularly in houses built longer ago. By contrast to this, he provides models for furniture exclusively in the ancient taste for opulent spaces designed more recently. What is most remarkable is the circumstance that the stylistic character of each, the Gothic cabinet as well as the furniture in the ancient taste, is kept as pure and unadulterated as possible. While the English mix the Gothic with antiquity, the logical and consistent Germans desire the two styles done only with historical felicity. We can understand how the series of "historical styles" in the 19th century expressed itself most bluntly and consistently in the German speaking areas.

English Gothic of the Empire was incidentally not without influence in Germany. Even the baroque style in the decorative variant of southern Germany was still such a strong influence at the beginning of the 19th century, particularly in the remoter provinces, that the unique rococo trend was able to succeed it in the 1830's and 40's. The internal ferment of German artistic life of the Empire period expresses itself in the furniture we have from that time, a number of very instructive examples of which were on display in the exhibition commemorating the Congress of Vienna.

Mood as the Subject of Modern Art[42]

I have sat down at an isolated mountain top in the Alps. Directly at my feet, the earth sinks so steeply away that there is not a single object that I might grasp. I am left to my visual sense alone, and this is a source for a great variety of many things. Hillocks are covered with grass and colorfully sprinkled with flowers of the season, which will be gone by the next. A dark pine forest with its countless rising points borders the meadows below. There is a soft breathlike gleam above it all since it is early summer and the young plants are continually breaking forth and multiplying the mass of the forest. Cows are grazing at the edge of the forest. As I know, they do not stand still for a moment, but for now they appear to me simply as white spots recording their existence. If I raise my eyes to the facing wall of rock, I first of all see the waterfall as it flickers over the high walls and thunders loudly to drown out all other sounds. This is the setting as I saw it and heard it at close range a few moments ago, but now it appears as no more than a bright silver band through the dark foliage. If I lower my eyes all of the way down into the green valley floor, then I see a small house with glimmering white walls and a small cloud of smoke hovering beside it as evidence of the industriousness of the people living within.

I am seized with a feeling of satisfaction, contentedness and

42 Originally published as: "Die Stimmung als Inhalt der modernen Kunst," *Die graphischen Künste*, vol. 22, 1899, pp. 47-56.

harmony when I reflect on all of this ubiquitous evidence of restless life, boundless power and endless movement, thousand-fold growth and decline all covered with a coherent sense of peace without the slightest dissonance. It is as if I have been liberated of a certain pressure and have finally gratified a sustained longing. What is this pressure casting such a dark shadow on our intellectual activity, and why does it yield to the sunny effect we gain from a gaze into the endless universe, or even into such a small portion of it, as it can be perceived through the imperfect human sense in a single moment?

The pressure arises from our learning, that ripe fruit from the tree of knowledge. We now know that laws of causality govern all of creation. Any form of growth causes something else to be displaced. All new life causes death in other quarters, just as all movement causes some sort of reaction. It is an ultimate and endless battle which brings much more anguish in humanity with its gifts of reason and feeling, than it does in the minute creatures that each human being kills by the hundreds with each of his motions. For thousands of years, the work of all culture involved the natural but brutal right of the strong in making way for a liberating world order. Now at the end of these long and arduous labors, our fate is inescapable and unavoidable. Instead of quiet, peace and harmony, there is endless war, destruction, and discord as far as life and movement reach.

What the soul of modern man longs for, either consciously or not, is fulfilled for the individual when standing alone on the peak of a mountain. He is not surrounded by the peace of the churchyard, but rather by the thousand signs of emerging life. What appears at close range to be an unrelenting battle, can seem at a distance to be a peaceful coexistence, characterized by concord and harmony. This allows us to feel liberated from the anxious pressure that never leaves us. We sense that far beyond the conflicts witnessed by our corruptible senses, there is something incomprehensible, a world soul, transfusing all things and unifying them into a complete harmony. This sense of order and regularity above the chaos, of harmony beyond the dissonances, of peace beyond the bustle, is what we describe as mood or atmosphere. It consists of quiet and a view into the distance.

My reverent gaze was interrupted by a sound. Close to me, a goat sprang up and shot away across the next hillside with vigorous jumps. With a jolt, my attention was torn away from the peaceful landscape toward the goat. My right hand jerked instinctively as if to reach for a hunting rifle. This was our predatory heritage erupting with the impulse to draw the weaker creature into the realm of my sense of touch. My hiking stick is my only weapon at hand and turns out not to be sufficient to the task. With an avid delight, my eyes follow the movements of the animal until it disappears behind the corner of a rock. And now? The beautiful atmosphere is gone, chased away, dissipated. This mood is such a subtle matter that the slightest stirring of nearby life can annihilate it. A single call of a bird in the air can have the same effect. A strong burst of wind can do the same if it causes me to feel cold and close my coat, or a strong ray of sun that suddenly hits my neck. These are not organic life, but also movements themselves eliciting further movements. Movement and a view at close quarters (Nahsicht) have reminded me of the struggle for survival.

Modern man does not find this redeeming mood exclusively on the Alpine mountaintops, which we enjoy visiting in such stark contrast to our ancestors in the ancient and medieval periods, who themselves fought battles in those valleys. When quiet converges with a vista into distance, this mood can also be reached at the lowest levels of dry earth, along the edge of the sea. This is most likely to occur in a quiet bay with the wavelets lapping at the pebbles, a boat resting half on the dry land, and the sun reflecting a thousand-fold flickering life on the surface of the water through the branches of the trees on the shore. The mood can even emerge on the open seashore when we are able to cast our eyes beyond the mighty repetition of the approaching and powerlessly receding breakers. It is the perfect image of worldly bustle seen at close range and into the distant surface, transfigured by the bright sunshine with a colorful streak lining the horizon, a billow of smoke above to betray the presence of a steamer beyond, and the fact that amid this desert of elements, human activity does not stand still.

There is no element of creation which can be completely excluded from the mood or atmosphere. We are not at all dealing here with the motif, since even the greatest enemy of the mood, human beings can themselves convey it. The only necessary elements are quiet and a view into the distance.

What nature can only occasionally reveal, art is called upon to perform at our behest. As soon as the arts progress beyond utilitarian and decorative functions, what we call the "higher" arts have never had another purpose than to convey the comforting sense of a certainty of order and harmony to us in our existence. In the narrow grind of our daily lives, we always miss it, and life would seem unbearable without it. In earlier times, humanity sought harmony elsewhere than today, and for that reason the goals of art were not in those days devoted to evoking mood. Such things shift along with the worldview of humanity or those aspects determining culture, and this has occurred three times in history. Allow us to briefly attempt to relate this process back to the human need for harmony.

The earliest and most primitive stage is the battle of each individual against all others. Humanity relied on nothing other than its own physical strength. Yet they realized that there are inconceivable natural forces to possibly overwhelm us. This causes discomfort. In the fetish, they created a visible vehicle for those opposing powers and honored it. It provided a sense of security and harmony free of discomfort. The fetish stood at the beginning of religion and of all the higher arts.

The second stage was defined by the dominance of the strongest. It is no longer the struggle of each individual for survival against all others, but a number of weaker members have banded together with a stronger individual. That was then considered to be the natural order. This phase included all of antiquity. The reasoning ran as follows: the struggle is disharmonious, but ends at the moment in which the stronger individual emerges victorious. This is the reason why ancient art celebrates physical strength and all that is victorious and significant, reveals the vivid movement of life, and is physically beautiful. This is the reason that they are shown in human form, because nothing in organic life is stronger and more beautiful than the human form. The human image is therefore the main subject of ancient art. Since the anthropomorphic gods are strong and beautiful, they also confer victory on those human beings who are also strong and beautiful. The weaker individual participates in this victory in that they have allied themselves to the strong individual.

This naive faith in the gods remained fundamental to all of antiquity. The harmony it craves consists exclusively in physical superiority. Just as the physical body inescapably includes the spirit, so is physical strength and power accompanied by ethical strength and power. This provides a factor which gradually entered human culture and determined its further development. For the ancient Egyptians, ethical power still had no validity. Its art does not reveal a single trace of moral expression. We can see it arise among the pre-Alexandrian Greeks, yet their gods are depicted as indifferent, and the emotions included in their art do not go beyond the most basic expressions of joy and mourning. The intellectual and spiritual element played a far greater part in the art of the Hellenistic and Roman imperial periods. It is here that we can see instantaneous expressions of emotion such as in the Laocoon, but also idyllic subjects which might be seen as direct ancestors for our modern atmospheric art. To explain the latter it is important to recall that the beginning of the Roman imperial period was simultaneous with that of the birth of Christ. From the point of view of cultural history, the emergence of Christianity presents itself as nothing more than the feeling of anxiety in having recognized the inadequacy of the pagan gods. The desire for an ethical world order became increasingly urgent. It was no longer the physically dominant person who should guarantee the peaceful use of the fruits of labor and life, but instead those with intellectual and moral strength. This view of the world was much longed for by all, proclaimed by Jesus Christ, and necessarily opposed for a long period by the Roman state as a threat to its existence.

The triumph of Christianity introduced the third phase, the Christian-medieval period. Both physically and spiritually, the harmony of life amid the chaos of life and the final refuge from the hostile forces is still found in the faith in God. This protection is now afforded no longer by a host of physically strong gods, but instead by a single God with moral strength and no physical existence, but rather pure spirit. Christian art never tired of underscoring the spiritual nature of God and the moral qualities of the saints. In spite of the purely spiritual essence of God, not only the saints, but also the three persons of the Godhead, were depicted as organically natural beings, usually clothed in human form. There is an internal contradiction revealing the inseparability of body and spirit and the inadequacy of a Christian world view built exclusively on morality. Throughout the medieval period, the human form therefore remained the central subject of art, just as it had been in antiquity. Since the goal is no longer the depiction of physical beauty but rather spiritual perfection, that part of the human body was now treated preponderantly which revealed the inner spiritual life most clearly – the human face. Each of the three world views which we have just outlined established a harmony by a quasi-personal intervention of an infallible higher power based exclusively on a faith in God. That of Christianity is doubtlessly the most complete and satisfying to humanity since it guarantees the protection of moral man by a moral power. As long as I have the solid faith that as a just person, God will protect me from a lightning strike, then the Christian view of the world will provide me with the most perfect harmony. This will change as soon as I install a lightning rod on my house. From that point onward, I am trusting more in my own knowledge, which allows me to expect the same protection from this particular device and not from my faith, which would make such an installation appear unnecessary. In worldly and material matters at least, faith alone can no longer offer the complete harmony. With the laws of nature, the Christian view of the world seems to have been abandoned and surpassed in those particular aspects decisively important for the visual arts. From this point onward, we can only hope for harmony through knowledge.

This is the inception of the fourth stage, which might most aptly be described as the world view of the natural sciences. By analogy to the polytheistic and the monotheistic views, it might also be called that of pantheism, but it would be mistaken to consider it at odds with the previous phase, since at the present time, most educated Europeans in fact combine both. The natural scientific view of the world seems to be based on an emancipation of knowledge from faith but not on an elimination of faith. Today it is widely recognized that there is no knowledge to explain the ultimate causes of being, and our need for harmony forces us to accept the explanations of ultimate questions from the revealed faith. Excepting a few deeply religious souls, we expect clarification to come exclusively through our knowledge in the matters of causal relations in nature. The knowledge we gain in this way can often be agonizing. We are frequently confronted with the thought that nations living under strict religions might have generally been more content than we are, and it is no coincidence that pessimism is a phenomenon peculiar to our modern intellectual life. Yet the same knowledge also brings us harmony in providing the purview over an entire chain of similar phenomena, and liberating us from the complications of conflicting details. The more phenomena we are able to survey in a single glance, the more certain, liberated and uplifted we feel in our conviction of their order and overall harmonious balance. Modern art, the art of mood or atmosphere, is essentially based on the harmony which is both provoked and presented by our knowledge.

Our modern knowledge no longer views natural phenomena in their individual isolation, an isolated expression of a personal God, as did the pagans of antiquity or the Christians of the medieval period. Instead, it sees them in a causal relationship with their closer and more distant environment. Modern art deals in the same way with those natural impressions which are beyond its scope, but which it recreates using its own means. This makes it clear that the modern need for mood or atmosphere can only be gratified and satisfied completely and directly by a type of painting based on purely optic perception, and made to be seen at a distance. That other type of "higher" art, the sculpture, as it dominated classical antiquity and challenged the sense of touch is immutably limited to viewing at close range. Today it is essentially practiced for historical and decorative purposes. What then are our uses for painting or two-dimensional imagery in the broadest sense? We do not expect beauty of proportions or linearity as they were prized in classical antiquity, nor the spiritual edification of the medieval Christian period. We expect a truth to life under all circumstances. The center of modern aesthetics in the visual arts and particularly painting lies in the strict observation of the laws of causality. We can accept the wildest things: red trees or green horses, so long as its reflected illumination seems well motivated. One thing not accepted from the artist is a bare miracle, which does not refer to poetry born of the imagination, but the negation of causal laws as we experience them, usually presented in all seriousness as occurring by "supernatural" personal forces.

In the final analysis, mood or atmosphere as the goal of all modern painting is identical with the soothing conviction of the universal nature of causality. Since the fundamental principle is overgrown and muddied by fortuitous details, this is difficult to demonstrate with concrete examples, and can only become apparent if an entire group of such individual phenomena are viewed at a distance. Before an individual painting, it is not so much clearly discerned as it is sensed and felt. For this reason, the illustrations accompanying the original publication of this essay were intended more as random samples from a pool of those available, than an exhaustive illustration of modern painting of mood. It might be more to the point to provide an assortment of individual observations as they frequently confront the spectator of modern painting. We must content ourselves with only a few examples.

The essence of mood is most directly apparent in the work of artists such as Max Liebermann or Carel Nicolaas Storm van 's-Gravezande, where a vignette from their surroundings is presented with all of the randomly perceived qualities of contour, movement, light and color. These coincidental details are necessities to the painter because they express the transfusion of all objects of nature and their unification in the laws of causality. The greatest difficulty for this is the depiction of changes of location. A human figure shown in the act of walking is an example that violates the laws of causality, which would demand an immediate continuation of the movement, as the medium of painting is unable to present it. Impressionist painters frequently resolved this by giving their figures repetitive contours suggesting motion rather than those of a more simple and firm character. Generally though, the goal of painting is not so much to represent movement as the potential for motion without its direct portrayal. It is obvious that this conception would lend itself wonderfully to the depiction of plants and inorganic nature such as rocks, water, clouds whose movements are not the result of free will, but rather of the laws of nature. This explains why landscape assumes such a prominent role in modern art.

Yet the modern artist does not allow the prerogative of the unfettered imagination to be taken from him. Neither the swimming mermaids by Böcklin nor the satyrs of Hans Thoma are being painted as a "slice of nature," but rather as children of fantasy to be understood as satisfying our taste for natural poetry. The artist is not attempting to make us believe in such biological hybrids, but if they were to exist, they would appear just in this way and no differently. They are also made to follow those natural causal laws that the ancestors of ancient pagan mythology, the ancient Egyptians, would have considered completely worthless. The same is finally true also of those works devoted to signs of human spiritual and intellectual life and the problems surrounding them. Our previous observations are decidedly confirmed by the fact that landscapes generally play an essential part in this. An example is the work of Max Klinger.

Is it true that this art of mood or atmosphere only arose in the modern period and particularly in our own time? Should its origins not reach at least as far back as the divergence of faith and knowledge? In fact, mood has been the ultimate goal of all modern art since the end of the Renaissance. Individual antecedents can even be found in the Hellenistic period – in a period when faith in the beauty and strength of the world of the gods was losing its grip, and the natural sciences first began to flourish. At that time, the categorical faith in the pagan gods was replaced by a no less categorical faith in the Christian God and the natural sciences went dormant for another millennium after having reached such a brilliant pitch in post-Alexandrian antiquity. Human intellectual life did not begin to preoccupy itself only with the study of nature again until the end of the medieval period when its divorce from faith could no longer be averted. It was a process developing unevenly but with constant reversions. It goes without saying that it transpired more quickly in Protestant areas where the Reformation immediately acknowledged the separation of faith from physical nature, and more slowly in Catholic countries, where the church still today officially denies the separation of faith from science. It is among the 17th century Dutch that we for the first time see an art of painting simultaneously and completely devoted to quiet and to the viewing point at a distance. Another quality of modern art also reveals itself. Humanity is no longer the center of art, but rather the entire breadth of nature with the artist moving at its center. Man is no longer the ruler as he had been in antiquity and even still in the medieval period, but only a link in an endless chain. As Christianity produced its first prerequisites, there was a leveling social effect typical and even definitive of our current culture. Directly beside the Dutch, a Catholic art also thrived concurrently in the work of Rubens. This was full of life and movement, but was decisively to be seen at a distance which neutralized and blurred the force of the motion, removing its un-harmonic character. Even if it was not officially admitted, the division of faith from knowledge was ultimately also factually complete in the Catholic countries by the second half of the 18th century. By this time then, there were no more obstacles to the art of mood in the Catholic territories. Humanity has always considered it uneconomical to seek out new solutions if an earlier one might suffice. This is clear from the renaissance which borrowed uncritically from antiquity, but also from antiquity itself which was equally unscrupulous in taking motifs from the earlier art of Asia Minor. Thus we can see a tangible need for mood or atmosphere in the repetitive cycle of previous and now historical styles since pre-Alexandrian antiquity. It did not occur as an end in itself or due to a blind helplessness, but with the relatively conscious intention of making extractions from the treasury of artistic monuments of previous centuries. This is the point of view from which it will someday become necessary to write the history of 19th century European art. It is far from coincidental that of all of antiquity, the art of Attica with its Olympian quietude was chosen instead of the Laocoon for instance, which Gianlorenzo Bernini still praised as the greatest surviving work of art. It is also hardly coincidental that the Venetian painting of solid conditions (venezianische Existenzmalerei) has appeared more sympathetic to us today than the pumped up manner of the Roman baroque painters with their lingering tendency to the ancient close view, or that we have taken the calm and detached Velásquez as a model, the only secular painter of the Spanish Habsburgs, but not his heated and ecstatic compatriots.

Mood and devotion are related to one another. Devotion is nothing other than religious mood. There is a profound reason for that, as far as we are able to survey human cultural history, mood always rises to be a supreme goal of art in those periods also moved by a deep religious agitation. This occurred for the first time in late antiquity, when the pagan faith in the gods was beginning to waver, and the faith in Jesus Christ was spreading. It occurred again in the modern period during that immense spiritual movement described as the Reformation and Counter Reformation. Today we are facing the same situation for a third time. Nobody will doubt that we are now living in a time of great intellectual change. Catholicism has renewed itself and generated a promotional power which many would not have considered possible sixty years ago. In terms of the moral world order, most people are today no longer able to place faith in the supernatural as they once did with the physical world. They expect a resolution to come from the numerous new disciplines studying the spiritual side of human nature, including psychophysics, ethnology, the social sciences, etc. As it always has in the past, art assists the spirit faithfully toward that particular redemption and liberation which it necessarily requires if it is not to abnegate its will to life. And thus it falls to our artists to draw the final, highest and most decisive profit from the knowledge of our time. In doing so they are able to provide a relief to our fellows in need of consolation where redemption is no longer available.

Essays from 1900-1904

A New History of Art – On Cornelius Gurlitt, Geschichte der Kunst, 1901[43]

When Bramante was commissioned by Pope Julius II to execute the dome of St. Peter, his impulsive excitement was so strong and caused him to work so quickly that when the first patron and architect died a few years later, the four mighty piers were already standing. There was an extended contemplative interruption after this, and the decision was then reached to proceed to the shell of the dome and complete the project. It is said that the piers were tested for their strength and found to be inadequate. A strong reinforcement was considered a necessary prerequisite to any further work. A half-century lapsed before Michelangelo and Giacomo della Porta could realize the lantern of the dome. In reflecting on the development of the history of art as an academic discipline, we are reminded of this history of the dome construction.

As we all know, the history of art is generally considered to have originated at the mid 18th century with the appearance of Johann Joachim Winckelmann. If the chronological tabulation and systematic description of works of art and biographies of artists are

---

43 Originally published as "Eine neue Kunstgeschichte Über Cornelis Gurlitt, Geschichte der Kunst 1901," *Wiener Abendpost*, "Wiener Zeitung Supplement," no. 15, Monday, January 20, 1902, pp. 7-8.

considered definitive, then we would at least have to include Vasari, the historian of the Florentine cinquecento among the art historians. Winckelmann also did not write with an interest in the art of his own period as it became historical, but rather chose an earlier one, and in this he had a predecessor in Pliny. What made Winckelmann the first art historian is the fact that he sought to recognize what was common in all of the ancient art works which he studied. He was not interested in the existence of an individual work of its own accord, but precisely for that which is common, what bound all of the isolated works and united them into an elevated whole, even if this was only conceptual. This made Winckelmann the first to conceptualize a style – that of classical antiquity. As a pure concept, this does not of course have an objective reality, something which can be perceived. His history of art shares this quality with abstract aesthetics. Yet every element of the concept can be perceived through the senses in the individual extant works, although they are also linked to other elements outside of this concept. This connects Winckelmann's history of art with the facts of experience. Since Winckelmann, the history of art as an objective activity seeks primarily to link the artistic phenomena according to their common characteristics, and to make us conscious of these and leave us with an understanding. The history of art seeks to make it possible for us to subsume each individual work of art, as we see it, within a conscious generality, the concept of style, so that the work of art will lose its disturbing character of strangeness and allow us to enjoy its specific, unusual, indeed unique appeal to the fullest.

A problem posed in this way can only be dealt with by dividing the entire overwhelming mass of the preserved monuments into limited groups of more or less consistent character. This has led to the distinction of stylistic periods which provide the foundations of a structure for the history of art. The first such attempt was begun by Winckelmann himself – that of classical art. The second main pier in constructing the discipline was to become the Italian renaissance, while an understanding of the third, the medieval period, had already been partially prepared during the period of romanticism. The most chronologically recent of these became our research of the so-called painterly styles, mainly of the 17th century. In the course of a hundred years, all of the surviving examples of visual art were largely divided into four enormous but well defined fields, and the task presented itself to create the crown of the structure by discerning what is common to all four groups and characteristic of its unity. At this point doubts arose about these foundations and they have led to questions about the entire stability of this structure.

Until then, works of art had often been assigned to certain stylistic periods on no more than superficial grounds, and one was forced to recognize that written sources demanded a completely different periodization. New and no less credible literary sources were also found to contradict those that had previously been trusted blindly. By the inclusion or exclusion of specific works from the one or other stylistic period, the image of the particular period and with it the concept of the style itself was also changed or modified. If the enthusiasm of construction had been all consuming, now things shifted toward a skepticism with apparently no bounds. The mandate arose: until the date and place of origin was determined for each individual work, or at least the most important examples, and a secure place within a given stylistic period could be decided upon, there can be no stylistic synopsis and no emphasis on common characteristics! This call rang out around the mid 19th century to reinforce the foundations for the history of art and its auxiliary sciences. It has dominated nearly all art historical research until the end of the [19th] century. In certain fields, such as classical archaeology, it has even remained strong to the present day.

However necessary such a reinforcement of the foundations has been, its lopsided preoccupation with isolated facts has led to an obsession with the foundations and caused neglect about the original purpose of the structure. Nothing could be more unfair than to deny or simply underestimate the continual successes we owe to research done in the later 19th century. During that phase, permanent and irreplaceable achievements contributed to a foundation, and offered a very important and real prerequisite for all scholarly research since Winckelmann. This has included the fact that every single work of art is worthy of scholarly attention whether it appeals to the individual observer or not. The auxiliary sciences of the history of art never did revert to purely chronicling enumerations as had been typical of the period before Winckelmann, but always sought to connect one work of art to another and to define common characteristics between one specific example and another. Its limitation lay in the fact that it always restricted its researches to only the closest neighboring works in space and time. At this rate there could be no telling if these foundations of the discipline would ever be completed. For this reason the question has arisen in the last ten years as to whether the soundness of our stylistic concepts would be too dangerously compromised if the birth date of a given artist chanced to fall a few months too early, or if a painting of the second order were attributed to the wrong artist within the proper school. A process was set into motion going beyond the local and temporal details of individual works, and began to search out more elevated shared essential qualities among individual works, allowing us to assess them in more than their extrinsic historical bearing. The need was again felt to recognize these unifying common aspects, because these alone can lead us to an actual understanding, not merely of the individual periods, but of the entire unbroken development. What is the detail involved in such change, and what is the force causing the change? This is the question now facing art history and presenting us with nothing less than the ultimate completion of the dome to crown it all.

There are two possible ways to reach this goal. The first is synthetic. It begins with the individual work and its profounder recognition, and relates to the common method of the historical auxiliary sciences. It is not preoccupied exclusively with distinguishing characteristics in relation to neighboring works, but in registering only the most obvious among them, so that the common qualities emerge more purely and unsullied. This presents an arrangement of energies allowing scholarship to more easily rise from the individual to the general. Using a concrete example, the phases of such research would run approximately as follows: a conception of the individual creative periods within the career of Albrecht Dürer, the entire art of Dürer, the entirety of southern German painting of his period, German painting of that time in general, all of the European art in the first third of the 16th century, and then the relation of art to the other cultural goals of the same period, including religion, philosophy, politics and social movements.

The second possible route is the analytical one. By positing a unity of the visual arts with the entirety of their contemporary culture, it accepts all of the conclusions of the previous method rather than viewing them as an axiom to be demonstrated. The new field thus presenting itself to scholarship is to be defined and occupied in a single bold step rather than incrementally. The advantages of this method are obvious. It, and for the moment only it, can immediately satisfy the urge for an absolute conceptual unity, while the synthetic method can at best point the way to a possible future resolution. The first route is the more deliberate, but more certain and more strictly scholarly. For this reason it is most frequently chosen by historians. The second is more apt for the educated layman who would like to feel a satisfaction in their need for a unity in art historical contemplation, without bothering with detailed doubts as to the certitude of their newly gained knowledge. The need for a formal unity is nonetheless truly artistic and must for this reason be especially brisk among practicing artists. For this reason, the analytical way is more often chosen by those art historians who are also practicing artists. The work we intend to introduce to the reader at present is a significant contribution of this type. *A History of Art* from the pen of Cornelius Gurlitt, architect and professor of history of art at the Technical University in Dresden, has recently appeared in two heavy volumes.[44] His name is preceded by a good reputation, and his conception of the universal history of the

---

44Cornelius Gurlitt, *Geschichte der Kunst*, Stuttgart: A. Bergsträßer 1902, vol. 1, 696 pp., 15 plates, vol. 2, 792 pp., 15 plates.

visual arts is already well known. His point of departure has been the criticism of individual works. This was the fundamental character of his History of Baroque Architecture which appeared approximately fifteen years ago, where general conclusions are still very much absent, but already showing a characteristically strong interest in political and intellectual currents running parallel to that of the arts. In this sense, the History of German Art in the 19th Century, published by Gurlitt one year ago provided a more mature resolution. This most recent publication now appears as a testament of his complete artistic views.

He states his reasons for doing this at the outset. He cannot discover unity in the current history of art. He takes the words out of the mouth of so many thousands, who stand clueless before the overwhelming presentation of jumbled individual facts as he himself once had, without being able to relate them to one another or within their own minds. There is hardly a modern art historian who would object when Gurlitt continues that this relationship can become apparent only when "the history of form is accompanied by the innermost impulses for the development of form."

Only then does Gurlitt set out on the analytical path that separates him from other scholars. He seeks the "innermost impulse" in the "faith of the people in their modes of expression, their religion, in the means of translating their forms from land to land, and ultimately in their thoughts about the essential qualities of art and their philosophy" [1902, vol. 1, pt. 1, p. IV] – rather than in certain tendencies incrementally derived from the artists, schools, nations or cultural periods. With the outward transfer of forms, Gurlitt thus concedes a mechanical aspect in development which had played a decisive role during the phase dominated by the auxiliary sciences, but with religion and philosophy also includes two intellectual motives previously considered unscholarly.

Gurlitt thus offers a careful survey of the important events of the history of art, particularly valuable due to his excellent eye in distinguishing what is essential from what is not. It is a survey made according to a coherent perspective, and this is exactly what many, particularly educated German laymen are desperate to read today. Gurlitt does not find the unifying principle in the development of art itself, but rather in a constant parallel with the political developments and intellectual life of the nations. For an idea of this, we have but to consider the chapter headings of the second volume: the middle class; Renaissance and Reformation; the Counter-Reformation; the period of the religious wars; mercantilism, the Enlightenment, the revival of folk traditions; the period of scientific objectivity. However often certain pedants will deny it, I am firmly convinced that this purported unity in fact exists. It strikes me as being nothing less than the unconscious prerequisite for all of our historical thought. It is doubtful however whether such a unity can be demonstrated objectively, such as that between art and religion for instance. I would not dismiss this, but it is certain that no evidence has yet been brought. Gurlitt does not present it either. The threads that he occasionally spins between the two convince us that the author intuits the cogency of such a parallel, but does not present them objectively as authoritative for all readers. Gurlitt seems to be aware of this, for his intention is rather to show how the development of the entire history of art is reflected by a given individual, this being himself. Gurlitt seems to be quite skeptical whether any generally applicable truths can be derived from the study of history and he almost reminds us of the fatal doctrine of the relativity of all so-called truths. If we admit the subjectivity of conception, then everything of potential interest for more general reflection revolves around the subject alone. Nobody will challenge so thorough a connoisseur and serious a scholar in such a pretension. So far as the great art historical questions of our day are concerned, this book must be considered unscholarly, although stimulating and debatable.

Finally, a word about the illustrations, for these also include a novelty which is symptomatic. They are excellently produced, but astonishingly few in number: only fifteen in each of the volumes. It is obvious enough that this is insufficient to demonstrate the development of the artistic styles. The purpose of the text appears from the outset to have been more to stimulate and entertain than to instruct us in the development of forms. The effect of the illustrations is to reduce the significance of the individual work in favor of the overarching relations and the general perspective, which can be conveyed only though words and not through images. The current literature frequently shows symptoms of a reaction against the predominance of the image. It is doubly significant that this can also occur in a book about the history of art written by a practicing artist.

Works of Nature and Works of Art[45]

I.

Our modern conception of the relation between nature and the visual arts is completely dominated by the idea of development. This was preceded by the idealist point of view which viewed the goal of a work of art as correcting nature, and believed this to have been achieved in classical antiquity. According to this, all other works of visual art can only be seen as sullied or incomplete in comparison to the pure idea present in ancient art. Our practical goal at the present must be to correct nature just as it was done in antiquity.

The idea of development conceded that the non-classical types of art have a right to exist, and began to take hold of modern intellectual activities around the middle of the 19th century. It entered the history of art as the exact opposite to the previous idealist conception, and denied that humanity could determine its own artistic expressions. According to this first period of the modern historical idea in the field of art, each individual work of art was strictly determined by the three physical factors of material, technique of the tools and the practical

---

45 Originally published as "Naturwerk und Kunstwerk I," *Beilage zur Allgemeinen Zeitung* (München), no. 13, Wednesday, January 16, 1901, pp. 1-5, "Naturwerk und Kunstwerk II." *Beilage zur Allgemeinen Zeitung* (München), no. 48, Wednesday, February 27, 1901, pp. 1-3.

function. These three factors are believed to exclusively determine the style, that is to say the external character of each work of art in relation to nature. The works of nature are only very general sources for the human creation of art. In creating a work of art, the artist must consider above all the character of the material, the tools and the conditions of use. Nature is only to be considered in a subsidiary way. A work of art can only be designated as true to style (stilgerecht) or beautiful if it acceptably satisfies the demands of those three factors. According to this, the aesthetic appeal of art would consist in nothing more than the successful use of the relevant material and functionality (Gebrauchszweckmäßigkeit).

It goes without saying that such an argument could most easily be made on the basis of those particular works, in the applied arts, where the three factors present themselves most clearly. This is the reason that the most prominent publication to have advanced these arguments, the monumental book by Gottfried Semper, Style in the Technical and Tectonic Arts or Practical Aesthetics, primarily involves the so-called technical arts, and among these most exclusively textiles. Semper's basic thought is best defined as the idea that every raw material and every technique led to their own most comfortable and malleable forms. The idea of development arose with the conception that originally, in the early stages of the visual arts, humanity had nothing other than technical arts at their disposal, and that the art forms emerging from the materials, techniques and functions were used only by their individual practitioners in isolation until they very gradually came to be transferred to one another by superficial imitation. This is considered to have occurred without the self-willed critical choice of any creative persons, and to have ultimately resulted in the putatively amorphous artistic mélange at the mid-19th century.

We must emphasize that this so-called Semper theory has been taken to explain not merely the applied arts but the history of art in its entire development. Its influence can be found not merely in the history of architecture, where it brought forth the noteworthy theory that the Gothic style was the product of stone construction dealing with lateral pressure, but also in the history of sculpture, where the flat archaic relief is interpreted as the result of stone cutting, but the later deeper relief is seen as resulting from a cross influence from the technique of driven metal.

Such a theory apparently assumes that the most perfect stage of all art must have been at the very beginning, and Semper indeed expresses this thought repeatedly throughout his book. All of the exceptions, such as the explanation for the high quality of figural tomb sculpture in the classical period, are in fact nothing other than subterfuge to conceal the inadequacy of the basic principle. The norm of idealism had been fortunately overcome, but then it was simply replaced with another, materialist norm. The so-called theory of Semper is ultimately nothing other than the metaphysics of materialism, taken from David Friedrich Strauß, Ludwig Büchner and the others, and applied to the history of art. Both philosophers believed that replacing the earlier idealism was tantamount to scientific precision, but overlooked that simply identifying the idea with material with no obvious connection is no less speculative than previous manipulations of the materials in the service of the idea.

Semper's theory has so thoroughly captivated notions surrounding the origin of the applied arts that it is still being espoused to some degree by numerous reputable scholars in spite of the fact that I refuted it on the basis of early eastern and Greek decorative arts in my book *Stilfragen*, published in 1893 [English ed. Questions of Style 1992]. By contrast to that field, the misconception that the entire historical development might have been due to a simple transfer of technical processes was not feasible in studying the figural arts. A virtue was initially made of necessity, and research on sculpture and painting considered it scholarly to avoid all questions of "aesthetics," and instead concentrate exclusively on the supposed matters of facts and figures. Authors limited themselves to determining the place and time of origin for individual works. Yet it was not possible to avoid comparing one monument to another, and value judgments as to the good, bad and mediocre are unavoidable. This was a practice of aesthetics that simultaneously denied itself for purportedly scholarly reasons. It did no more than prevent a reflection on the meaning and justification of those judgments of value. Actual scholarship was subdued by sham scholarship. It was inevitable that such an intrinsically fallacious cult of individual facts would be recognized at least indistinctly as such if not clearly. It is true that the broader public has still not recognized this today. Another theory, the second modern attempt, was then introduced to deal with the historical judgment of the two figural arts. It consists in nothing other than accommodating the relation of nature and the visual arts to a certain influential mode of thought, as this had already been espoused during the later 19th century.

This trend sought to create the sorely absent link between

material and idea by a psychology based on physiology (Wilhelm Wundt, Gustav Theodor Fechner and others). It attempts to approach the essential expressions of human intellectual life without departing from the obvious material appearances. For the history of art, this current brought a theory that declares the figures appearing in a work of art before our eyes to be simple material reproductions and mnemonic images of actual figures – works of nature. Human beings necessarily store impressions from the outside world in their consciousness which they have absorbed through their sense of sight. They are also possessed with the urge to reproduce these impressions by hand for our senses either on a surface or in the round, or to see them reproduced by others in this way. It is clear that this theory combines two diverse elements. The first is a mechanistic idea that the works of art are strictly determined by external sensual impressions such as the image from memory, and the second is a teleological element proposing that a purposeful aesthetic urge exists and demands the reproduction of the objects of nature in works of art by means of the image from memory.

We come to the question of how there can be any development according to this theory. It is generally supposed that the earliest sensual impressions, and along with them the memory impressions and the art works determined by these, remained completely foggy and indistinct in relation to the manifest natural appearances. In the course of time, the senses became sharper and provided a more faithful record of appearances in detail and the relation of details to the whole. In this way, the works of art were held to have become increasingly naturalistic; their vague psychological impressions ever closer to physiological cognizance, myth became knowledge, idealism yielded to naturalism, although such a process also included occasional reversals. As far as the figural arts are concerned, this has been the general point of view behind the practice of art history over the last twenty to thirty years. As we have already noted, the decorative arts continued to be judged according to the theory of Gottfried Semper. The result of this was a dualism all the more surprising since the motto of the "unity" of all the arts continued to make the rounds. While the development of the applied arts was conceived to have been essentially mechanical, that of the figural arts was seen as half mechanical and half teleological.

It is striking that until very recently, no attempt was made to account for the monuments of even a short historical period of the visual arts on the basis of such a psychological theory. Of course, there were continual isolated references to memory images with the suggestion that they played a part in all works of art. Yet these authors always shy away from consistently applying their historical model to entire stylistic periods. Could this restraint be a result of the materialist cult of individual facts and figures that arose in the period of reaction against Hegel, or was it the result of an uncomfortable impression that the new theory would not sustain itself in every case? By now, this is only of historical interest and we are no longer obliged to deal with it. What had always been lacking has finally been very recently fulfilled. In his relevant publication about the archaic and strictly classical figural art of the Greeks up to Lysippos, Professor Emanuel Löwy has only dealt with a short period systematically.[46] The development within this

---

46 Emanuel Löwy, *Die Naturwiedergabe in der älteren griechischen Kunst*, Rome: Loescher, 1900. [English transl. John Fothergill, Loewy, *The Rendering*

period is treated according to the psychological theory of mnemonic imagery.

Aside from the numerous apposite and stimulating individual observations, this book will primarily retain its value as an example of what can be gained from linking intrinsically inanimate individual facts from a well informed point of view. Details surrounding the place and date of origin for an individual artistic monument have no more than an antiquarian interest. Since this art was not made to appeal to our own tastes, if we are to understand it, it is indispensable for us to delve into the assumptions necessarily accompanying its production. For us today, these prerequisites can only be gleaned from the internal historical coherence, and it is therefore important to properly recognize this connection. Since the mechanistic theory has long ago proven itself incapable of providing a resolution to this, we must welcome wholeheartedly the emergence of a scholar who has been able to establish this connection on the basis of the far more suitable psychological theory.

Of course we can never claim that the psychological theory is able to provide a convincing explanation for all art historical phenomena. Even in so narrow a space of time as he has studied, the excellent book by Löwy demonstrates this. It is already awkward that the earliest works presented here cannot themselves be considered primitive, and the author himself admits this. We would imagine the earliest foggy mnemonic images to have been flat. Contrary to all of our expectations, the earliest known works of art, the early Egyptian sculptures, reveal not merely a strong conception of relief, but also the

---

of Nature in Early Greek Art, London: Duckworth, 1907.]

most refined imaginable observation of nature – and I would like to stress this particularly since it is usually overlooked. The reason that we normally ignore this latter quality and feel Egyptian sculpture to be flat and inert is due to the fact that it was not made to be seen at a distance in the more extreme optical terms we are accustomed to, but rather at the strictest close range, so that the complete effect of its unsurpassed finesse of modeling is frequently only accessible to the touch of the finger tips. The original mnemonic image which is supposed to have been the source of it all turns out to be nothing more than a construct which cannot be made to jibe with the historical monuments whatsoever.

Löwy was also forced to list a number of works that could not be harmonized with his image of the sequence of development. He described them as exceptions with only a symptomatic value in face of the overwhelming number of examples supporting his theory. It is true that anachronistic phenomena are not uncommon in other periods either. The anticipation of a post antique conception as it can be seen in the Vaphio cups is completely unique in the history of art, while the additional circumstance must be borne in mind that Mycenae as an artistic region was quite isolated from the dominant contemporary trends of the earlier eastern Mediterranean, and appeared more barbarian and artistically regressive in comparison. Are we not forced to assume that another second development ran parallel to the eastern trend already in the earliest period and later merged with archaic Greek art? Such an assumption would challenge the psychological theory of all developments based on a hazy memory image.

The difficulties of this theory become completely insurmountable when it is called on to explain the final phase of ancient art in the late Roman imperial period. An inexorable development is supposed to have occurred toward a constant increase in natural observation. Occasional small reversals also cannot stand in the way of it. How could this have been the case if the natural observation accrued over millennia were jettisoned and based on the most nebulous image from memory? Could there have been any sort of coherent development whatsoever? And yet, this is what faces us at the end of the ancient period. Traditionally, the situation is explained as having not occurred intentionally, but that this "reversal" was brought about by the violent invasion of uncivilized barbarians. Not long ago, I believe to have sufficiently exposed this hypothesis as a compromise excuse and that it is not justifiable either intrinsically or extrinsically.[47]

The psychological theory fails no less when it is applied to the other arts, which naturally relate to one another. We would concomitantly expect the development of music to more closely approach the sounds as we hear them in nature, yet if anything, the opposite is certainly the case and natural sounds have probably never been a goal of music even by a presumed detour through a presumed mnemonic tone.

Psychophysics and the other related psychological movements

---

47 Alois Riegl, *Die spätrömische Kunst-Industrie nach den Funden in Österreich-Ungarn, Im Zusammenhang mit der Gesamtentwicklung der bildenden Kunst bei den Mittelmeervölkern dargestellt von Alois Riegl*, Vienna: K. K. Hof- und Staatsdruckerei 1901 [reprinted Vienna: Österreichische Staatsdruckerei, 1927, English trans., by Rolf Winkes, *Late Roman Art Industry*, Rome: Bretschneider, 1985, Italian trans., by Lioia Collobi-Ragghianti, *Arte tardoromana*, Turin: Einaudi, 1959].

based on experimental observation have often been criticized as basing their conclusions too exclusively on the subjective experiences of the individual observers or researchers. This circumstance is also relevant in our present context, since it might account for the great success of the psychological theory in the history of art over the last two or three decades. This was the same period in which the visual as well as the other arts were dominated by the idealist trend. Art historians noticed that their contemporary artists were primarily striving to paint perfunctorily done color imagery of subjects from nature to be seen optically at a distance. Somewhat over hastily, they declared a certain modern phase in the recent development of art – the optical art of Impressionism geared to be viewed at a distance – to be the fundamental principle of the entire development of art, much in the way that Semper had earlier believed to have found the principle in the development of the textile arts and supposed it to be the basis for that of all art.

If the psychological theory were applied completely consistently to the history of art, it would necessarily place the optical art of Impressionism at the beginning and the more sculptural conception later on. This because the latter more clearly reveals the relations of the bodily parts and the individual figures among themselves. Yet the history of art transpired in precisely the opposite way. The arts of Mesopotamia were based on an explicitly sculptural conception and objective observation of nature, while the subjective and optic element only gradually emerged. One branch of earlier ancient art, that of Mycenae, showed an optic tendency at an early date, and since it is not definably but undeniably related to later Greek art, this gives us an indication for the source of the "naturalist" forward impulse in early Greek art which was otherwise essentially sculptural and relating to the east. As we have already observed, this would mean that there were two existent contradictory trends simultaneously working upon one another. The one sculptural to be viewed at close range of eastern origins, and the other more optically oriented and to be viewed at a distance, presumably coming from the Indo-Germanic nations. Taken in isolation, each of these would have become tedious and petrified, but in a reciprocal and often antagonistic interpenetration, they have led to a development which has even remained fruitful into our own time.

The reason for the untenability of the psychological theory is ultimately the trace of materialist metaphysics contained within it: the view that artistic creation is determined by the memory image. This was calculated as a known quantity, and yet it is nothing more than a materialist bugbear, an obscure metaphysical concept. The path along which the future lines of completely impartial research must run can only become clear once this is acknowledged and this last vestige of materialist metaphysics is done away with.

Today there is a widespread line of philosophical thought devoted to the exclusive use of observed facts and the complete rejection of all metaphysics. It is called positivism in the broadest sense. If the principles of this are applied to the history of art, we would have to say that the creation of art is reduced to nothing more than an aesthetic urge. On the one hand we have the artists depicting the objects of nature emphasizing some and suppressing other qualities. On the other, the public views these objects from nature in just the same way as the artists of their time. For us, the possible determining factors of this urge are unknown and might necessarily remain unknown. We are left with nothing other than the will to art as the only solid fact.

The question is how historical development is possible within this will to art. From our study of the monuments in their well-known chronological sequence, the development is not related to the natural objects themselves, which have after all remained essentially unchanged, but in the way humanity wished to see those natural objects depicted. At this point, I can give no more than a general sketch of the decisive impulses for the development in the will to art, as it reveals itself through the stylistic periods as currently known and distinguished. In the book mentioned just before, *Die spätrömische Kunstindustrie*, I have done so with greater precision, on the more limited subject of late antique and early medieval art.

Human vision perceived the objects of nature as isolated figures, yet linked to the universe as an infinite whole or an apparently infinite section of it. The figures are defined by their contours, but dissolve more or less fluidly into their surroundings. They possess a definite local color and yet participate in the general hue of their environment. The development of the human will to art is attached to this double apparition which the objects of nature present to the human eye. We find two extreme possibilities. These are on the one hand, the furthest possible isolation of the objects of nature from one another, or on the other their greatest conceivable interrelation. In either of these cases, the individual figure is annihilated, and with this, the possibility of its reproduction in the work of art. In the first it is atomized and in the latter it dissolves into infinity. On the inestimable scale between these two extremes there is a tremendous latitude for development.

Depending on whether the will to art is directed more to the appearance of the isolated single figure or to its connection with the outside world, the human subject projects nothing into the natural object to be depicted, but instead intensifies the isolating or unifying qualities while suppressing the others. Both directions were present from the very beginning. We have already identified the isolating tendency as probably descending from an early eastern source, and the unifying tendency as probably of Indo-Germanic origin. The latter has always been the more projective and the former the more receptive. From this, the discernible development within the known material generally shows the progression from a strict isolation to an ever-growing confluence. Observation of nature and the precise rendition of the objects of nature which we call naturalism have always and without exception been a guiding principle for the visual arts. Various characteristics, all of them reducible to contour and color, were at various times deliberately emphasized, while others were as deliberately subdued depending on the manner in which the figures were isolated or combined, isolated or joined to the surface, and isolated or joined to the pictorial depth. This intensification and suppression embodies the unnaturalness, the exaggeration, and the idealism which is as common to all works of art as is their particular naturalism as contrasted with the objects of nature themselves.

We also note another fundamental aspect. An object of nature, which is as isolated as possible in its contours and color appears to our perception as a self-contained unity. If its contours are unclear or blurred, then additional conscious experience is necessary to clearly understand its isolated essence. Since, as we have observed, the development tends to move from strict isolation to increasing interpenetration, it follows that the earliest artistic creations, essentially those of the near east, were devoted to an evident rendition of objects, while later phases increasingly incorporated conscious experience as an intellectual factor in the perception of the art work.

Finally, we must bear in mind that the ultimate confirmation for the isolation of a given object can never be gained through the sense of sight, but only through the sense of touch. As we perceive it with our eyes, the isolation is itself already no more than a reminder of our experiences by the sense of touch. The earliest important examples of art consist in near eastern sculpture and thus appeal to our tactile experience, while the tendency of art since then has, with occasional reversals, been consistently in the optical direction.

We have already seen that the monuments from the Mycenaean culture-resisting placement according to psychological theory might be explained in this light. It is significant that the first archaeological scholar to attempt a single coherent account of the earlier ancient period already sensed that the Mycenaean artifacts would play a significant role in resolving the question. He lamented that previous scholars had neglected them. Löwy (op. cit. p. 16 note 1 [ed. 1907, p. 30, note 33]) has said: "Except for its ceramics, I cannot see that the history of Mycenaean art has begun to be written." In light of the richness of the material this is indeed remarkable, but those familiar with the situation will understand why. Mycenaean art resists being fixed in place and time, and its iconographical aspect does not leave much latitude for the scholar either. When faced with the artistic qualities of individual works, most of our archaeologists are clueless. The vexing thing is that this perplexity emanates artificially from places of authority in the name of putative sound scholarship. From my critical remarks above, it should be clear that this cult of isolated individual facts in the name of objectivity is self-delusional. What might have been a healthy self-restraint in the time of Semper has by now become the worst sort of stumbling block to progress and the development of archaeological scholarship.

It should not have been, but was accepted in the past for art historians and archaeologists to simply tell us that a particular painting or statue is good or bad, but in the future it will be incumbent on them to reveal how they arrive at such a judgment. Why did an individual work of art give pleasure when it was made, but no longer does so today? These are questions which it is possible to answer on the basis of the monuments themselves, and they must for this reason be answered in due course. In fact, this strikes me as the most pressing task facing art historical scholarship in the near future.

Metaphysical presumptions could be marshaled to determine why the aesthetic urge stressed or subdued either the isolating or congealing aspects in rendering natural objects, but these are not the domain of art historians. On the other hand, it is probably possible to create a sounder basis for a deeper understanding of this will to art. If we go beyond the realm of the arts and consider one or the other of the great human cultural endeavors such as the state, religion or science, we will realize that these are all based on a relationship between the individual and the collective. In studying the volitional trends in these pursuits for certain periods among given nations, we will inevitably discover that it is completely identical with their contemporary will to art. If this common volition in all cultural fields is combined under the rubric of "world view," we might find that the visual arts are not determined by the concurrent "world view," but that they develop in tandem.

To demonstrate the relationship between the visual arts and the worldview would not be the calling of the art historian, but rather the actual future role of the cultural historian. Yet the art historian cannot revoke their collaboration on this task, because their interest in its conclusion is too great to simply wait for it to be accomplished by others. All of the non-artistic cultural fields affect the history of art by providing the artwork with its content or subject matter, which never occurs without an external purpose. It is clear that the art historian will not be in a position to properly judge an individual work of art when they have recognized that the will generating the impulse to a particular motif is identical to that which aroused unique choices of contour and color in the individual figure. In other words: the current trend to study the original place and date of individual art works, which along with iconography, is being practiced so exclusively, will only become valuable to the history of art when it is recognized as congruent with the patent appearance of the art work as form and color in surface and space. The determination of location and date of origin can only become truly interesting when we are able to recognize why this particular work could only have been created there and then.

So much for the positivist theory of artistic will as the exclusive driving element of artistic creativity for art historical scholarship. This might allow philosophy to arrive at an empirical aesthetics. What the followers of Semper and G. T. Fechner have identified as such can at best be seen as no more than a preliminary step. Neither of these have yet attained a stage of completely pure empiricism.

II.

In an earlier essay with this title, I have attempted to show how three theories of the relation of nature to art had succeeded one another since the middle of the 19th century. The pure materialism of Gottfried Semper yielded to the semi-materialism availing itself of the memory image, and then also the positivism based exclusively on the aesthetic urge, the will to art, as the exclusive extant positive fact. What these theories had in common was the basic principle of the capacity for development. Otherwise, it would not have been possible to account for the colorful sequence of stylistic periods.

For a number of years now, an artistic doctrine has been gaining approval in Germany which the German sculptor Adolf Hildebrand has conceived and published in a book *The Problem of Form in the Visual Arts*, which has quickly become famous and recently appeared in a third edition.[48] The author felicitously combines three qualities in a way unprecedented in any modern artist since Gottfried Semper. He is a significant practicing artist, a thinker able to give an exact account of his work, but also gifted enough as an author to be in a position to explain the results of his reflections to the public. It is definitely worth closely considering how such a reflective artist imagined the relation

---

48 [Adolf Hildebrand, *Das Problem der Form in der bildenden Kunst*, Dritte, verbesserte Auflage, Strasbourg: Heitz, 1901, as *The Problem of Form in Painting and Sculpture*, transl. Max Meyer and R. M. Ogden, New York: Stechert, 1907.]

of works of nature to works of art. The reason that, in spite of this, I did not include this in my previous essay is because Hildebrand has posited a fixed rule without leaving room for historical development.[49] Compared with Semper, who stood at the beginning of a retrospective period, Hildebrand is a member of the younger generation which has lost its respect for earlier art and is bold in expressing its own artistic views. As we can expect from so progressive an artist, Adolf Hildebrand has reached an opinion of his own and has become unflappably convinced of it. It follows compellingly that Hildebrand rejects not merely the contemporary artistic trends which do not concur with his norm, but also older developments which have become simple historical facts – such as that of Canova for instance. Hildebrand never intended to understand the intrinsic necessity, the developmental conditions of earlier artistic styles differing from his own. His exclusive concern has been to establish a norm universally applicable in judging earlier art. His theory has this in common with that of Johann Joachim Winckelmann, and it separates him from the three theories we have discussed above.

In spite of this fundamental difference in the basic intention, there are a number of threads connecting them in both directions. It is worth pursuing these connections in order to broadly recognize the relation of this deservedly popular theory of artistic creation to the predominant theories of art historical development. Such attention

---

49 This is not to say that Hildebrand denied any possibility of artistic development. His words about ancient Egyptian sculpture imply it directly. His book nowhere mentions a principle behind such a regular development, while he strictly repeats his basic principle is generally as an immutable formula.

should promise to be illuminating and profitable for both sides. It could be as illuminating for those following Hildebrand in their search for a norm in judging earlier art as for the others who would like to know why the art of earlier periods does not look like that of their own time.

Both posit a single basic principle, which the theories of development were as unable to escape as the absolute theory proposed by the artist. Fundamentally, the doctrine of Hildebrand holds that the essential difference between the work of art and the work of nature lies in its architectonic content, while the imitative content is common to both. Since it is only able to develop the imitative content, this negates any decisive influence of a memory image on the artwork, and Hildebrand states this explicitly (p. 37 of the third edition [English ed. 1907, pp. 42-43]). He has also unequivocally said that the architectonic content of the work of art is inconceivable as determined by material factors such as its raw materials (p. 85 [pp. 91-92]). This would appear to include a rejection of any connection to the theory of Semper. He sees the architectonic content as conditioned by an aesthetic urge described as an "instinctive need" (p. 7 [p. 12]). Since this compulsion is nothing other than the "artistic will" of the positivist theory, it follows that the theory of Hildebrand is fundamentally identical with that which we have called the positivist theory of development.

If we pursue the Hildebrand theory of architectonic content into the final detail, its agreement with what I have called the positivist theory of development would emerge on several other points. According to Hildebrand, the architectonic content consists in the fact that the natural objects within the work of art should appear as three-dimensionally developed and self-contained, but also as freely moving in infinite space. Among the numerous variables, this definition includes an unvarying factor. The consistent aspect lies in the proposition that the function of all artistic creation can be found in the establishment of an overtly evident and unified relation between the individual objects and their surroundings. It is not difficult to recognize this as the double appearance of all natural objects, between individual enclosure on the one hand and dissolution into their surroundings on the other, which the positivist historical theory attaches to all artistic creation. The rest of what Hildebrand says is in his definition only valid for his own artistic creativity, and by extension perhaps to contemporary sculpture or even to all of contemporary art. It can only be applied to earlier art forms with relatively sharp limitations and caveats.

This refers to three special and variable relationships within the given general and immutable factors as we have them: the relation of the individual objects to the surroundings generally. They are the relation of the individual forms to their surroundings in particular, the relation of these things to the three dimensions, and then the relation of the ambient space to the three dimensions.

As far as the first is concerned, Hildebrand imagines this in the ideal instance to be a state of balance. The individual objects should be completely and clearly delineated unto themselves and should also not drop out of their environment in any disturbing way. This betrays the sculptor in stone, whose material itself does not allow overly loose contours and makes certain modern artistic trends appear anathema, such as in Italian sculpture of the early modern period. We might see this attitude of Hildebrand as something of a reversion to antiquity. This point of view can neither accommodate the existence of the art of the ancient near east, archaic and late Rome, nor of the medieval period, which had all strictly isolated the forms against their surroundings. It conversely also fails with some of the modern periods in which the contours were rendered too softly, as would be the case of Rembrandt and his chiaroscuro. There was almost no sculpture produced by Rembrandt's contemporaries. Nonetheless, for centuries and millennia, these arts served humanity as the pure and complete satisfaction of their aesthetic needs.

According to Hildebrand, the relation of individual objects to the three dimensions should be registered in such a way that the development of its parts ideally remains completely clear and coherent in all three dimensions, and particularly also into depth. This definition again can neither allow ancient Egyptian art which suppressed the third dimension as much as possible, nor late Roman art and some of the most recent artistic developments which strive to evoke living appearances without any tactile-plastic edges, but exclusively using the colors and contours from our conscious experiences.

Finally, Hildebrand imagines the relation of the spatial ambient to the three dimensions as identical and appearing freely and evenly extended in all three dimensions. This is the point at which Hildebrand is most shrill and one-sided as a modern artist. To conceive the surroundings of the individual figure as an infinite three-dimensional space did not begin strictly speaking until Lorenzo Ghiberti and the Renaissance. If it ever included the surroundings of the individual figure at all, antiquity considered only the two dimensions of height and breadth, in other words a surface. Even the advanced Roman paintings of the later imperial period, with their apparently deep planes, accumulate figures and motifs beside and above one another, but they consistently suppress precisely those characteristics which might have conjured depth in the mind of the spectator. The figures in these images are bound within the various planes before and behind, all of them equally large and with equally clear contours.[50]

As it relates to the art historical theories of development, that of Hildebrand can be summarized in terms of the consistent and generally valid characteristics of artistic creation, as remaining completely within that which we have called the positivist theory.[51] This is true in his acceptance of the concept of an artistic will as the ultimate tangible impulsive factor, as well as in defining the role of the artistic will, which he sees as establishing a unified relation between the individual form and its surroundings. As soon as one seeks a greater precision of definition, the paths of the artist and the art historian diverge. The artist can only conceive the imaginary relationship in a single way, that being the way in which he himself would pursue it in his own artistic

---

50 The theorists of the memory image felt themselves forced to attribute such "shortcomings" in the rendition of nature within art to an insufficient or undeveloped capacity of observation among the people of the ancient cultures. This example demonstrates how preconceived notions have led to some of the coarsest and most tangible errors. In their observation of nature, the ancients were as superior to the moderns as the Indians were to the Englishmen who subdued them. The overwhelming domination of nature which characterizes our current situation is essentially based on intellectual work. Among the "intellectual nations" of Europe, the predominance of people requiring spectacles for their vision makes it obvious that the senses have not benefited from this. When the ancient Greeks and Romans did not use aerial perspective in their art, they had good reason to suppress it and were doubtlessly as aware as we are today.

51 That is to say not in the sense in which Hildebrand himself (p. 39) has used the term "positivist."

work. This is his own right, and we can only take pleasure in his strong convictions. The art historian cannot assume this attitude, for it would forfeit the idea of development and remove any possibility of doing complete historical justice to any earlier period, such as that of Canova for instance, which Hildebrand has explicitly rejected.

All of these difficulties which I have attempted to delineate in the previous essay appear to be allayed by the positivist theory. On the one hand this theory includes the Hildebrand doctrine of art with its valid and enduring aspects as fundamental principles and its specifics as peculiar to a certain modern trend. On the other hand it goes beyond it in conceiving the fundamental principles more broadly, and thus creates space to completely accommodate all past manners of style.

The Place of the Vaphio Cups
in the History of Art[52]

In the following pages, we do not intend to contribute one more study of these much discussed monuments from the point of view of classical archaeology, indeed, do not feel competent to do so. The intention is rather to subject the significance of the Vaphio cups to a more rigorous general art-historical examination and discussion than seems ever to have occurred previously.

In every work of art depicting objects of nature it is necessary to distinguish between the idea which led to the choice of the particular natural models and the mode and manner in which these models from nature are reproduced by the hand of the human artist. It is the latter which is artistically essential. We might even ask whether the idea, the original vision of function is not a rather extrinsic consideration to be strictly distinguished from the actual artistic purpose. We would like to leave this question aside, and express our doubts about the ideas behind the reliefs on the Vaphio cups in a merely formal way at the end after all of the rest.

---

52 Originally published as "Zur kunsthistorischen Stellung der Becher von Vafio," *Jahreshefte des Österreichischen archäologischen Institutes in Wien*, vol. 9, 1906, pp.1-19 based on a lecture held in 1900, transl. as "The Place of the Vapheio Cups in the History of Art (1900), by Tawney Becker" in Christopher S. Wood ed., The Vienna School Reader: Politics and Art Historical Method in the 1930's, New York: Zone, 2000, pp. 104-129. Illustrations: Google Images.

For this reason we immediately turn to the second of these main questions: the mode and manner in which the given ideas have been embodied. This essentially addresses two aspects of our observation, first about the composition and then the relation of form to surface. The specific will to art expresses itself in both. The natural barriers to an art just beginning to struggle with materials and technique seem to have been overcome to such a degree in the Vaphio cups that we might leave them aside as subordinate factors in the sources of their style.

Composition is defined as the unification of numerous parts into a coherent whole, be it the limbs and elements of a single figure or numerous figures into a group. Early eastern art, specifically that of the Egyptians never actually reached that stage. It has been observed long ago that the segments in the Egyptian figures are carefully recorded and organized in a crystalline way, that is to say clearly enclosed and symmetrically arranged, but that, to the modern spectator at least, they lack the compelling connection and with it the convincing impression of a necessary cohesion of the elements as a whole. They lack the proficiency to fulfill the imagined movements. The same is true of the depictions of groups in Egyptian art. The figures all have the same height and are placed in an even row but without the dominant accent that might at first glance unite it to a recognizable whole. It was the Greeks or rather their Indo-Germanic predecessors of the pre-Homeric period who invented relief sculpture. With its one-sided sequence of figures, the warrior vase from Mycenae does not seem to show an advance beyond Egyptian art (although in other aspects it certainly does). Yet the Vaphio cups reveal that an incalculable development has already taken place. It strikes me that this fact has not yet been properly recognized in its ramifications and that this is largely due to the original but not always impartial remarks made about these monuments by Heinrich Brunn in his *Griechische Kunstgschichte* (vol. 1, Munich: Bruckmann, 1893, pp. 46-52). Brunn believed that the origins of Greek compositional art lay in the crystalline grouping with a dominant center as it occurs on the Dipylon vases. By comparison, he felt the Mycenaean composition of the Vaphio cups to show a cruder and less refined preliminary stage of development. This is something we must first analyze in the two reliefs on the cups.

Just facing the handle at the center of the one cup, a single bull is seen rolled together into a hemispherical mass in a net. There are individual bulls to its right and left, each of them having escaped the trap. One of these turns about and runs away in a full gallop with its hind legs in the air and fore legs stretching forward. The other has broken through the net and overrun two of its hunters in a leap with its hind legs below and fore legs raised. Both in unmistakably material and ideal terms, this includes a clear distinction between the center and the flanks, as well as the flanks from one another. A bull is rising on the side and descending on the other. In contrast to the general downward movement, the one throws its head upward, while other does the same downward. As unobtrusive and natural as it appears, the movement of all their tails follows the same law. This is not merely a composition with a sense of unity, but also one quite consciously constructed in terms of contrasts. In a word, it is a contrappostal composition as Greek art did not attain it until its classical period at the earliest. How refined so studied an intention has been concealed and depicted so naturally! In the case of the left bull, the two men divert our attention from the hidden scheme. To the right, the tree performs the same function. It has also been noted that the even placement of the bull in the net at the center is based on contrapposto. Its forelegs are to the left and its hind legs to the right, and yet this strange distortion does not strike us as noticeably studied since it is explained by the momentary situation of the animal in the trap.

By a stroke of fate impossible to fully appreciate, a second cup was discovered and allows us to examine and confirm our previous and our later observations about the first. We are already struck by the contrast in the total composition. The one depicts the greatest imaginable energy and wild movement while the other exudes a reflective stance or peaceful stride. This cannot be a coincidence, but for the moment, we are interested in the details of the second composition. Again the center is clearly distinct from the two flanks. While the one was dominated by a single bull at the center in close relation to another object with the net tied to two trees, here it is two bulls at the center. This Mycenaean artist seems already to have felt that a single point would provide an all too rigid constraint to be used as a dominant motif. Who is not reminded that later classical Greek compositions prefer a couple rather than a single central motif? The Aldobrandini Wedding [Vatican Library, Sala delle Nozze Aldobrandine] is only one of the best-known examples. In our imagination we might also be reminded of the double kingships and double consulates, as they existed in ancient political systems. We see a single bull on each of the flanks of the second cup. They face one another in contrappostal movements. The one to the right is grazing with its head lowered. That to the left is bellowing with its head raised in the air, and the bellowing is further motivated by the fact that a man is tying one of its hind legs. By the placement of the trees, the deliberateness of the composition is somewhat indistinct. Since our own modern art attempts to conceal anything intentional from the work of art, this might well be a factor contributing to the popularity of these reliefs today.

The central group of the two bulls on the second cup has other relevant characteristics. We are only able to see the front part of the bull's body to the rear. It is nearly completely covered by the bull before it. Egyptian art fundamentally avoided any such overlapping and treated it as a necessary evil in those instances when it became unavoidable. In depicting a quadriga for instance, the Egyptian artist would completely delineate the foremost horse and merely suggest the other three by their outlines. This is very different in the case of our Mycenaean artist. He has depicted not merely the complete front half of the bull to the rear, but also included elements of the rear legs and tail, deliberately showing them rising above the back of the bull before it. The restlessness expressed in the tail is motivated by the parallel upheaval expressed in the pose of the head to which we shall return. In comparing this with the quiescence of the bull at the front it becomes clear that a principle of contrast is again at play within the central group itself. The full import of this deviation from the Egyptian custom of avoiding all overlapping will later become apparent.

Art historians must be particularly struck by the almost spiritual relationship that appears to be indicated between the two bulls. That to the rear turns its head almost caressingly to its mate, which is in turn gazing out toward the spectator. We shall later concern ourselves with the truly epochal importance of the latter pose of the head for the development of relief sculpture. Suffice it to say that the entire corpus of near eastern sculpture provides us with no comparable example of two animals relating to one another in what we might call such a cozy way. The closest subjects might be obvious blood relations such as a mother and her offspring. In Egyptian wall decorations, sexual coupling, which was a popular subject for obvious associational reasons, was depicted as a material and not an ethical relation. Even among human subjects, Egyptian art rarely admitted such a thing, and then only grudgingly. The Mycenaean artist did not shy from expressing this in a very basic way even among animals. Could we be blamed for succumbing to the temptation and interpreting this as an Indo-Germanic impulse toward participation in nature by contrast to the ancient Near Eastern tendency toward practical utilization?

Allow us to return to the tangible elements of our observations! We are already able to conclude that the reliefs on the Vaphio cups do not represent a crude preliminary stage to the Dipylon compositions as Brunn proposed. The artistic goals of the artifacts from the Dipyon had already been achieved in the Vaphio cups – the unification of a scene with multiple figures around a single dominant motif. Our only question can be which of the two do we esteem as the more artful: the simple stiff repetition to the right and left of a central axis or the ingenious dissolution into contrasting lines and movements with a balance of weight? The answer comes to us from classical art itself, which adopted the latter as its own. We can be satisfied.

Furthermore – in some respects, the composition of the Vaphio cups even goes beyond that of classical art. Strictly classical art before Lysippos never achieved an actual landscape. When the subject demanded elements within the image we consider to have the character of landscape, such as trees, bushes, houses, animals and the like, they were always rendered in the same manner as the human figure in its objective self-enclosed existence. A full millennium earlier than such attempts among the Alexandrian artists, the Vaphio cups include a true landscape, almost in the modern sense. It includes a common ground line with all of the humans and animals moving on it and with only one exception, the trees growing from it. This ground also does not include a sculptural division for instance among objective, complete and individual things such as rocks, clumps of earth or cliffs. Even less does it involve a mathematical line, as it was common in Egyptian art and the examples from the Dipylon. Its ground line is made in imitation of its actual appearance in nature. On the first cup with the impetuous figural actions we recognize its moving grasses, while on the second the growth of grass is indicated by abrupt punctuations on the rocky clumps that anticipate the late antique technique of drilling. The trees and bushes are not stiff vertical protrusions like semi-geometrical configurations, but diverge from the normal vertical as if they were subject to the random effects of nature. An example would be the palm tree with the bull fleeing behind it. Its broken line at the center reveals nature in its evanescent and random state, the precise opposite of all archaic-crystalline art. This bit of nature nonetheless has the highly refined artistic function of dividing the movement of the bull into two pleasing parts, accompanying the direction in which the bull moves with its broken line. However unusual and un-classical it might be, we must not read too much into this since a similar agreement between the main figure, in our case the bull, and an ancillary landscape motif, here the tree, also occurs in the completely artless composition of a relief in the temple of Ramses III at Medinet Habu.

There is only a single factor in which this Mycenaean landscape disappoints us today. Of the two trees to which the hunting net is tied, only the foremost is rooted in the ground while the other hovers in the air behind. The artist seems to have faced a conflict between two aesthetic goals of equal importance to him. On the one hand, the unity of the landscape needed to be maintained for its optical impression, and on the other, the narrative required clarity. Since both could not be achieved simultaneously, he decided in favor of the latter. A modern artist would not hesitate for a moment to do that which the Mycenaean artist shied away from and allow overlapping in the tree to the rear. Even into the latest phases of the Roman Empire, antiquity could never reconcile itself to compromising the clarity of the optical unity, that is the objective existence of things by their subjective appearance to the human retina. In spite of having developed beyond the general self conscious objectivism, this Mycenaean art nonetheless concurred with that immutable paradigm of ancient art that had governed all of the early art of Asia Minor and, as the Vaphio cups demonstrate, was taken over by the predecessors to the Greeks at an early date. It was consistently maintained until the very end of antiquity.

The artist of the Vaphio cups surpassed all of ancient art in another way and must be recognized for this. We refer to the strange stalactite forms as they protrude into the upper portions of the relief ground. Their artistic purpose is clear: they serve to fill the empty space. This is the same tendency that presents itself also on the grave stelae from Mycenae and differs so fundamentally from earlier Near Eastern art.[53] These show a horror vacui that remained completely unknown to Egyptian art, mollified by regular composed spiral lines, that is to say semi-crystalline elements. What is the meaning of the conglomerated masses on the Vaphio cups? Since they lack any regular compositional quality, they cannot be considered ornamental. This means that they must be imitations of natural objects, and there seem to be only two possibilities. They could either represent the mountains on the horizon or the clouds on the firmament. Whichever we prefer, either remains completely unprecedented until the latest phases of ancient art. Even if ancient art after Lysippos made great concessions to the subjective feeling for space, the eye of the ancient artist never penetrated that far into depth that it recognized and recorded space as far as the horizon. And yet we are forced to decide in favor of one or the other explanation. There can be no doubt for us. Only clouds and no mountains could explain the raddled effect and interruptions in the hanging masses, particularly as we see it on the second cup. If they are supposed to suggest mountains, they would present a complete inversion of the optical impression that we have seen the artist to be pursuing, and this

53 The stiff conception of objectivism in the ancient Near East necessarily led to a tendency to remove anything which might remind the spectator of space and time. This included the ground in relief sculpture as well as in painting, which the Egyptians clearly felt, if ever acknowledged, would ultimately lead to the emancipation of space. This accounts for the assiduous inattention and even denial of the ground in Egyptian art, as it is expressed in the relief *en creux*, the sunken relief, and then in the contrived disproportion between figure and ground. By contrast, the Mycenaean artist immediately filled the empty ground with ornamental motifs. This was not necessary in the Warrior Vase since the many lance points in the air already provided a satisfactory resolution in the relation of figure to ground. From this indication alone, one could guess that this art would soon recognize depth in space.

without providing any clarity comparable to the treatment of the trees supporting the net.

Our second conclusion can be summarized in the fact the Vaphio cups depict a landscape which first of all includes a segment of the earth's surface designed to be seen as a momentary subjective view as it remained alien to earlier Near Eastern art and was never reached by Greek artists until after Lysippos. The cups also include the appearance of clouds above the earth as it never again occurred during antiquity and never reappeared until later medieval art.

The second purely artistic element of this work of art is the relationship it shows between form and surface. It is true that all objects of nature include form and are limited by surfaces. Yet, it does not follow that this relationship is simply replicated in artistic imitations of these originals. Changes in the times, in the nations and the sequence of styles directly express this relationship. In what way do we see it in the Vaphio cups?

This again calls for a survey of the previous historical developments. Earlier Near Eastern relief sculpture had been of the flat relief type, with the figures sharply circumscribed in their height and breadth, but timid and shy in the dimension of depth. This is explicable from a fundamental tendency based in the world view of the ancient Near Eastern nations which interests us only in regard to the visual arts. Egyptian art strives to depict things as they appear objectively and independent of the confusing and depressing randomness of our visual perception. The Egyptian artists examined the objects precisely at close range with recourse to his sense of touch, and carefully modeled part for part. Only in the height and the breadth did they attain complete clarity both of the whole and the individual parts. Depth always remains unclear to the eye, and yet it is a given, a necessary evil, and must for this reason be taken into account, though reduced to the lowest possible level of intrusion. This is expressed equally in Egyptian sculpture in the round with its surface bound frontality, as well as in Egyptian flat relief sculpture, and certainly most strikingly in Egyptian painting with its silhouetted and unmodelled contour drawing. In every case, shadow, as a sign of form, is avoided as much as possible since shadow is incorporeal and would only create unclarity. With a typical sense for objective material reality, the ancient Near Eastern artist added part for part to the art work as most strictly visible at close range with corrective recourse to the sense of touch. He never manages to visualize the entire figure or groups of figures in a single moment as an optical unity from a personal and subjective point of view. All of early Near Eastern art is objectivist, spaceless and timeless. It consists of silhouettes in painting and only very shallow swelling in sculpture, with the shadows kept as weak and wide as possible.

The earliest monuments known from what later became Greek soil already reveal a completely different character. A spinning wheel found at Troy includes an image of linear engraved stags on the surface of a knob with nothing comparable to be found anywhere in early Near Eastern art. In this image the element of depth has not merely been suppressed, but in fact everything is reduced to the exclusive dimension of length. The engraved lines do not indicate the edges of volumes with surfaces extending between them, but instead they delineate the volumes themselves. These stags have certainly not been observed at close range and tested against the sense of touch, but are images made

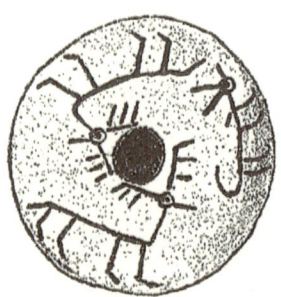

Fig. 1.
Troischer Spinnwirtel.

from memory on a purely optical basis at long range. Their forms
are imaginary and vague with no reference to the tactile dimension.
These Greek artists, if that is what we might call them, worked in a
way precisely opposite to those of the ancient Near East. They saw the
parts of the image and combined them into a whole. In this way, the
precursors of the Greeks looked above all at the whole in the way in
which we still recognize it today, with the parts losing all significance.
While the Egyptian worked along objective lines and sought to
render things as they would exist beyond the contingencies of optic
appearance and tangible to the hands, the Indo-Germanic artist took a
subjective approach in rendering the most prominent traits according
to a momentary optical impression. It is clear that such a conception
of art as on the knob of the spinning wheel from Troy could never rise
to higher perfection of its own accord, and that it was a blessing that
these artists came into contact with the objectivist art of the Near East.
It is also no less obvious that the objectivist art was bound to soon
reach insurmountable barriers in all directions, which could only be
overcome with the help of a subjective and imaginary form of art. In

fact, Egyptian art reveals how they did indeed reach those limits. In sum, we are presented here with the confrontation of ancient Near Eastern Semitic and Indo-Germanic culture as it has characterized the entire development since. The consistently retardataire influence from the east always came to the aid of the west at the right moments. True progress and the ultimate political and cultural domination always reverted to the Indo-Germanic elements in the end.

From what we have said, it is clear that an expansion of eastern influence was absolutely necessary for the later development of Greek art, and we can recognize these conditions fulfilled in the so-called Mycenaean art. An eastern as well as another non-eastern influence has long ago been discerned as a factor of this art. At present we are interested in relief sculpture. In Mycenae, the flat relief on the tomb stelae is the earliest known type. It is probably Egyptian, and at first glance even seems to present an exact copy of Egyptian flat reliefs. The spiral ornament also seems to confirm this. Yet an interesting distinction emerges upon closer scrutiny. In Mycenae there was no modeling whatsoever of the third dimension. Egyptian artists did not believe in completely eliminating this since it was an objective property of objects and would not escape close range viewing. The Mycenaean artists reject even such slightly raised modeling as used by the Egyptians. Their figures present us with an absolutely flat surface appearing to us exclusively optically at a long range. From the single dimension of the spinning wheel knob from Troy, the Indo-Germanic artist has moved to two dimensions, presumably under the influence of Egyptian art, while the third dimension is still completely disregarded since the artist was accustomed to the subjective optic mode of viewing.

To understand the astonishing anachronism presented to us by the reliefs from the Vaphio cups it is necessary to bear in mind this apparently primitive stage of development and basic feeling common to all of the nations. After seeing nothing but the flattest possible reliefs among the Egyptians and Mycenaeans, we suddenly come across a deep relief without precedent. It is a deep relief not merely due to its depth throughout, but also because of the sculptural treatment of its tangible surface. There is no longer any trace of hesitancy regarding the dimension of depth and no anxious avoidance of shadow, but instead a deliberate accumulation of mighty rising, sinking, folding and buckling forms with conscious contrasts of light and shade. The manner in which the heads and limbs of the animals and bodies of the humans are modeled can only be described as painterly (malerisch). Instead of the scrupulous clarity of the wide and flat elements, we are shown a stormy conflict of incorporeal lights and shadows! Instead of the flatly swelling half shaded transitions such as on the ribs of the bull on the second cup, there is a linear engraving like the latest phases of antiquity with their stress on viewing at a distance! Where in the history of art does another comparable relief appear? All of early Greek art from the Homeric period onward produced nothing other than flat reliefs in the Egyptian sense, and where there is an early deeper relief as at Selinunt, then this is only due to the simple depth of carving and not the treatment of the surface, which remains flat and goes to great length to avoid modeling. Of course the deep relief was thoroughly developed during the classical period, but such a predominantly optic painterly conception of the surface as on the reliefs of the Vaphio cups does not even occur in the Alexandrian period or even in the last phases of ancient art. The necessary prerequisites for such an uncompromising triumph of the optic qualities did not emerge until modern art.

We should recall in this connection that two of the bull's faces are turned outward from the relief plane to face the spectator directly. Early Near Eastern art avoided this outright, which had its reasons first in the objectivism which basically ignores the spectator, and then also in the tendency to avoid both the dimension of depth and foreshortening, where the difficulties of depicting noses and "facial protrusions" became prominent. In early Near Eastern art, the exceptions to these rules are extremely rare. When it occurs in Egyptian art, it is only in painting and never in relief sculpture. Can it be a coincidental exception that the frontal depiction of a head occurs in these two cups?[54] The problem of foreshortening was not dealt with until the transition into the classical period, yet it appears here in Mycenaean art and has been resolved without regard to the resulting lack of clarity. One thing must be considered peculiar, and since it also occurs in other Mycenaean

---

54 Two of the human heads on the cups are shown in profile, but that of the figure being cast over reveals a bit more. Unfortunately, the galvanoplastic cast at my disposal does not allow me to distinguish the smaller details of the face. This is because the Mycenaean artist sought a primarily painterly effect in the heads. The absolute profile in the body of the man flipping head first over the back of the bull is all the more important as a contrast to the Egyptian postulate of a clear frontal presentation of the body including both arms. This motif of motion which literally places the human form on its head, is absolutely distinct from all early Near Eastern art. An optical conception of the whole provided the prerequisite to the success of such a figure. Such a secure hand in depicting so eruptive a motion does not occur again in Greek art until the optical qualities had been rehabilitated in the Hellenistic period, where baroque qualities arise with a general similarity to the Vaphio cups. This seems to be based on the escalation of motion in the forms that is common to both.

artifacts, cannot be considered a coincidence: the heads of these two bulls are foreshortened downward toward the plane, not in the usual vertical but moved horizontally. We can only explain this by a desire of the artist to avoid direct eye contact between the bull and the spectator. This is doubtlessly an influence from the objectivism which still characterized classical art in a similar way after it had ultimately admitted the use of foreshortening. In classical art, the heads are shown looking out of the picture with foreshortening, but usually in a three-quarter profile and generally not facing the spectator. It was not until Christian art that the contact between such a head and the spectator became a well-considered feature.

After specifying the position of the Vaphio cups within the development of compositional and relief art we are left to consider the idea they express. In the earliest historically discernible periods in which the entire vision of nature and the conditions of life are dominated by intractable religious conceptions, the idea plays the smallest part in a purely artistic appraisal since it leaves very little or no latitude at all for the artist. Egyptian art for instance contains ideas that are of greater interest to Egyptologists than to art historians. Among the Mycenaean artifacts, we can also expect to find allusions to the gods and their worship in all aspects. Is this true of the scenes of capturing bulls on the Vaphio cups? It would appear unlikely although we cannot exclude the possibility out of hand. From the joy with which the various adventures are depicted in all of their random and passing details it strikes us as unlikely that they might have been essentially made to evoke religious thoughts. It is notable how comparatively recessive the religious character actually is when we survey the mass of other Mycenaean monuments.

This is obvious when they are compared to Egyptian art. Not only are the most important decorative motifs of Egyptian art, such as the lotus, papyrus, scarab or uraeus taken from Egyptian religious practices, but also the apparent genre scenes in the Egyptian tombs, which share certain objective details with the reliefs on our cups and relate to the well known sepulchral beliefs of the Egyptians. The battle scenes from the period of Ramasses present an isolated exception, but since they allude to the deeds of the king in the same way as the Assyrian battle reliefs, they are also actually simply glorifying another of the local gods. Mycenaean art presents a fundamental difference to the creative arts of the ancient Near East in shifting from the eastern religious imagery toward decoration. This is generally admitted to have been the case with the typology of plant ornament. Why should it be any different with the figural scenes of bulls being caught? This would make them genre images in the true sense. From the history of art we know that genre imagery only flourished in periods devoted to the optical unity of the image and with either no interest in adequate religious imagery or else very little. We have already seen how well these cups fulfill the first of these conditions. By the emphatic abdication of its religious character, Mycenaean art also confirms the second condition in an indirect way at least. If the reliefs on the Vaphio cups are indeed genre images, as they appear to be, then this presents an early advance in a direction which only again became possible in the Hellenistic period after the end of the system of the gods from the period of Homer and Hesiod. I have not found as gripping and instantaneous a conception of a quotidian activity in any other artifact of antiquity. The closest analogy to the conception of the Vaphio cups can be found in the more recent art of the Germanic nations – above all the Dutch of the 17th century. The two are most closely related in the intimate preoccupation with the nature of animals. This leads us to another remarkable aspect of the peculiar character of these two cups.

We have already referred to the somehow emotional relation evoked between the two animals at the center of the second cup. Even a cursory glance at the two cups shows that the primary subjects are the bulls rather than the humans. Particularly on the second cup, we see an image of bulls completely in the sense of Dutch 17th century painting. Human figures also appear, but they recede in significance in two ways.

First of all in their dimensions. The bulls are shown much larger than the human figures or the trees. To our modern point of view, it strikes us as a great shortcoming, the only one beside the tree shown hovering in the air.[55] This seems again to result from the tendency to clarity which runs through all of ancient art. The main subject may not be obscured by secondary features or attributes, but should be grasped immediately. Or must we assume that this omission in terms of the optical and distanced momentary image was not apparent to the artist? If this were the case, how then could he have captured the bulls, as well as the humans and plants in their isolated unity with such a masterly

---

55 Brunn, loc cit., voices criticisms of the treatment of the fore legs of the fleeing bull and the projection of that caught in the net, but is completely unjustified. His other reproach seems to be based on inadequate photographic reproduction, since the galvanoplastic cast shows that the line of the back from the head to the tail is rendered completely correctly. Regarding the former, one must wonder whether Brunn has ever seen a running bull.

rendition of their momentary motions – unprecedented in early Near Eastern art, and comparable only to much later Greek examples?

The second and no less important aspect in which the human form is subordinated to the animals lies in the subject matter itself. The entire order of the ancient world was built on the right of the strong. The victor was not merely considered to be right in all matters, but was universally admired. In the visible world however, the strongest protagonist is the human being, and all other creatures serve his needs. In the scenes on the two cups, the humans are also the stronger. In one case the bull is caught by human craftiness, and in another is being transported away restrained with ropes. It almost seems as if the overarching artistic theme is to illustrate the ultimate physical superiority of human intelligence over the realm of the animals. Does it not appear to do justice to the massive basic power of the animal when the artist shows the bull overcoming two men at once? This presents us with another characteristic of the Indo-Germanic nations in contrast to those of the Near East which stands out as all the more typical when it is unalloyed with eastern influences. The Semitic and the Germanic nations comprise two poles in this, with the Romance cultures situated in between.

We might summarize the conclusion of our observations. We would expect the earliest Greek monuments to reveal isolated individual traits of their later national development, and we found the cups from Vaphio to include all of the relevant characteristics, including composition, the treatment of the relief and the idea. They seem completely independent from those of the ancient Near East, but also in a developmental stage more advanced than that of post-Homeric early Greek art, and in some sense even surpassing the classical and Hellenistic artistic character. We might explain such a puzzling situation as follows.

Greek art had developed not as a continuation of earlier Near Eastern examples but in an opposition to them which it displayed from the very beginning. This contrast can be seen most clearly in the approach to the relation of form to surface. In the east, this was done in an objective manner based on a view at close range with the parts recognizable to the sense of touch and mechanically assembled to a whole. Among the Greeks, or their Indo-Germanic predecessors to be more precise, the whole was from the very outset conceived subjectively and optically as seen at a distance, originally as a mere image from memory in the imagination. This contrast was also apparent in its very earliest compositions. In the east there was a choice of a purely material organization of the parts on the basis of a crystalline parallelism of lines and surfaces. The Greeks loosened the lifeless inorganic crystalline quality to allow for organic movement, first in the physical sense, accepted by the Egyptians only as a necessary evil. It also later did so in the emotional and intellectual sense which Egyptian art had completely eliminated. Finally then, on the level of the idea, this contrast is no less apparent. In the ancient Near East, all art was identical with religion, which is to say that all phenomena and actions related to an objective personal deity. The Greeks had a subjective interest in the objects of the world in their relations and causality to the spectator as well as among themselves. Already in the Mycenaean period, we can recognize the nation that would later invent philosophy, natural science, and give birth to the insight that man must be the measure of all things.

On the knob of the spinning wheel from Troy, we recognized the earliest expressions of a conception at odds with that from the east. This primitive art, which art historians call Indo-Germanic on the basis of analogies among Celtic and Germanic examples, soon took notice of eastern models and learned from them. It then made use of what it had learned and brought its own creation to a breakthrough in a more elevated and monumental way. This occurred in Mycenaean art, and the cups from Vaphio are evidence of it. In relief sculpture at least, very little was lacking in this art for a complete rendition of optical and material appearances. We have already noted that one of our own contemporary sculptors would have very little to add. We must identify what it is that was still missing from this art in spite of its perfection in this particular aspect, and why it could not have led directly to classical art. In Mycenaean art it would hardly have become possible to make the human figure the vehicle of ethical or moral ideas. As an inescapable condition, such a quality requires a close range record of the human figure and above all of the face.[56] This was the point in which early Near Eastern art with its exclusively close view of objects assumed a decisive importance. Early Near Eastern art itself had eliminated all thought and emotion from its figures, but it did indeed create a type of the physical appearance of humanity with crystalline quietude and objective being. It was this rather than a more or less imaginary image from memory that became the point of departure for the Greeks in

---

56 It strikes us as characteristic in this light that Mycenaean has left us with no large scale human images as they were so common in Egyptian art, and which would have demanded an approach viewed and made at a close proximity to the models. The more recent history of art has also shown that predominantly optical problems are better treated in terms of small figures.

creating the corporeal and intellectual beauty, and then by extension also the perfect rendition of emotion.

This explains how it was possible for this puzzlingly fascinating Mycenaean art, so well developed in particular ways, to disappear and yield to that of the Dipylon. As much as I recognize that this was a necessary transitional phase in the development of classical art, in its figural aspects at least, I can still only see the Dipylon essentially as a regression in the development back to early Near Eastern qualities, just as I stated it seven years go [*Stilfragen*, *Problems of Style*, 1992, cf. Glossary "Dipylon style," p. 400]. While the Mycenaean Warrior Vase sought true optical appearances and did not depict the rear arms behind their bodies, the art from the Dipylon showed both arms to either side of the body – according to the same human objective habit that governed Egyptian art with only very rare exceptions. While the Bull Fighter from Tiryns [National Archaeological Museum Athens] had included the thigh and calf muscles drawn in their contours, creating a degree of modeling that Egyptian art abhorred in its avoidance of depth, and post-Homeric art only developed very slowly in the course of centuries. The Dipylon figures show a return to silhouettes following the Egyptian example. Compositions approach the stiff sequential rows of Egyptian art and the religious content of the Dipylon paintings is also closer to the Egyptian sepulchral scenes than to the cups from Vaphio. There is of course no lack of typically Greek details in the Dipylon art, and the essential one of these is certainly the fact that the dominant center of the compositions was not relinquished. Nonetheless, we are left with the pervasive impression of symptoms of regression, and a resumption of qualities from Near Eastern art.

Allow us to say a few words in conclusion about the antithesis we have been describing, and its life in the later development of ancient art. The second phase after assimilating the eastern achievement was a glorious and unique balance of the existing contrasts in the great period of Attic art, with composition, form, surface and idea predominantly returning to the specifically Indo-Germanic mode. When another, the Italic national group with less contact to the eastern influences, began to create art during the later development of the ancient period, it was natural for the specifically Indo-Germanic qualities to predominate still further. This included the viewing from a distance, painterly composition and the rendition of objects outside of traditional religious functions. In comparing this Roman art to the early Near East and to the Greeks as well, we should bear in mind that it is not the Greeks in and of themselves who strike such a distinction to the more gradual than habitual character of Italic art. It was the Greeks under eastern influence that was compelling and useful to them. What Italic art achieved during the first century of the Roman imperial period, had in principle already occurred among the Greeks some thousands of years before, in very different circumstances and in a far more radical way as we have just seen in the Vaphio cups. If another proof were necessary that in spite of its innate tenaciousness, the Indo-Germanic trend perpetually required revitalization by eastern impulses, then it can be seen in the development of late antique art. Another wave of eastern influence in politics, government, culture and art began with the Antonines and gripped not merely the Greeks who had long ago assimilated eastern elements, but also the Italic populations. It would take another thousand years until the artistic level of the Vaphio cups would again be reached, but this time crucially surpassing it. The role of advanced development this time fell to the Germanic nations while it was now the Romance cultures that assumed the role of the eastern trends, just as it had previously existed between the Italics and the Greeks, the Greeks to the Egyptians and the Near East.

The Origin of the Early Christian Basilica[57]

I.

In the territory of Austria-Hungary there are still intact monuments of early Christian basilica architecture which can be counted among the most complete and best preserved in existence. If we add to this the results of recent excavations, such as those at Salona, then we can claim without anticipating any objections, that aside from Italy, the Austrian monarchy possesses more, and the most important surviving examples of early Christian basilica architecture in Europe. This might explain why we attempt to resolve the persistent question surrounding the origins of the early Christian basilica in a periodical such as this one devoted to the description of Austrian artistic monuments.

If we recall that colonnades with hemispherical niches were quite characteristic both of profane and sacred pagan architecture, then it is obvious that the Christian basilica was not an innovation (around the 3rd century AD) occurring independently of Roman architecture of its time. This fact has always spawned the correct deduction that in creating a house of worship for the specific needs of their cult, the Christians

57 Originally published as "Die Entstehung der altchristlichen Basilika," *Jahrbuch der K. K. Zentral-Kommission zur Erforschung und Erhaltung der kunst- und historischen Denkmäler*, new ser., vol. 1, 1903, pp. 91-110.

did not invent unprecedented architectural forms, but used examples then already current in the Roman Empire. The problem was posed in the materialist, purely utilitarian terms as they dominated all of the later 19th century research in artistic questions. It was assumed that the Christians looked among the pagans for the system of architecture that might best serve the practice of their creed and particularly the celebration of the Eucharist. According to this, they found what they were looking for in the market basilica on the one hand and in the private basilica on the other. The functional model for the Christian cult then developed to accommodate the needs of the new religion. The earliest of these hypotheses on the basilica – which remains the most likely if we follow the functionalist argument – declared that the Christians modeled their basilica on the secular market basilica, and for practical reasons simply eliminated the columns from the two narrow ends.

Such an explanation omits an aspect that could be considered purely antiquarian, and that is art. It was natural that such things would be overlooked in the period of artistic materialism: beauty was then simply considered the necessary result of practicability, and the work of art nothing more than a mechanical product from the conjunction of purpose, material and technique. In the course of the last century, the distinction has become clearer between what is practicable in accommodating human needs, and what is beautiful because of its appeal. We can barely find our moorings in this dualist conception when the question already arises: how could the basilica have appealed to the Christians in such a way for them to perpetuate it throughout Europe for a good millennium?

We might undercut the justification of the entire question by recalling that the early Christians expressed indifference to the visual arts at best, but usually outright hostility. It is true that the first Christians were possessed with eschatological conceptions, and that later on when they began to reconcile themselves to the world and built a church for themselves we still often see ascetic tendencies, a lack of interest or even open rejection of the visual arts. It would be wrong to lend too much weight to these objections. Polytheistic paganism, which could in some sense be considered to have deified the visual arts, itself brought forth spirits from its own midst who not merely denied any cathartic function for art, but even its very right to exist: these included not merely the Neo-Platonists, who might be discounted as a phenomenon from the later period, but also the great Plato himself, who represents the pinnacle of Greek culture in so many ways. The opulent funerary art of the early Christians should actually preclude any assertion that they objected to the visual arts. We have but to compare the graves being designed in our own time when we are experiencing something like an intense cult of art, and then recognize that even at its best, none of it can compare with the artistic quality of some of the early Christian tombs. Quite to the contrary, the early Christians felt the pronounced need for the arts and the enjoyment of creativity. As such, the majority of them assumed their place as fully entitled participants in creating the art of the Roman Empire alongside the pagans who are all too often seen as its only contributors. We are left with the question as to what distinguishes this putative Christian artistic will from the pagan temples of the time. How did the two relate to one another?

If we look for answers among the monuments themselves, the current state of research will not help. As has been the case over the last decades, our publications are still primarily limited to iconographical distinctions in the poses of figural compositions. The most obvious characteristic here is the suppression of objectionable pagan motifs, although even that was not pursued with any rigor. While iconographic comparisons of that sort cling more to extrinsic qualities such as the content and subject matter, nobody is in a position to clarify the possible differences between the treatment of form and color. Even this negative state of affairs does not fail to enlighten us. If the differences were in fact as prominent and profound as it is claimed, then some of the scholars would probably have recognized them. Other more general considerations also suggest this.

I am deeply and ineradicably convinced that our ethical and aesthetic will is intimately related. This is clear from the fact that we are consistently tempted to make comparisons between phenomena in the history of art and those of contemporary cultural history, and always consider art to be conditioned by culture. It is an easy matter for rigorous critics of this comparison to reject it wholesale and simply ask for the evidence. This only demonstrates that humanity is simply following an irresistible and therefore presumably natural compulsion, something like an electrical current we might say, which could achieve its connection forcibly in a short circuit if the normal avenues become too circuitous. We might even claim that every single one of these intelligent and careful critics has at some point indulged in this in one way or another. It might even be possible by now to demonstrate the close relationship between the early Christian artistic will and that of contemporary paganism, as well as that of the early Christian religious intentions and pagan religious volitions of the time. This can already be seen in those extreme cases where the mutual relations reach an intensity with the one negating the other, as in iconoclasm. Something like this would be far too involved in the present context, and we can only appeal to the instinct of the reader. How does current research evaluate the relation of the early Christian to the pagan religious practice?

What has prevented an unbiased assessment of this relationship has primarily been the doctrine of revelation, and less of its own accord than by some of its close associations. The idea of a communication that could only come from heaven, and which humanity was incapable of finding on its own, has led to the assumption that early Christianity was separated from contemporary pagan religion by an unbridgeable gulf. Progressive research has narrowed this chasm without actually harming the creed based on the revelation. This also remains unaffected by the proposition that the pagans of the Roman imperial period were pursuing the same goal as the Christians, but that the latter had the advantage of having found the coveted salvation in revealed truth. Too much documentation has come to light to continue denying the common religious and ethical goals uniting all of the nations within the Roman Empire.

Religious life during the first three centuries of the Roman imperial period was characterized by a growing sense that the traditional polytheistic faith was inadequate to the ethical redemptive needs of the civilized humanity of the time. The more educated groups had already begun to feel this centuries earlier when Greek philosophy applied reason to the questions lingering where faith had failed. By the second century AD, these educated people had arrived at the stage of skepticism and doubt surrounding the possibility of any sort of salvation through philosophy or science. The largest parts of the population felt the necessity for an imperative faith in their lives, lost their trust in the religious system of the twelve Greek gods and looked to other cults. Romans of the imperial period continued to worship the traditional deities of the state and family much in the way they performed their duties of citizenship. For its most intimate emotional distress and needs of redemption, they no longer looked to Zeus or Hera, Apollo or Athena, but rather to Isis or Attis, Serapis or Mithras etc. All of these deities were superficially transferred from eastern religions and had certain things in common. They had a tendency to monotheism, a cult practice centered on ceremonial mystery, and finally also an aspiration toward immortality, which the people of late antiquity increasingly came to consciously see as their salvation. Each of these aspects includes both differences as well as an affiliation that existed to the classical polytheistic view and that of Christianity.

We thus recognize common religious goals among Christians and pagans of the early imperial period, but can see that they merely sought them by different means. By analogy then, we might assume the same about its artistic intentions (Kunstwollen): Christians and pagans generally pursued the same goals through the arts, only by differing avenues. We do not have to look far for an example of this – the basilica presents itself as just such an example. By the great similarity of most of its parts, it is clear that the Christian and the pagan (forensic) basilica are closely related if indeed they did not fulfill identical basic aesthetic needs. Yet there is also a difference in the fact that no Christian basilica is completely like a market basilica or vice versa.

II.

These observations were simply intended to allay the obstacles which an obsolete, materialist view poses for an understanding of the essential meaning and the origins of the Christian basilica. The implication had been that the early Christian used the arts like clothing that might be worn or removed depending on the warm or cold weather, without the slightest consideration of whether it might have appealed to the owner or to others. The most important result is that we are not under an obligation to find a certain architectural system among the pagans, which the early Christians adopted without alteration to satisfy their practical needs. We can recognize the Christian basilica to be an independent artistic creation on the part of the early Christians, interpreting and dismembering elements common to the pagans, with whom they had shared certain artistic volitions.

We must first of all consider the practical purpose the Christian basilica was intended to serve. Even if its function does not generate beauty along mechanistic lines as the doctrine of artistic materialism would have assumed, it does nonetheless provide an outside impulse for the introduction of beauty, and provides at least one of its conditions. In order to appreciate those aspects of the artwork revealing the actual artistic will, then we must eliminate those from consideration that serve exclusively practical purposes. Before the purely artistic analysis can begin, we must therefore recognize exactly which were the practical functions of Christian ecclesiastical architecture. In doing so, we can completely omit the earliest period which was consumed by eschatological expectations, and has been felicitously described as one of communism. Among the Christians, the conditions for a general type of church architecture only arose once they began planning to spend the remainder of their lives on this earth until its unknown end. For a variety of reasons, this did not occur before the second half of the second century AD. We shall see that this shift brought with it an internal consequence for the religious practice and had a significant effect on the general design of the church structure.

Since approximately the end of the second century, the Christian cult architecture emerged as the place where the community conceived themselves as participating in the redemptive actions of the priest. Less from a desire for secrecy than for cleanliness as it were, this activity was to take place within an enclosed space since none were supposed to witness the sacrament unless properly prepared to do so – not even accidentally from a distance. By contrast to those of the polytheistic cults, the Christian sacrifice had a distinctly mystic meaning, like among others the contemporary pagan Mithras sacrifices. Characteristically, this mystery never physically excluded the individual believer, who participated in the sacrifice in spite of the fact that as spiritual leader of the community, only the priest handled it. Isolated from the outside, they contributed only the appropriate inner devotion within this space. This arrangement began to have an effect on the design of the church in the course of the communistic period when the physical presence of each co-religionist was mandatory at the presentation and reception of the sacrament. With such changes in conception, the role of the priest was bound to become more distinguished and respectful in relation to the congregation than that of a functional mediator – if such an inaccurate term is acceptable – as it had previously been during the communistic period. In this situation, the Christian religious architecture required one space for the priest to consecrate the host, and then another attached but respectfully distinguished from this, accommodating the community, with both protected by solid walls on all sides from the eyes of the uninitiated or those lacking the honor to participate.

The one of these spaces was the semicircular apse, covered with a half dome and originally without windows, where the mystery is enacted at the sacrificial altar by the priest. It was in no way distinguished from a domed half rotunda, derived from the centralized construction, one of the best known Roman architectural forms. At this point, we should digress slightly and reflect on the meaning and significance of the Roman centralized plan (whose presumed Hellenistic sources are too little known for us to speculate).

The round plan resulted from the emancipation of the perspective of depth in ancient art. This emancipation expresses itself not merely in the external tactile surfaces marked by strong light and shadow appearing to the viewer to either bulge inward or outward, but also in the admission of empty space as an aesthetic factor – and this is the basis of its actual epochal significance. Only at this point, after the classical period was over, was there a move to treat the interior space as an artistic element. Only after this moment can we speak of monumental art based on space. The centralized plan resolved the problem of a balance between intangible, endless, formless depth on the one hand, and limited tactile relatively symmetrically enclosed space on the other. In entering the Pantheon in Rome for instance, we immediately sense that the immeasurable and therefore disturbing depth of its space is approximately equivalent to the measurable width and height. By including the same radius, the round dome balances out all uncomfortable angles and completes the impression of certainty in the viewer. The extrinsic, tactile and enclosed form is also felt in the interior, and the firm encompassing form causes us to forget the impression of immeasurable open space. As is the case with all of classical art, the basis of the centralized plan is symmetry, but no longer symmetry in a plane, but the symmetry of space which Gottfried Semper has given the name of eurhythmy.

The centralized plan became the typical monumental form of Roman architecture. This is manifested by the fact that the most overt monuments to have that name, the tombs of the most influential nobles of the republican period were designed along these lines. They are monuments or memorials like works of sculpture, presenting themselves only to the exterior as self contained, tactile and yet eurhythmic bulging forms. Only when they came to be covered with centralized domes did their interior spaces assume a monumental meaning. In the ancient world this was true of all sacred functions, and there were many of these, since its daily life was completely permeated with sanctity. Spaces built with a simple functional purpose and no monumental intention were often given an added space with some sort of sacred meaning, usually using the favorite motif of a malleable open space. In many of these cases, it seems as if this was done out of an artistic impulse, and that the sacred meaning provided no more than an excuse. These appended round structures could not of course be completely round, but only half circles: hence the semi-circular niche surmounted by the half dome.

Since the addition of a second connected space was a given, it becomes clear that the Christians could choose no other architectural form than the centralized ground plan for their space, the apse, and that this was to house the mystery itself and to be the place of the priest as its agent.[58]

The other space was conceived as the meeting place of the community. This function was distinctly subordinate to the place of the mystery. Generally speaking, the faithful had no direct relation to the mystery itself. If their space had also been given a monumental character, this would have obscured the significance of the place reserved for the mystery. The place of the faithful was therefore designed along the lines of the average meeting places of the time: a space accommodating the circulation of people, coming and going with no monumental closure. The hall with colonnades provided such a space.

The ancient form of the hall (στοά, *porticus*) had been an aisle articulated with a row of columns on at least one, but often also on all sides. The thought was to create a space that would allow people to converge and perambulate without creating the impression of an enclosed space. The eye was intended to meet only with columns:

---

58 Among other reasons, baptisteries were regularly built with a centralized form because this was reserved for interior spaces of a monumental nature. They presented a monumental housing for the "piscina," the sacred spot at which the acceptance into the Christian community was performed. It can come as no surprise that the round form was also used for tombs and churches built over tombs.

limited, tactile, individual material elements, standing on a flat ground, but rising above it, and pushing back the emptiness of space so as to suppress it artistically, much as the relief sculpture does with its open background. The market basilica-type in architecture makes it clear that halls such as this existed in the Roman imperial period as ordinary spaces for the congregation of people.

In its basic constituents, the Roman market basilica was composed simply of four colonnaded halls opening onto a common oblong court. The artistic element of the basilica consisted in the columns on the interior – tangible limited material forms repeated rhythmically. For reasons that have not been documented for us, the idea of the open court was at one point replaced with a roofed space. Adherents of the materialist theory of art would presumably be content to explain this decisive change from the fact that the space was supposed to be used during the summer, the winter, and in all weather conditions. In superficial terms, this might easily have been one of the reasons. Yet there was certainly also at least one artistic consideration running parallel to any such practical factor. It seems likely that the increasing tendency to choose enclosed spaces, as it had characterized the centralized structures, was also applied to more strictly functional architecture. The Mediterranean nations of the classical period all considered the even ground of an open space to be the foil for the tangible human individual, that this was the only valid aesthetic subject, and all of them began to feel the need for an enclosure within a limited space. Expressed more plainly: they began to feel embarrassed that unwanted spectators could observe their movements in the market place, and not only built walls around the sides, but also covered it with a roof, creating a question of lighting which called for the walls to be raised higher than the columns. This undeniably left the court no longer open, and meant that even the latent introduction of an enclosed space with colonnades created the basis for a new and essentially un-classical development. When this was originally done, presumably in the Hellenistic period, there was no thought of the possible consequences so clear to us today. During the Roman imperial period, the roof over a court seems to have been considered a provisional solution, since it did not include vaulting in a single instance, and was not made of permanent materials, but always as a flat, wooden roof.[59]

We can also understand now why the early Christians created their meeting place before the apse as a horizontal space with three (or more) aisles. The current type of such spaces was the columnar hall, and there was no reason to change it. Since their cult demanded isolation from the outside world, the roof over the hall presented a necessity. It is obvious why it was necessary to eliminate the colonnades at the narrow ends, so differently than the market basilica. There could be no direct relation between the space of the mystery and that of the congregation, while the space of the mystery needed to open independently onto

---

59 The basilica of Maxentius on the Roman forum with its vaulting is a completely isolated example, has a ground plan with fundamental differences from the typical basilica scheme, and can only be seen as the rudiment of a development that was never followed – much as Diocletian and his party broke off relations with Maxentius in religious matters and his approach ended immediately. Numerous monuments prove that the Romans might have placed vaulting over an oblong ground plan if they had wished. They normally divided monumental horizontal spaces (particularly their bath houses) into square subdivisions with individual cross vaults.

the free space of the (roofed) court. At the opposite narrow end, it was not necessary to eliminate the columns, and occasionally they remained. It is natural that these halls which led toward the mystery would be favored and that an entrance at the side would not have an actual purpose. This created a directionality that had been only latently present in the market basilica and now became pronounced in the Christian basilica. We must dispute the notion that this directionality was embodied in these naves with a perspectival connotation. This was only expressed artistically in the corridor forms of the side aisles with their extensive length in relation to the breadth. It is essential not to project the artistic intentions of later basilicas onto the basilica of the early Christians.

This suggests that the constitutive element of the nave originally included only the two side aisles. Of course, this does not mean that the worshipers did not also walk into the central aisles, or certainly not also into the atria, which indubitably included an open area surrounded by four colonnades – and as accessible as the halls themselves. It is known that at least a part of the central nave was off limits to the congregation, that area closest to the altar, the "schola cantorum." It was still the columns which provided the most prominent artistic element of the early Christian basilica. The artistic effect of the nave in the early Christian basilica was not achieved by the perspective view down its length toward the altar, but rather from the side aisle across the covered court to the front of the other side aisle with its colonnade and paintings on the wall above. Not a single example of the many early Christian basilicas known intact or in remains in the east or the west has vaulting or even a ceiling with cassettes: they all have a simple wooden roof, sometimes paneled, which contrasts starkly with the semi-dome of the area hosting the mystery.

What then is the relation of the early Christian basilica to the type of the market basilica? Was the latter the direct and conscious model of the former? It was certainly not the case in the sense that the early Christians made a thorough survey of the available architectural types and then chose the market basilica. This would appear to be contradicted by the complete unity of form existing throughout the entire Roman Empire to the extent to which Christian communities built churches at all. It is so natural that variations of one sort or another would have occurred that the opposite would be easier to understand. However the type with the combination of the apse, two colonnades separated by a court became so widespread within such a short time, that it is inconceivable that the market basilica might have been first imitated in a particular location (even if this had been Rome) and then spread from there to the remainder of the empire. This strong persistence is more an indication that the conception of individual architectural forms we have mentioned was universal within the Roman Empire, and that without any sort of necessary impulse, the identical church design was therefore destined to be adapted everywhere. From what we know, this would also not have sat well with the reserved attitude of the church toward the arts during the first centuries. On the other hand, the early Christians could not have overlooked the similarity that existed between their basilica and the market basilica, for this could be the only explanation for the fact that the name of basilica was adopted for the church structure in the first place. The similarity was not only based on the colonnades around a central court, but extended also to the apse. The market basilica also required a monumental part relating to the whole, but set apart by its distinguishing shape. This was the judicial tribune corresponding completely to the apse, but in keeping with its far more limited significance it is kept much smaller, and by no means commanded the attention of all present, for which reason the colonnade was not interrupted before it.[60]

III.

In the view of the origin of the early Christian basilica and nave as we have just presented it, it might at first appear strange that the central nave should not be given the greatest importance. What are actually present are the two side aisles. The central nave is actually only a relief ground, architectonically a void, a formless, empty space,

---

60 From what we have said, it should be clear why we have not dealt with the question of where exactly the early Christian basilica first took shape. As they were presumably first made by Greeks, colonnades and apses occurred all over the Roman Empire. When an international Roman art is then mentioned, it includes the fundamental elements of Roman architecture. The question of "Orient or Rome" which is currently being so emotionally discussed, seems to be completely indifferent from the point of view of the sources we are studying here. What would be the result for research if we were to replace the general term "late Roman" with "Eastern," when there can be no question of the art of the 4th to the 8th centuries AD being identical with ancient Egypt, Mesopotamia or Persia? What would it help us to know if a given motif appeared earlier in the eastern or the western provinces of the Roman Empire if we cannot understand its artistic meaning in terms of its artistic origin? The state of our knowledge of early medieval art is still remote from any such distinctions. Over the last decades, it has been my own far from simple task to work on this problem. Neither the repeated emotional attacks of some or the disinterest of others will divert me from the dogged and confident pursuit of a truly historical understanding of late antique art.

covered only provisionally. In our own time, we are so accustomed to the central aisle as the actual center of the church space, and the side as merely providing access to the lateral chapels that we have difficulty understanding the reverse arrangement. During the consecration of the host, we today congregate in the central aisle to allow a view of the main altar and the celebrating priest, and even if our eyes are in the prayer book, we feel confident that an upward glance could at any instant confirm which moment of the sacrament is transpiring. How can we imagine that the early Christians crowded mainly into the side aisles so that almost only those beneath the arcades were able to see the consecration with their own eyes!

As far as the cult aspect of this objection is concerned, we should consider that in the Greek Church, the congregation is still today separated from the altar and the priest by the iconostasis, and a view of the altar or the priest has never been a necessary part of the Christian celebration. This would also seem to be confirmed by the fundamental quality of mystery that emphasized internal contemplation over external sensual perception.[61] The galleries, actually also nothing other than flanking aisles, further confirm their intended design to be occupied by the congregation, although today they strike us as subsidiary. Since the galleries were conceived to be occupied by the members of the one sex, it is at least highly probable that the two side

---

61 In spite of a number of meritorious observations, this is also a reason that the explanation for the origins of the Christian basilica offered by Felix Witting, *Die Anfänge christlicher Architektur: Gedanken über Wesen und Entstehung der christlichen Basilika*, Strassburg: Heitz 1902, is mistaken, because it presumes a "visual impression" suggested by modern habits which are not historically documented.

aisles on the ground floor were originally designed to separate the two
sexes and used in that way for some time thereafter.

Our own interest is in the artistic aspect of the question. Whether
it be conscious or not, we fully experience the spatial effect of the
central aisle as a self-contained experience of space with the effect of
perspective leading our eye toward the main altar. It seems natural to
us that the early Christians should have desired and enjoyed the same
effect. Yet historical examination does not support such a preconceived
notion.

I myself can vividly recall the hours I spent during my student
years at the portals of S. Paolo fuori le Mura and S. Maria Maggiore
in order to experience the effect of their central aisles and to draw
conclusions about the artistic intentions of their original authors. Of
course, I was also looking for an effect of space and of perspective.
At least one aspect of the perspective effect seems present in S. Paolo
(which although it is only a reconstruction, still preserves the original
spatial relations): according to the handbooks, the round arcades were
supposed to lead the eye toward the main altar. If this is the case,
why was there such a massive wall above the arcade and such a very
heavy immovable ceiling? I attempted to allay these impressions with
explanations of "barbarism" or "antagonism to art" on the part of the
early Christians. Such explanations felt very inconvenient and untrue
as soon as I set foot in other interior spaces from the late imperial period
such as S. Maria degli Angeli or the basilica of Maxentius. In S. Maria
Maggiore, even the arcades seemed to fail. And then came a strange
phenomenon: when I stood at the center of the nave, the foreign and
oppressive effect began to disappear, the columns began to have their

effect, the massive perforated upper walls seemed less heavy and even harmonious in their alternation of wall and opening with the columns and intervals below. Even the ceiling appeared to lose its rigidity and weight, possibly because it did not seem to obtrude on the eye from this vantage point. This might have led me to realize that the artistic effect is not to be sought in the perspective of a closed space, but rather in the flat fronts of the lateral walls. However, the prejudice in favor of the central nave as the presumed vehicle of the fundamental artistic intention was so strong that I then became discouraged and curtailed my studies with the conclusion that I had been pursuing a problem in vain.[62]

Of course, the explanation soon became apparent. Aside from the iconostasis which we have just mentioned, the barriers and ambos, Easter candles and other details would have blocked the perspective view toward the altar so that this could not possibly have been the view originally intended. If it is possible to draw conclusions for a parish church from an abbey church, then it might be especially clear from the plan of the abbey church of St. Gall, where the entire central nave is filled with altars. In studying the art historical development of the entire medieval period, I was soon led to the opinion that the perspective effect could not possibly have been a goal of the early Christian basilica because there was not yet any understanding of such things at that time. The effect we generally attribute to the early Christian basilica is not known to have been fully developed until the 15th century: in the

---

62 I hope that the personal manner of this description can be forgiven, since the difficulties of imagining the experience of the late antique viewer are difficult, and conveyed most graphically and convincingly in this way.

churches of Brunelleschi, the reliefs of Donatello and the paintings of Jan van Eyck. An intended perspective view of a longitudinal interior can be seen in baroque churches since Giacomo della Porta – the same baroque style that removed the viewing impediments from the early Christian basilicas, closed the windows in its upper walls and opened others to increase the painterly effect. The nave of the early Christian basilica could neither have been calculated for an enclosed spatial impression nor for a perspective view of the altar. What could have been its significance?

Five years ago, when I wrote the relevant paragraph in *Die spätrömische Kunstindustrie*,[63] I was already confident that the central nave was originally simply a central court like the central space of the forensic basilica, an open space serving as background for the surrounding colonnades. I was then so inhibited by the prejudices of modern practice and opinion, that I still did not dare to take the final step and to completely eliminate the nave from the list of artistic factors, but in contrast to what I have just said, this posed the question as to what artistic intentions other than the effects of space and of perspective might have led to the configuration of the nave. Our observation seemed relevant that the Romans of the imperial period did not use heavy walls to enclose even the most contained spaces such as centralized plans, but instead left them with a limited open spatial sphere similar to the framing shadows of late antique reliefs, as we see it in the development from the Pantheon and Minerva Medica to Sta. Costanza. I believed the opening of the nave walls with the colonnades

---

63 Alois Riegl, *Die spätrömische Kunstindustrie nach den Funden in Öster-reich-Ungarn*, ed, 1901, pp. 30-31 [ed. 1927, pp. 55-58, ed. 2014, pp. 95-102].

to be the result of a similar thought, revealing the open space behind. Already then, the fact that the narrow ends and the ceiling were not treated this way led me to believe that my hypothesis was inadequate. I have since that time completely abandoned the idea, because it does not explain the doubling in the number of side aisles that occurred in the largest and most monumental of the basilicas. If the side aisles are recognized as the constitutive element, then their multiplication can be explained simply and naturally, especially in those cases where greater space was required for large communities. If the central nave had been serving that function, then it would have sufficed to lengthen and widen that. What is true of the lateral expansion of the side aisles is equally true of the extension upward, that is to say into the galleries.

The emancipation of the central nave from its subordinate function as a foil or the ground of a relief began at that moment when the "schola cantorum" was moved there from the apse. It intensifies with the proliferation of altars as seen in the plan of St. Gall, and reaches its pinnacle in the phase that built double choirs. Only when it was covered in vaulting was the central nave perceived as an enclosed interior space: the vaulting is nothing other than the monumental expression of that change of conception in the architecture of Christian churches. The space for the community achieved the same monumental significance as the altar space that had been given such covering from the beginning. The medium is closely related to that used by the Romans for similar purposes: the division of the nave into square cross-vaulted segments assuming an intermediate place between a centralized and longitudinal plan. The medieval period only conceived of directionality upward and not as longitude.[64] During the Gothic, the central nave was continuously aggrandized, and the tendency emerged to reduce the side aisles into mere rows of chapels. This was then pursued to the fullest in the Baroque: the Roman churches of the Baroque consisted of a single vaulted space including the altar as the point of perspective. The side aisles have completely disappeared and are replaced by chapels, similar to the spaces in the Roman baths. It is no coincidence that Michelangelo transformed such a space into the church of S. Maria degli Angeli. In the churches they later designed, his followers then replaced the cross vault with a unilateral running barrel vault.

As we have traced it, the progressive emancipation of the community space was achieved far earlier in the Christian east. Here also, the dual basilica had originally been the church type. This is apparent from the examples in Syria, published by Melchior de Vogüé.[65] The caesaro-papist movement seized the east and did not allow the division between sacred and secular to become as pronounced as in the west.[66] For this reason, the community space in the east soon merged with the Presbytery, and both found their place in a common central

---

64 Allow us to correct the statement in *Die spätrömische Kunstindustrie*, ed. 1902, p. 29, [ed. 1927, p. 54, ed. 2014, p. 95] that Romanesque art already sought perspective effects.

65 [Eiugène Melchior de Vogüé and W. H. Waddington, *Syrie centrale: Architecture civile et religieuse du Ier au VIIe siècle*, Paris: Baudry, 1865-1877.]

66 The transept seems to have no other function than to further emphasize the strong distinction between the monumental space of the mystery and the profane space of the congregation, and its use seems characteristically to have been limited to the west. – As evidence for the derivation of the basilica form as I have traced it here, I feel I might also mention the earliest mosque layout (such as that of Amr and of Ibn-Tulun in Cairo).

space. While the distance between the priest and the congregation diminished in the east, that between man and God grew proportionally. In the east, the altar became the place where the deity revealed itself and was hidden from the eyes of the congregation by the iconostasis. It has often been stressed that there is a relation between the Byzantine centralized church plan and caesaro-papism. Our study shows a series of tangible links demonstrating what has previously only been vaguely intuited.

The Situation of Salzburg in the History of Art[67]

The unique place of Salzburg in the history of art has long been well known and articulated. Aside from numerous modern buildings on the outskirts, it has a strong Italian element still determining its character today. Of course this is also true of some other Austrian cities. The difference is that the Italian quality presents itself in Salzburg in a far purer form than in other cities further to the south, such as the episcopal seat of Bressanone (Brixen) or the commercial city of Bolzano (Bozen), both of which have always had much closer secular and ecclesiastical relations with Italy than Salzburg.

In Salzburg we meet not with the slow, normal, automatic, and unconscious transition from the southern-Romance to the northern-Germanic forms, as in southern Tyrol, but rather with an abrupt, purposeful transplantation of southern forms into the north for which Salzburg provided conditions better than any other city of the former Holy Roman Empire of the German Nation. If we were set down in Salzburg with a blindfold and removed it, none of us would believe we were in an Italian city. We could not doubt for a moment that we had arrived in a city north of the Alps and not in Italy. The

---

67 Originally published as: "Salzburgs Stellung in der Kunstgeschichte. Vortrag," *Mitteilungen der Gesellschaft für Salzburger Landeskunde*, vol. 45, 1905, pp. 1-22, and reprinted as *Salzburgs Stellung in der Kunstgeschichte*, Österreichische Kunstbücher vol. 18, Vienna: Hölzel 1921, 26 pp., 10 plates.

German aspect cannot be overlooked alongside the Italian. While the transition is gradual and unnoticeable in the German language area of Tyrol, it presents a sharper contrast in Salzburg. Both the Italian and the German factors are purer here. Since we are accustomed to the German qualities from other cities, we are more struck by the unusual Italian element, which generally appears stronger. The entire history of art in Salzburg is characterized by so unique a relationship between its art and the Italian art of the same particular period that it is best understood in light of this connection. I would like to speak to you this evening about this relationship more systematically than it has previously been done.

The fundamental Italian character already expresses itself in the fact that the artistic profile of the city is thoroughly dominated by the baroque style. In this regard, Salzburg recalls the great cultural center of all Romance culture, Rome itself. Amid the churches and secular architecture of the 16th to the 18th centuries, medieval monuments such as the interior of the church of St. Peter almost completely disappear to the extent they have not already been almost completely remodeled during the Baroque. This lack of medieval monuments corresponds to a lack of documentation of a predominantly Germanic artistic will, much as the Baroque had predominantly belonged to the Romance cultures.

Yet the Italianism of the art in Salzburg is not limited to the art of the baroque period. It did not begin in the more recent historical periods. The most prominent symptom of this is the absence of a large Gothic cathedral, indeed the absence of any trace of the pure Gothic. Since the Gothic is nothing other than the climax of the medieval artistic development among the Germanic and semi-Germanic nations, the indifference of the people of Salzburg to the Gothic also reveals how little they could relate to this efflorescence and fulfillment of Germanic medieval art. This raises the level of interest for the medieval period in terms of our attention to the Italianate elements in the art of Salzburg. Perhaps these monuments can provide a clue as to why the artistic development of the city consistently showed so pronounced a trend toward the Italian taste.

The origins of Salzburg as a settlement of a coherent civic character occurred in the ancient Roman period. For centuries, Romans or a Romance population inhabited the city. It is very tempting to attribute the trends of taste among the people of Salzburg to this circumstance, and this has in fact been proposed for a long time. Yet this hypothesis has also been denied with equal consistency. The basic assumption would be that the Romance population of the ancient period had maintained itself in such strength through the medieval and modern period that they continued to predominate over the waves of Bavarian-Germanic immigrants. We know from reliable sources that the Roman city lay completely dilapidated and in ruins during the lifetime of St. Rupert, indicating that, presumably at the end of the 6th century, it had been destroyed and not reconstructed. This makes it unlikely that the original ancient Roman population survived in sufficient numbers to support that hypothesis. On the other hand, there are documents to prove that such a population survived in the region around the city as late as in the Carolingian period. We remain ignorant of the size of this group in relation to the Bavarians. The fact that documentation suggests that the freedmen and nobles of this period seem to have had predominantly Germanic names is not critical to the argument. The same relation existed in France and northern Italy, and did not lead to a Romanization of the Franks, the Burgundians, the Goths or Lombards. Only since the high-medieval period do we have documentation suggesting an urban character that was purely Bavarian-Germanic. For this reason it would be untenable to deny any influence from a clear Romance element in the Salzburg population on the later Italophile tendencies. Today, the tools available to scholarship are simply too blunt to illuminate and determine the role of the Romance population any more closely.

The monuments themselves also provide no information here. The by no means negligible discoveries from the Roman period reveal the same uniform character typical of the entire area from the Danube to the Rhine and far beyond. It is not possible to confirm the precise date of origins for the oldest chapels on the Mönchsberg traditionally said to have been in use during the early Christian period. We can only confirm that as remains of the early Christian period, pagan conversions to Rome, these mirabilia continued to be venerated as was usual throughout the entire medieval period and into modern times. Even the Prince-Archbishop Wolf Dietrich von Raitenau [1559-1617], who was completely free of any such sentimentality, preserved the Chapel of Maximus.

We turn to the medieval and to the Romanesque period. In the Romanesque style, the church type that had arrived from Rome, the early Christian basilica, was developed along the lines of Germanic preferences, in other words it was articulated and heightened.[68] This

---

68 The term "Romanesque" is a misleading term in the sense that it alludes

Germanic development was resisted only in the city of Rome and in southern Italy. In Rome, there were basilicas built as late as the 12th century precisely repeating the type of the 4th century. Tuscany had taken up this articulation and heightened it, however hesitantly and compromisingly. Northern Italy, with its large Germanic population, proceeded decisively, even extending the articulation to the ceiling and developing an independent system of vaulting in the basilica, like the French and the Germans.

It can come as no surprise then when the people of Salzburg did not lag behind this development being led by the Germanic cultures. During the term of the Archbishop Konrad in the 12th century they used such forms as had been carried demonstrably to southern Germany from Saxony, a purely Germanic territory. I refer to the Hildesheim system of alternating supports used in the nave of St. Peter [in Salzburg] and now invisible beneath the baroque mantling. And yet, how small must this church of the mighty abbey of St. Peter have appeared in comparison with the monumental monastery churches in the rest of the German speaking area, to say nothing of France. All over France, Germany and northern Italy, the question of vaulting had been discussed since the 11th century: not as a technical problem, since this, in spite of its providing the basis for books and large publications, did not in fact exist, but rather as an aesthetic question pertaining to an extension of the ceiling articulation. In Salzburg, this question of the Germanic changes to the basilica did not exist. We know of no such

---

to the origin but not the actual goal of the development, which was more Germanic, as the Italians of the Renaissance sensed more clearly than the more recent critics, when they coined the term *maniera gotica* or *tedesca* for medieval art.

thoughts before the second half of the 12th century. By this time, many a less important church in Germany had been vaulted. This shows that during the period in which the Germanic taste advanced and predominated, there was no predilection for architectural activity in Salzburg. We might conclude that in a time when the city was governed by energetic and significant archbishops, the fashion of the period was not felt to be provocative or attractive enough in Salzburg to inspire any particular achievements.[69]

During that period, sculpture and painting seem also to have found little patronage. It is quite characteristic that there is evidence of a scriptorium but no school of book illumination during the Carolingian period while Bishop Arno [ca. 750-821] was active there. There is also no surviving evidence of sculpture in stone or ivory, or of bronze casting. Compared to the numerous northern German 10th and 11th century dilettante priests who worked in the techniques of the applied arts, the Bernwards, Egberts, Meinwerks etc., Salzburg has nothing more to offer than the semi-legendary figure of the Blessed Thiemo [ca. 1040-1101/2].

An increase in artistic activity did not begin before the late Romanesque period. At this time, the large cathedral was finally given its monumental form, as it had been considered appropriate in a series of episcopal seats along the Rhine a full century earlier. This late Romanesque cathedral of Salzburg was torn down in the late 16th century, but drawings and other preserved evidence reveal that

---

69 It has been argued that this was due to unfavorable circumstances of the times (the investiture controversy), but the validity of these has long been refuted.

it had been modeled on the example of Lombard vaulted basilicas. It seems typical that Salzburg only then decided on a large Romanesque experiment once there was an Italian model to follow. It is all the more apparent that the systematic examples along the Rhine had already existed for quite some time, and had been followed as far afield as in Heiligenkreuz in Lower Austria. The parish church (today Franciscan) was constructed according to the same southern system, with its nave still preserved and stands as a testament – however badly it has been restored in modern times. The polychrome portals in white-red marble, as they are preserved on the Franciscan Church and St. Peter, reveal the Romanesque influence even to the most cursory observer, and have their source in the cathedrals of Verona, Piacenza, Modena etc. Since it can also be seen in churches of the German areas of Tyrol such as Bolzano (Bozen), this custom might equally well have arrived in Salzburg along the normal lines of influence, while the Lombard system of vaulting cannot be documented in spite of the fact that the cathedral of Trento includes it. It must have come from a single impulse, exactly as it arrived in northern Switzerland, Bavaria and at Klosterneuburg, as a direct and conscious borrowing from Italy.

In Salzburg there was no taste for the independent development of the Romanesque style. Places with no variants of the late Romanesque are also precluded from examples of early or high Gothic, which in some sense developed further away from the Roman basilica. There seems to be a deeper reason why Salzburg never built a Gothic cathedral, as they came to adorn most episcopal seats of the German speaking area. It is not possible to object that the presence of a recent cathedral from the later 12th century would prevent its being torn down and replaced within 100 to 150 years, since fire damage had forced repairs throughout the 13th and 14th centuries. This had provided sufficient external opportunities for the introduction of at least some Gothic elements. As we shall see, this was done with the addition of a remarkable Gothic choir on another late Romanesque structure in Salzburg during the 15th century.

In general, it is conspicuous how little Gothic architecture there is in Salzburg. We see no great churches of the mendicant orders, so common in the German cities, and built particularly in the 14th century during the high Gothic. There is also a lack of the final result of the Germanic Gothic development – the hall church, where the three aisles are coordinated in their height, in contrast to the tradition of the Roman basilica where the two side aisles were consistently subordinated to the higher central nave.[70] These hall churches whose character and artistic intention is particularly clear in those examples including only two aisles, are widespread throughout the Alpine territories, particularly in Germany and Carinthia. As far as we know, Salzburg did not produce such a work of architecture. There was only one hall choir to be built here in the 15th century, but this is so exceptional as to be unique – the choir of the present day Franciscan Church. It is worth a closer look.

It is striking that only the choir of this late Romanesque parish church was rebuilt during the 15th century in the Gothic style, specifically late Gothic, which has its reason, as we shall see. The nave was left in its late Romanesque forms without the mediation of a transept, so that the late Gothic hall choir with its ambulatory and surrounding chapels immediately abuts upon the Roman-basilical nave. Today, the

---

70 The largest cathedral in Austria, St. Stephen's in Vienna, is a hall church.

spectator is struck by its enormous narrow round columns shooting up to the vaulting, forcefully drawing the eye upwards, almost an extreme example of the tendency to heighten things, as it was characteristic of the Germanic areas. Standing at the back of the nave and viewing the length of the church as a whole with the nave and choir together, it appears completely unique. The nave comprises a narrow dark corridor emptying into a broad, brilliant space radiating with light, although only isolated parts of this space can ever be seen at a single moment.

These are two effects that remained alien to the medieval period, and which it never pursued. The view from the dark into the light, and the contrast of the two makes an unusually strong impression. Painterly effects (chiaroscuro) did not begin to be exploited until the shift towards the Baroque in the 16th century. The division of the field of vision into distinct randomly drawn compartments toward the choir is unprecedented. No more than an individual part of the whole can be seen at any single moment, and this animates the imagination to supplement the rest. Within limits, this also has a painterly effect as would later emerge in the Italian Baroque, but even Dutch painting never introduced it so trenchantly. That was reserved for more recent art.

The composition of a Romanesque nave with a Gothic choir was calculated for a painterly effect. This is a trend we know from the mature Baroque, and one achieved by the baroque rebuilding of so many Austrian medieval churches, where a bright presbytery was cunningly added to the dark nave accommodating the congregation or laymen.[71]

---

71 Until recently, the best example of this was the church in Altmünster, where the victor over the Protestant peasants used the occasion to introduce the

It is completely surprising to find this trend present in Salzburg as early as in the first half of the 15th century. It is inconceivable that this should have been done without an idea of its tremendous effect, and can therefore only have been intentional. The baroque calculation of contrasts in light and shadow within interior spaces was later developed in Italy and only then transmitted to northern Europe, where it was then well received. The composition of contrasting light and shadow in the 15th century rebuilding of the Franciscan Church presents no imitation of an Italian model, but rather an anachronistic precedent for the later Italian development, unique in the history of art.

The second surprising feature, that of visual compartmentalization, appears as an even greater anachronism, and has a source not in the Italian, but rather in the Germanic taste. Italian baroque style called for spatial unity. Its half-concealed stimulations to the imagination are limited to lateral coulisses and never extended into the nave. Such a zesty apparition as we face it in the Franciscan Church presents a system virtually anticipating modern art.

As we have said, this places it in a completely isolated position. Even as such, it shows itself to be a true product of Salzburg in the stark confrontation of both an Italian and a Germanic tendency. We know the architect who designed it – Hans Stettheimer, born in Burghausen. He received no further commissions in Salzburg, but led the architectural lodge of Landshut to great heights.

In its style, the choir of the Franciscan Church is far removed

---

Counter-Reformation to Upper Austria. This unique historical monument has in the last few years been unfortunately disfigured when the windows of the nave were again opened without authority or understanding.

from the strict Gothic. It is normally referred to as Late Gothic. This style developed in the German areas parallel to the Early and High Renaissance in Italy. On the one hand it involves an intense escalation of Gothic and Germanic tendencies, but also its fragmentation and dissolution, and with this a return to Roman and Italian qualities. In northern Europe, the Late Gothic style represented a great intensification of the articulation and heightening, the central qualities of the medieval Germanic trend. This extreme intensification embodied a transition into its opposite – unification (a unified mass replaces diverse articulation) and horizontalization (with everything being raised vertically it creates a new form of horizontality). There is a foil for either the articulation or the height. Unity and horizontality are the characteristic heritage of Italian art. They became an element of the Italian Baroque since the middle of the 16th century, in a form appealing to the northern European taste, particularly with a heightened activity in the interior.[72] It thus becomes clear that Salzburg showed an understanding of the Gothic once it had reached its last, final phase, which led into the Baroque, since northern Europe cannot be said to have had a Renaissance.

The Chapel of St. Margaret in the cemetery of St. Peter is a relatively pure Gothic monument. By contrast, the rebuilt church of the Nonnberg is completely in the Late Gothic style. From this example it becomes clear that a sense had begun to develop for closed interior spaces. The innumerable ribs no longer have the articulating effect of

---

72 The fluttering loincloth of Christ provides an example of a motif, not caused externally by a wind, but instead set into motion from an internal subjective and mystic impulse.

a cross vault. Yet the eye follows the piers, supports and ribs, as this had been usual throughout the medieval period, and is diverted from contemplating the space in and of itself.

Although Salzburg showed an understanding of Late Gothic architecture and became a center of its eager application, this enthusiasm never rose to a point of taking the lead before other cities. One Gothic question remained to be resolved, more in a negative than a positive way. For the specific art of Salzburg, the great moment only arrived when the Gothic had disintegrated and Italian art came to replace it in a pure and unmitigated form. The choir of the Franciscan Church did not contradict this since it presented an anachronism that was not imitated. By contrast, the Nonnberg Church is one of many examples of its kin throughout the southern German speaking area.

Things were no different in the Late Gothic sculpture and painting of Salzburg between 1440 and 1540. An increasing number of names and works are being discovered as the emerging evidence of the local art of Salzburg, but no unusually gifted master has yet been discerned. Masters such as Melchior Pfennig, Conrad Laib and Rueland Frueauf, who have been connected to Salzburg with a degree of reliability are none of them comparable in quality to the south German masters of Nuremberg and Augsburg, of Ulm or Nördlingen. The situation is nowhere more overt than in the case of a particularly important commission – the high altar of the newly rebuilt Franciscan Church. In this case, the decision was made to commission an artist who was not local, Michael Pacher from Tyrol, one who also happened to be well acquainted with northern Italian art. During the period of the Late Gothic, Salzburg developed a more active and lively relation to the visual arts than had previously been the case. Yet there still seemed to be a lack of the inner stimulus we see among the citizens of other German language cities, and particularly the southern German free imperial cities with their relatively independent charters.

In Salzburg there was great activity in the field of applied arts, particularly pottery and goldsmith's work. In spite of this, when the Prince-Archbishop Leopold von Keutschach [ca. 1442-1519] desired a tiled stove of particular quality, he commissioned it in Nuremberg. The goldsmith's work in Salzburg has predominantly popular and decorative quality, particularly the silver, and not unlike the ceremonial vessels that made Augsburg and Nuremberg so famous. The decorations of the noble quarters in the Castle of Hohensalzburg, and we should not forget that they are heavily restored, also fail to reveal a particular artistic understanding on the part of the Salzburg archbishops of the time – with Leopold von Keutschach and Matthäus Lang [1468-1540] being the most active and enterprising among them.

Slowly but inexorably, we can see the insurgent Italian baroque style emerge during the 15th century. It remained absent from church architecture for the entire century. Salzburg did not possess any purely Gothic works that might have aroused a contradictory aesthetic response. The more recent examples of the Late Gothic gave a tolerable image of the altered taste, while the Romanesque still recalled the old Roman ecclesiastical style.[73] No new churches were built during that century, but the old ones were also not torn down. During the

---

73 It is in the same sense that Albrecht Dürer for instance depicted Romanesque capitals and arches in the architecture within his paintings of sacred subjects. In the Romanesque, he recognized something roughly similar to what the Italians saw in antiquity.

16th century, the shift toward Italian models appeared in secular architecture, and already did so during the first half of the century.

German urban domestic architecture typically faced the street with its narrow side, allowing the least possible amount of the interior to face outward, and was topped with a gable providing its most striking feature. During the medieval period, the gable is steep and pointed, and often broken by steps and crennelation. Beginning in the 15th century, it tends to be formed more sinuously, rounded or with a wave. The façade with the gable survived in its typical individual articulation and verticality, rising from the uniform horizontal emphasis of the street. By contrast to this, Italian domestic architecture did not include a gable, and since at least the 15th century tended to be built with its longer side to the street and as many windows as possible opening outward. Its roof is horizontal and thus harmonizes with the direction of the street, but it lacks individual characterization. This exemplified the differences in Germanic and Romance tastes. The houses in the center of Salzburg were built without gables. They are horizontal at the top and conform to the Italian custom as much as they differ from the German. Houses further to the south in Tyrol were nevertheless built with the Germanic form of the gables. The transitional character of the region is apparent from the fact that their gables are less steep and façades wider. In Salzburg on the other hand, the only Germanic characteristic of the houses lies in the fact that their façades are comparatively narrow and often protrude from the line of the street at the corner, as well as in the relation of the fenestration to the wall. We cannot see the roof from below, and the top level is generally an artificial space intended to conceal the roof analogously to the attic in Italian Renaissance houses.

In looking down at the roofs from the Mönchsberg we can see that they are aligned in a low row. This tendency to shy away from revealing the roof is also specifically southern.

Domestic architecture in Salzburg certainly acquired this Italianate character before the middle of the 16th century. This is suggested by the Late Gothic arcades with round and low arches on decorative octagonal columns of red marble as we can still see them in the courts of several of these houses. It is confirmed in a drawing with a veduta of the city, made in the year 1553 and preserved in the abbey of St Peter. The houses in the center can already be seen to have the lowered roofs hidden by the raised wall of the façade, while the residential streets of the Gstetten, am Stein, and at the foot of the Nonnberg still include gables, which today have been largely replaced with long unified horizontal fronts. This de-individualization of the houses in the center of Salzburg must have begun before the year 1553. – This must also explain the lack of projecting alcoves, which only occur very rarely in Salzburg, while they are very common in the German speaking areas of Tyrol and widespread in Germany, where they are considered one of the characteristic features distinguishing local architecture from that of the south.[74] In Salzburg there are also almost no pergolas. This in spite of the fact that the pergola must have been widespread in the medieval period, even favored in Italy before the Renaissance, and

---

74 The only configurations recalling such alcoves are to be found in the castle of Hohensalzburg, but this important structure for the art of Salzburg must be omitted from our consideration. It was built for the purpose of fortification and therefore shows less of the Italianate trend. It is for the same reason that Italian castles also include an intricate articulation and verticality more markedly similar to the northern European preferences.

used in northern Europe well into the 16th century. This aversion to pergolas, as we see it in Salzburg, shows an anticipation of the baroque preference for closed masses of walls, particularly characteristic of the Roman (and Tuscan) Baroque. During the Late Gothic, secular architecture of Salzburg shows itself already leading in an Italianate direction.

We have noted that monumental architecture experienced a hiatus in the 16th century. Of course this was generally true of the entire Catholic portion of the German speaking area. It was only at the end of this century that the time was considered ripe to replace the traditional style of ecclesiastical architecture, particularly the Romanesque, which had determined the profile of the city churches, with another more appealing style. As in the remainder of the German areas, and even in the Protestant territories, Italy became the source. Salzburg is distinguished in this process first for having chronologically preceded most of the other German speaking cities, and then also for adopting the Italian model relatively unchanged, with no thought of altering it to accommodate northern tastes. The Italian taste could be applied only forcefully of course, as this was the case in Salzburg. It is significant that it was attempted particularly in Salzburg and that it was relatively successful here. This required an unusually energetic, even inconsiderate personality to be realized, and fate found just such a figure in the Archbishop Wolf Dietrich.

This nobleman of the cloth, who is especially interesting in light of modern personality cults, seems to have been born into the wrong historical period. He recalls to us the Roman popes, more the renaissance popes such as a Julius II who saw their principality as the end and means of their activities, and less those such as Sixtus X, Clement VII or Paul V of the baroque period who never overlooked the fact that they were primarily vicars of Christ and first shepherds. In other words: this relative of Pope Pius V and the Borromei, born on Lake Constance of both Italian and German descent, pupil of the Collegium Germanicum in Rome, desired to Italianize the city of Salzburg both externally in terms of political and ecclesiastical power, as well as internally in regard to its intimate cultural, religious and artistic life.[75]

Wolf Dietrich and his ambitions were of course inhibited by everything already present, and this made him a destroyer above all else. Entire blocks of buildings were demolished, particularly around the cathedral to make way for palaces in the Italian manner, or on the right bank of the Salzach to accommodate architecturally designed gardens along the lines of the Roman villas of the Aldobrandini, Borghese and others. His most memorable deed in this regard was the destruction of the time honored earlier cathedral. The fire of 1598 had lent him only a superficial excuse, since the wooden winged altarpieces had not even been damaged. The populace expected him to restore it. It was similar to the case of Old St. Peter's basilica in Rome, where the need for structural repairs was exaggerated in order to sooth the misgiving of the pious population weaned on the early guide books, and devoted to the older monuments. In this aspect also, Wolf Dietrich matched the impiety of the renaissance popes. Along with the previous

---

75 Of course his personal origins and education do not and cannot explain his actions in an external sense, for these were trends of the time, but they do assist in understanding why this man was suited to execute this particular mission.

cathedral, the Karner, the original cemetery and even some of the tombs of some episcopal saints, disappeared without a trace.

What did Wolf Dietrich desire to see in place of the old Romanesque cathedral? A variation of the new basilica of St. Peter in Rome, albeit not on a centralized plan, but with a nave as it was being executed by Maderno in Rome just at that time. The architect given the commission by the archbishop was a northern Italian, just as his agents in all-important matters were Italian. The plan was too ambitious. In this as in politics, Wolf Dietrich overestimated the means at his disposal, and he himself failed along with his artistic vision. The designs by Scamozzi remained unrealized, just as those for a villa on the other riverbank were stopped at the initial stage.

Wolf Dietrich was successful in the realm of secular art. He introduced the Italian palazzo to Salzburg. Before then, the type had not been known in southern Germany. Isolated examples began to appear at the end of the century beginning with a small structure in Munich: the former Jesuit college with a character less palatial and more like barracks. Wolf Dietrich desired actual secular palaces for his court and his bureaucracy, and by giving them an Italian form; he wished them to define the image of Salzburg. On the drawing of 1553, it is possible to make out the appearance of a German palace in the medieval tradition, the archiepiscopal residence which Wolf Dietrich began to demolish. It included a number of individual structures of varying height and fulfilling diverse functions, with elements protruding and receding, as well as a large hall at the center with a stair tower, clearly the "palas" of the medieval period. It is a composition as we see it with greater size and complexity in the castle of Hohensalzburg.

The Italian palazzo forced all of these spaces with their various functions into one single architectural body. Outwardly, it presents a single ceremonial façade composed strictly, symmetrically, and divided into two subordinate wings by a central portal. It has a marked horizontal emphasis in the floor levels, articulated in breadth by bands and cornices, and stressed by the proportions of windows and wall, carefully suppressing any vertical emphasis, especially the eschewed gable. An example of such a façade would be the present day central customs house in the Kapitelgasse. It was in the same spirit that the archbishop began rebuilding his old residence. Its regular design around the court before the cathedral and its symmetrical connection to the cathedral itself by the arcade is born of the same spirit of unification and subordination.

The new cathedral was completed under the successor of Wolf Dietrich, Marcus Sittich von Hohenems [1574-1619], a relative with a similar disposition in many ways, who employed another north Italian, Santino Solari. For him also, St. Peter in Rome provided the model. This variant was completed with less opulence and detail. As an interior space, it is the most purely Italian monument in the German speaking area, or north of the Alps generally. The interior has a comfortable breadth. The pilasters are set on low bases, and bear the vault at a moderate height. The nave is dark, with the space of the dome and the apse light in a pure expression of baroque composition in light and shadow. The dome is dominant even to those entering at the far west end of the nave. It provides a strong contrast to the medieval crossing dome of St. Peter which we notice only upon arriving beneath it. Each of the lateral chapels can be seen openly and freely rather than in forced partial views. There is a refreshing clarity throughout the entire plan. We can still feel an echo of the majestic calm persisting from its Renaissance model, the central plan by Michelangelo. The greater emotional activity of the Baroque is evident only in certain details such as the multiple superimposed pilasters and bent cornices. On the exterior in the two side towers of the west façade there is an almost jarring tribute to the northern taste. In a strictly Italian conception, the side façades being treated subordinately, and the east side, could never have been presented so openly to all sides as they are in the cathedral of Salzburg.

Italian artists dominated Salzburg during the 17th century. There were certainly many local architects, sculptors and painters employed, but southerners always set the tone, and significant commissions were executed by them. This was true of the courtyard fountain designed by Antonio Daria in the spirit of the gifted Roman fountain architect Gianlorenzo Bernini, whose rocky fountain on the Piazza Navona and Triton fountain provided some of the inspiration. It was probably also more than a coincidental intersection when the most active 17th century archbishop who did the most for the city, Paris von Lodron [1619-1653], was himself a native of the south. Authentic Italian culture was seasonable at that time for Salzburg in every sense.

In Salzburg, this turn to purely Italian art reached its climax under the Archbishop Max Gandolph Khuenburg [1668-1687]. During this period, the archbishops hired southern architects to build in a completely southern style. The busiest architect was Gasparo Zugalli. It is necessary to see his church of St. Kajetan in order to understand the architectural reaction, which was achieved by Johann Bernhard

Fischer von Erlach. The church of St. Kajetan is supposed to have a central plan, but it is agitated as called for by the Late Baroque, and therefore includes a diagonal oval dome. This created such a lateral effect in the interior that it was necessary to extend the choir in order to preserve the centralized feel. In any case, the dome dominates the entire interior. On the exterior, the actual façade is visible as if squeezed by two symmetrical wings of the abbey buildings with gables on theatrically colossal pilasters. It is a projection of outward show and a unified effect that even includes illusionism! Such a unification might create an impression of profanation and could almost strike the pious German sensibility as objectionable. The dome also dominates the façade, and the low gable below it almost completely disappears as such. This tendency is further escalated in the church of St. Erhard im Nonntal. All of this presents such an exaggeration of Italian and non-Germanic artistic elements that it could not ultimately persist even in Salzburg.

The patrons of the church of St. Kajetan were Theatine monks and Italian nationals. The architect could have been confident that his work appealed to them. Yet the citizens of Salzburg would never themselves become Italian, even if they remained pleased with this Italian aesthetic through the entire 17th century. The time would inevitably arrive when their native northern European taste would assert itself, and this arrived when Salzburg lost its interest in monumental architectural projects. This critical shift occurred under the Archbishop Johann Ernst Count von Thun-Hohenstein [1643-1709] at the turn of the 17th and 18th centuries. His conscious emancipation from the south has even been documented. Zugalli was its particular victim. His intention was nothing less than to replace the Italian with northern Germanic elements. It might have been more of a personal aversion against Italian style on the part of the archbishop than a feeling that a change in style was necessary. This meant that Italian style would not be given any precedence, and that there would be a change toward the well known northern characteristics of articulation and verticality, as well as internal movement rather than the outward and showy tranquility of Italian taste. For the realization of these plans, the archbishop required the proper architect. Since this question was in the air, he was able to find this architect in the person of the elder Fischer von Erlach, the leading protagonist of the so-called Austrian Baroque style.

The art of [Johann Bernhard] Fischer von Erlach thrived primarily in Vienna, the older provinces of Austria, and in Bohemia. His presence in Salzburg was never more than a phase, but it became an episode of eminent importance to the history of art. Johann Bernhard Fischer von Erlach created his early monumental works in this city, and developed his own Austrian Baroque style though them. It was only after this that he was given the chance to develop his great creations, particularly in Vienna. For the appropriate monumental commissions, he required a patron who was deeply familiar with the Roman Baroque style while desiring an emancipation from this very thing, and this is exactly what he found in the archbishop of Salzburg. Two examples should suffice.

In the Church of the Trinity (Priesterhauskirche), Fischer still followed the Italian models closely. Its façade is squeezed between the wings of the seminary, but while Zugalli expressed this as a flat surface at St. Kajetan, Fischer lends his façade an independent articulation, has it protrude massively, and then places it in a curve based on that of his model, the church of S. Agnese in Piazza Navona in Rome. On the interior (a centralized plan), he extended the dome to an oval, just as Zugalli had, yet not laterally, but as an oval extended into the depth, with the rear transept including the apse heightening the impression of depth (by comparison to the tranquil breadth of Zugalli).

In the climax of his activity in Salzburg, Fischer further emancipated himself from the Italian models: the University Church [Kollegienkirche]. In terms of the history of art, this is the most fascinating single work of art in Salzburg. In entering the interior of the University Church, the sense of extension into depth and height is so strong that it is difficult to recognize that it has a centralized plan. Indeed, the dome hovers quietly and firmly above the whole, and yet we feel the depth and height more strongly than the breadth. Its nave appears far narrower than that of the cathedral in spite of the fact that the latter has a longitudinal plan, while the University Church is supposed to have a centralized plan. The pilasters are on high bases and seem to rush narrowly upward. Between them, the niches push upward and abut the entablature. Along the walls of the transept, the peaks of the altars cut directly into the round arched windows above them. Vertical oval windows (the so-called "ox eyes") appear on the axes at all four terminal walls in the spot where Zugalli placed horizontal ovals. The walls and ceiling are devoid of color. There were probably plans for this, but the very fact that it never came to be executed is significant in itself. The deep and heavy seriousness of the architectural design was considered sufficient. The attractive, playful and cheerful additions that seem essential to Italian conceptions of perfected harmony were not necessary to the Germanic baroque sensibility.

On the exterior, the main façade presents the central point of interest completely in keeping with the Italian Baroque, but the lateral façades reveal a certain joy in protrusion and recession, typical of Germanic art, as well as an increased articulation by comparison for instance to the unified masses of the receding cathedral walls. The dome no longer plays any part in the effect of the façade. The façade is autonomous and independent of it, as is the articulation. It is dominated by that favorite Germanic motif, the pediment. It is flanked by two towers no longer as strongly subordinated as at the Church of the Trinity, since they are somewhat higher than the pediment, which nonetheless predominates due to its greater breadth. What is most striking are the terminal parts of the towers. They neither have roofs nor spires, but singular attachments with the artistic function of revealing the movement in all dimensions. Like much else about the façade, this seems overly studied and pedantically refined, grasped only gradually through a brooding sort of guesswork. In Italian architecture, the entirety is normally apparent at the first glance. Material factors and relationships, pressure and counter pressure, structural, neutral, intermediate are their primary means of expression. German artists felt the need to introduce complex thoughts and intellectual allusions into their formal language. While the Italian creates a tranquil image on a horizontal plane, the German tends to strive for a movement into depth and height, which is not as simple to convey as the broad surface.

This ends the period of purely Italian art in Salzburg. Works such as the fountain by Antonio Daria were no longer possible. We have but to compare the two horse ponds with their models in the monumental

Roman fountains such as the Fontana Trevi. Significantly, one of the last great monuments of some ambition, the Neutor (or Sigmund Gate), is a predominantly technical achievement, anticipating modern interests and needs. The work of Fischer von Erlach also embodied the final great phase of architecture in Salzburg. As the times progressively distanced themselves from the Italian school, which had dominated the north for two centuries, Salzburg also showed less interest in cultivating the visual arts. The people of Salzburg were no longer interested in these questions. They turned to music, literature, and the sciences.

This ultimately confirms what our entire study has shown. In periods of advancing Italian influence, Salzburg was always in the vanguard of the development and willing to assume the southern qualities (das Welsche) without qualification. As soon as the movement tends toward an emancipation from Italian influence and a balance with the Germanic artistic tendencies, the interest dies down and the artists trained in Salzburg orient themselves toward other artistic centers. When Italian models are completely rejected, then artistic patronage in Salzburg stagnates completely. In those times, the unavoidable gratification of the continual need for art is satisfied without any verve and with no pretensions to the higher forms of monumentality.

The importance of Salzburg in the history of art lies in its character as a persistently receptive gateway for Italian artistic taste, assuming a particular importance in times when the northern European development, in its endless fragmentation and random individuality, had reached a dead spot, and required fertilization from the unity and normative regularity of Italian art. As far as we can see, such a fertilization never took place in Salzburg itself, and when this seemed to be occurring, as in the case of Fischer von Erlach, its riper fruits were not reserved for the city of Salzburg, apparently because it no longer demanded it. Count Franz Anton von Harrach [1665-1727], the successor of Johann Ernst Thun-Hohenstein, quietly dismissed Fischer von Erlach from service in Salzburg. Salzburg no longer had a commission to offer the figurehead of the Austrian Baroque.

In Salzburg we cannot see anything like the continuing interest in the originality and shifting attraction that is apparent in Nuremberg for instance. On the other hand, Salzburg offers a glorious abundance of relatively pure Italian impressions, greater in number than any other city north of the Alps, and just of the sort that have always appealed to the northern taste. And yet, modern man would like to know nothing of historical or exotic appeal, nothing of the subject, its function or historical significance, and remains preoccupied with exclusively optical and coloristic stimuli more related to music. Such a person is still able to find more than one object of the greatest interest among the monuments of Salzburg. Let a single example stand for many others. The Capucine abbey on the Imberg is an unprepossessing complex of buildings from the period of Wolf Dietrich and lacks even the ornament of a tower. When we see this in the setting sun from a vantage point such as the Höll brewery it provides quite a pleasurable chromatic chord. Yellow walls protrude from the greenery, capped by the red roof, cutting into the blue sky with each of the colors contained by tranquil horizontals and verticals. It is a quiet and pure aesthetic impression, conveying a soothing and contemplative mood to the viewer. Anybody who has seen the Müllner Kirche with its Late Gothic choir and baroque tower as a silhouette against the afternoon sun from the upper quai of the Salzach will never forget this impression.

This is how the monuments of the past periods deeply and directly affect us today, and for this reason if no other, we must cultivate, protect and preserve them with pious care.

Jacob van Ruisdael[76]

According to current art historical scholarship, the Dutch painters of the 17th century presented us with the earliest actual landscape painting. As long as contemporary taste is able to pass judgments unchallenged, there will be no convincing arguments to the contrary. The landscape painters of our own time pursue the unity of all individual things above and below the earth, all drawn together by the ubiquitous connection through the open air, something which had first become a clear and conscious goal to the Dutch of the baroque period. They no longer followed the earlier styles in unifying their imagery by means of contour lines and to a lesser degree the closely corresponding local colors evoking the tactile limits of individual forms. They did so instead with a harmony of coloristic appeal based on an exclusively optic stimulation. Their goal of depicting the open space of the sky is something that cannot be grasped by the sense of touch. It can only be introduced into the image by tactile, tangible, objective-physical objects treated the same way as optical stimuli and spots of color within them, and which the viewer from their own experience then can reconstruct as a constellation of individual objects. An optical stimulus is exposed to more subjective fluctuations than one from the sense of touch even

76 Originally published as: "Jakob van Ruysdael," *Die graphischen Künste*, vol. 25, 1902, pp. 11-20.

when the latter are perceived circuitously through the visual sense as in the art of painting. For this reason, Dutch and later landscape painting necessarily depicts a subjective conception of the individual objects, contrasting with the objective image that is so central to ancient art, and to some degree still to that of the renaissance. This art is no longer geared to the objects themselves, but to the viewing subject, expressed by the existence of a single point of linear and aerial perspective.

The difference between the [17th century] Dutch and the modern landscape paintings is essentially only one of quantity. We have become more sensitive to certain mistakes in draftsmanship and illumination that have gone unnoted in even the most celebrated Dutch painters. Where Dutch and modern landscape painting differ fundamentally is in the conception and representation of the open space of the sky.

The Dutch of the 17th century conceived the space of the sky as something autonomous, sharing nothing in common with the objects around which it circulated, and therefore laying itself like a colored veil between them. It appears as color derived from the various manifestations of light, either as sunlight or an artificial flame descending in all possible degrees into the deepest shadow. The modern painters go further with the associative tendency, by showing the individual objects as affecting one another, and the aerial space, colorless in and of itself, as reflecting the objects: the tone of the air is no longer merely light, but also includes reflected color from the individual objects depicted in the painting. This is the reason that the objects are given far more attention in modern painting than ever occurred among the [17th century] Dutch, who subdued them within the autonomously colored aerial space. It becomes clear from this that the Dutch landscape painter to be most valued by our more recent contemporaries would be the one who left most of the separate coloration to individual objects in their relation to the air's unifying tone. This is Jacob van Ruisdael. He also embodies the highest and the most mature stage which Dutch landscape painting reached in the 17th century.

This development went through three stages. The earliest is exemplified by the tonal painters surrounding Jan van Goyen. In their paintings, the sky is always colored by the light in a single monotone color ranging between a straw yellow and grayish-green, covering the local colors of all of the individual objects in the painting. The impression made by the color of these paintings is so unnatural and mannered that some have explained it rather gratuitously as a result of the hazy atmosphere of the Netherlands. The individual objects have not been observed properly, the optical appearance of their details does not emerge with the same vivacity of conscious experience. The objects are still recognizable on the basis of their contours, just as they had been in earlier periods of art. On the other hand, these painters attempted to introduce interesting and amusing motifs into works by way of content. Instead of ceremonial and political actions, they included human beings and their activities, involving intricate detail of life on the banks of rivers and in towns. While the eye of the beholder is not primarily preoccupied with the color and its character in the painting, it is vigorously entertained by the content, much as in the art of antiquity and the Renaissance which had on their part excluded suggestions of mood.

Rembrandt and his contemporaries embodied the second

stage of the development. He had overcome the monotone character with his chiaroscuro, which is nothing other than spatial shading (Raumdunkel). With this, he broke through the tactile and limiting effect of the local color and contours. He was able to match the depicted objects with the optically most effective details, limit space into legible segments rather than an endless euthanizing depth, and to restrict the objective interest in the individual objects. Although the landscape paintings by Rembrandt are universally and properly esteemed most highly, they are not among the greatest achievements of Dutch landscape painting. When we regard nature today, what we see is no more the brown of Rembrandt's landscapes than the straw yellow of Salomon van Ruysdael. By contrast to this, we feel far more convinced by Rembrandt's landscape etchings with their lack of local color in the brown chiaroscuro. As a history painter, Rembrandt was never able to completely overcome the urge to subordination. His shrill isolation of certain parts by direct lighting while others remain shrouded in shadow seems to militate against the absolute equality of motifs within a landscape, as it is necessary to the genre of the mood landscape (Stimmungslandschaft). For this reason, it is not surprising that the human figure and its inevitable objective interest to the human viewer still assumes a greater role than is tolerable to our modern extremely subjective demands of absolute subordination of the human figure to nature. Rembrandt has been done injustice in this matter. Humanity is entitled to assume its deserved place in nature, and Rembrandt might have discovered the perfect degree to which the human form can participate in a mood landscape without irrevocably threatening the effect of the mood.

Each of these points has been lodged against Rembrandt by our modern subjectivist trend and was corrected by Jacob van Ruisdael to the degree permitted by the medium of the lit aerial space without reflected color. His landscapes are definitely bathed in a certain greenish or brownish tone, but never so monotone that the individual motifs seem unnaturally discolored as in the paintings by Jan van Goyen or Rembrandt. Nor do they appear as random as in some more recent painters, and this is a reason that many a conservative art lover, and many of those attuned to modern values are inclined to rate Jacob van Ruisdael above all later examples. He never loses himself in unclarity and indeterminacy, neither in the extension into depth, nor in his characterization of individual motifs. He treats the sky and the earth as of completely equivalent value. Eugène Fromentin's observation is true that Ruisdael became the first to record the cloudy sky as a part of the landscape, but this might lead to the misconception that earlier Dutch painters, as had generally been true at least since the 15th century, conceived the space above the earth as little more than a neutral relief ground, something like the artists of antiquity. Van Goyen and Rembrandt had not treated it simply as empty sky animated with clouds, but also gave it an incremental linking function, the former by the use of color tones and the latter with chiaroscuro, usually involving a storm. The individual motifs are always coordinated in the landscapes of Jacob van Ruisdael and none of them emphasized at the expense of another. We shall see that examples apparently violating this rule date mostly from his later period and can be explained by particular aspects of his development. He immerses the human figures in the whole of nature, particularly in plant life. When staffage figures were called for, so as to clarify distances or relations of format, he employed other painters to add them. This has been explained rather naïvely as a sign of inability on the part of the great landscape painter, as if a master able to evoke the optical appearance of a tree in the most enthralling manner with only a few strokes, would not have been able to fix a small human form as staffage. To the contrary, he conceived his landscapes as devoid of human beings, and as soon as the artistic conception stood before him in its completed state, he considered it to be perfected, and left the necessary evil of staffage additions to friends specializing and amusing themselves in painting human figures.

Although Jacob van Ruisdael did not live much beyond the age of fifty (born toward the end of the 1620's and died in 1682), he nonetheless left us with an unusually large number of paintings. In spite of such a restless productivity which might have brought greater wealth in another profession, documents reveal his income to have been austere, and we are left with the image of an ideal artist whose urge to express his "inner vision" consumed his entire being. Such a rich creativity was possible only through a step-like development, and in fact the dated paintings reveal just this. It ran in the same direction as Dutch 17th century painting generally, from a relative objectivity to an ever stricter subjective conception. In the last period of the master, we can finally observe a reversal into the opposite extreme, only appearing to return to the point of its inception.

The earliest period, which begins in Haarlem around the mid 1640's is exemplified by compositions such as the town in the forest behind dunes in the Dresden Gallery (cat. no. 1503 [Slive no. 86]).[77]

_____

77 [Seymour Slive, *Jacob van Ruisdael: A Complete Catalogue of His Paintings,*

This still displays the comfortable artistic device of the monotone painters, placing the most important motifs so deeply in space that their tactility, borders and impenetrability are evaporated, an effect most easily achieved by the view from a distance. This is no longer provided by the endless distance of the tonal mask which causes the horizon to blur indistinctly. The terrain rises slightly from the unobtrusive grassy foreground to the rear, so that the main motifs of houses and trees appear at the highest spot and form a silhouette on the horizon. The trees no longer create a uniform wall, but are instead arrayed as a series of individual treetops, without one predominating over the others. We see a house with its façade, a windmill with blades crossed frontally and a church tower with an open window facing the lower ground. Two or three human figures are present to signify the depth in space. Their absence would be odd around such a town. There are clouds in the sky above, individualized in their form and movement. If anything is lacking to prevent the present day viewer from a simple dispassionate view (interesseloses Schauen), then this is due to the distance and small size of the motifs – house, mill and church, their relative lack of a relation to one another and resulting objectivity, and finally by the strong linear motion in the details which are not properly dominated by any straight emphasis.

A second phase is found in the view of a village at the foot of a wooded hill in the Berlin Gallery (cat. no. 885 F [Slive no. 555]). This image is already more contained and moved closer to the spectator while also calmly constructed by many verticals and horizontals. It is anchored at the front by a still body of water that does not lose

Drawings and Etchings, New Haven: Yale University Press, 2001.]

itself in an immeasurable distance, but instead turns to the right and disappears behind an imaginative cover of growth. On its banks there are two anglers. This is the most fitting motif imaginable for Dutch 17th century painting to express its basic tendency to suppress any activity that might encourage the sense of touch, but instead to arouse our impulse to view optically and intellectually. The landscape paintings by Rembrandt also repeatedly include the angler, whose activity evokes the most intent viewing and absolute physical stillness. Almost all of the houses of the town face the spectator with their facades with windows, as if in silent observation. The background is taken up with higher ground, and each of its individual trees distinguishable up to its top. A small tower affords a view into what we presume to be the continuation of the valley with the stream.

This painting was made in a period when the greatest landscape artists were preoccupied with the problem of depicting broad surfaces so that the individual details emerged clearly and the distance of terrain could be indicated securely without sacrificing their unity. Hercules Seghers had preceded them in this. Undoubtedly with a knowledge of Hercules Seghers, Rembrandt discovered the solution in his etching, the "Gold Weigher's Field," dated 1651 [Bartsch 234]. This sheet certainly reveals the greatest conception of Dutch art of this sort, with the size of the challenge and its success corresponding to the nature of this master, whose works often combine intimacy with the character of absolute greatness and timelessness. Jacob van Ruisdael would have seen this as a danger to the quiet intimacy of his purely subjective atmosphere, and this led him to never use such an extended vista in his landscape paintings. The furthest he went in this regard are the views of his native city of Haarlem from the dunes of Overveen, which he repeated frequently and therefore certainly for the edification of patrons. One of these is in the Berlin Gallery, with others in the Rijksmuseum, Amsterdam and the Mauritshuis in The Hague [cf. Slive numbers 35, 36, 37, 40]. A mountain or high trees does not form the horizon in these paintings, but instead the houses and towers of the city in the plain. That part of the painting which normally provides the only relevant pictorial content, the earth with its products and human industry, is now so low and barely fills a third of the picture surface! Two thirds of the height of the painting are consumed by the sky with clouds, whose vehemence appeared appropriate to effectively balance the human activities and their interruption of the mood (stimmungsgefährliches Menschenwerk). Zones of light and shade are distributed across the breadth of the painting so as to clarify the unifying progression into depth. Yet they are never taken to that degree of darkness used by Rembrandt to so often goad our imagination to supplement and even thwart the mood, that pure vision devoid of interests that provided the ultimate goal of the painter. A number of gables protrude from the array of houses; the Grote Kerk which dwarfs all the others is still no more than the first among others, larger but not artistically more significant than they. When the eye is led along the row of houses, whose optical size matches that of the church, its effect is weakened within the pictorial whole. From the church towers rising vertically above the horizon line and the intersecting straight lines of the foreground, we can see how conscious the painter has become of their extrinsically sedative effect since making the early paintings such as that in Dresden. During this period, Rembrandt also showed the same tendency to evoke the impression of a flat succession rather than placing the individual motifs variously to suggest depth, as they had done earlier.

The third developmental phase which appeals most to our modern preferences and already dates to the Amsterdam period of the painter around 1660 is exemplified by the large beech wood forest in the Vienna Gallery [Inv. 426, GNr.1337, Slive no. 437]. All traces of human activity have been omitted; there is almost nothing other than trees to be seen, and yet each of these appears to us as an individual, and all of them lure us irresistibly into their shade.

Any of those who might still require such a lesson can learn from this painting why the direct view of nature can never convey the complete and unsullied mood exuded by art. Not one of the trees emerges with that plasticity exciting the tactile sense which we experience each time we take a walk in a forest, with the eye poking around it (das Auge daran spießt) without perceiving the whole at once. With a hundred eyes, the light of the sky is gazing down upon the spectator between each of the trees. The only sign of human activity is the path with deep ruts no longer leading into depth as in earlier paintings, but instead disappearing vertically around a corner and following the picture plane along the front, crossing a shallow stream exhibiting the typical secrecy of darkness in Jacob van Ruisdael's landscapes. The staffage consists of a traveler resting introspectively and a couple walking in the shade of the giant trees further back, with the waves of an ocean of greenery closing around them.

As we have seen, the development of Jacob van Ruisdael reveals a movement toward an increasing reduction and purification. Motifs that might arouse the viewer's interest in a particular object and divert attention from the pictorial whole were increasingly omitted until we are finally left with nothing other than the pure joy in looking. The apogee of this specifically Dutch development is achieved in this painting of the large beech wood forest. The last traces of any narrative, as an expression of will have been obliterated. What the artist depicts and the spectator experiences is pure sensation. Yet this sensation is not one of reception. By approaching them with attentiveness, the viewer still relates actively to the objects of vision. With the exception of its final phase, all of Dutch 17th century painting can be described most succinctly as an art of attentiveness. We have reached the turning point here where the sensation ceases to be active, and becomes passive. This transition was an unavoidable result of the continual intensification of subjectivism. As long as the artists and spectators focused on the external objects, these retained a modicum of objectivity. Ultimately, subjectivism must aspire to a more intimate effect of the objects upon the subject (the spectator and the artist). This cannot persist merely on the basis of attentiveness, but the emotion must enter in (es muß der Affekt platzgreifen). The sensation must become passive (eine leidende). It was the unavoidable internal fate of Dutch 17th century painting to make the transition from Rembrandt to Van Dyck, which our present day taste might lament, but must be accepted in the interests of a progressive universal development.

In the artistic development of Jacob van Ruisdael, the beginning of this shift makes itself apparent with the emergence of new motifs addressing more than pure vision: while this had previously been a negative and reductive process, it now became positive by introducing new elements into the landscape. The things Ruisdael painted had been available to him in his immediate vicinity, such as the example of the great beech wood forest in the Haarlemer Hout. By and by, we find motifs that could not possibly have been observed by a Dutch landscape painter in such a composition. We can see a reversion to the composed landscapes as had been current in the 15th and 16th centuries. Of course the master had no intention to arouse an objective interest in the spectator. As modern viewers considering ourselves to be independent of the intellectual preoccupations of Ruisdael and his Dutch contemporaries, we sense something intentional in these elements that alienate and obstruct the mood (stimmungsstörend).

This change in the master which might be interpreted as a decline, is already discernible in the much praised forest paintings with trees reflecting vaguely in dark almost eerily swampy ponds. The same tendency gave rise to his paintings of waterfalls, while the frequently posed question whether he saw these himself or was inspired by Allaert van Everdingen is of very minor importance. The extreme of this hyper-subjective conception, bordering almost on the sentimental, can be seen in the Jewish cemetery in Dresden (cat. no. 1502, [Slive no. 180]). The works of human industry are here again allotted a large space within nature, but they lapse and revert again into nature. Nature even annihilates the monuments created by humanity to perpetuate its evanescent individuality, and returns them to its bosom. From elements such as the dark stormy sky, the longing movement of the tree to the right – contrasted to the craning trees of the beech wood forest – we are made aware that an objective interest has again entered the process of pure and attentive viewing, and that these are not objectively given, but are rather the result of an increased attraction to sentiment in both the painter and viewer.

Some of Ruisdael's seascapes and winter landscapes reveal this escalation of sensation into emotion, in which the tautly spun sense of feeling begins to burst, and modern tastes sense a lack of atmosphere. Some of the paintings, which by their technique and composition ought to belong to the second period, still include much of the enchanting balance of mood typical of his middle period. Among others, this is true of the View of the Dam at Amsterdam in the Berlin Gallery (cat. no. 885 D [Slive no. 1]). It is a view of the city, but made within the city and omitting any form of vegetation. The balance that leads to unity is achieved only by the elevated space of the sky with the clouds. We see the city scales in the foreground while the characteristic gabled facades of houses to the right along the Damrak and in the narrow street to the left provide a background. In this case, the foreground is filled with the unavoidable staffage by the hand of a painter similar to the Kleinmeister. These are people either alone or in groups. They are not bustling with any particular activity but rather looking around, quietly conversing or attentively listening, and this very well befits human beings within the landscape.

The Modern Cult of Monuments
Its Character and Origins[78]

1. The Values of the Monuments and Their History

A monument is defined in the oldest and most original sense as a work made by human hands to serve a given purpose in commemorating a given human deed or situation (or combinations thereof) for the consciousness of later generations. It can be a monument of art or made in writing, depending on whether it evokes the occasion for the spectator with the expressive qualities of visual art or by the inclusion of an inscription. Most often the two are combined on an equal footing. The erection and cultivation of such "intentional" monuments which reaches back to the earliest known times in human history, has by now almost ground to a complete halt. In speaking of the cult and protection of monuments today we barely think of those "intentional" monuments, but rather of "monuments of art and history" as the official expression runs in Austria at least. This expression has seemed appropriate from the 16th to the 19th century,

78 Originally published as *Der moderne Denkmalkultus Sein Wesen und seine Entstehung*, Vienna: Braumüller, 1903, reprinted in Ernst Bacher ed., Alois Riegl, *Kunstwerk oder Denkmal? Alois Riegls Schriften zur Denkmalpflege, Studien zu Denkmalschutz und Denkmalpflege*, 15, Vienna: Böhlau, 1995, pp. 55-97, with a list of previous translations into other languages, p. 289.

but might lead to misunderstandings in relation to our most current connotation of artistic values, and we are therefore obliged to make an attempt to understand what has hitherto been meant by the expression "monuments of art and history."

A work of art is generally defined as any human artifact with artistic value, available to be touched, seen or heard, and a historical monument is the same possessing historical value. The audible monuments (those of music) can be completely omitted from consideration here, since they belong to the class of hand written monuments to the extent of their relevance to us presently. With regard to the tangible and visible works of visual arts (all artifacts made by human hands in the broadest sense), we must pose the question as to what constitutes artistic and what constitutes historical value?

Historical value is the more widely flung of the two and should be discussed first for this reason. Historical refers to anything which once was, and is now no longer. According to the most current opinion, this is combined with another view that something which once occurred can never recur, and each historical fact presents a unique link in a chain of development. In other words, everything later is conditioned by the previous, and could not have transpired in precisely that particular manner if it had been preceded by the other link in the chain. The nub of every modern conception of history has been the idea of development. It follows from the modern conception that without exception, a historical value clings to every human activity and aptitude to have left a record for us. Each historical fact is unique and irreplaceable. Since it would be impossible to consider the overwhelming mass of historical incidents as accounted for directly or indirectly, it has been necessary to limit our attention predominantly to those records appearing to commemorate particularly conspicuous stages in the development of given sectors of human activity. Such records can consist of written remains arousing certain associations in our consciousness, or an artistic monument calling for direct visual or aural experience. It is important to realize that without exceptions, every monument has historical properties, since each embodies a particular moment in the development of the visual arts and strictly speaking remains irreplaceable by any other. All historical monuments are transversely also monuments of art, since even so inconspicuous a record as a torn piece of paper with a short written note of little importance has historical value as a record the production of paper, the development of handwriting, the utensils used for writing as well as an entire series of artistic aspects. This includes the outward form of the scrap of paper, the shape of the letters and the way in which they are joined. Of course, these are such unimportant elements, that we will not take note of them in thousands of cases, since so many other monuments preserve roughly the same information more richly and elaborately. If such a scrap of paper were the unique surviving monument of the artistic activity of its period, we would be bound to consider it as an indispensable artistic monument in spite of its paltry nature. The art confronting us there is primarily of interest for its historical location. The monument presents itself to us as a necessary link in the chain of development constituting the history of art. In this sense, the "artistic monument" is actually an "art historical monument" and from this point of view, its value is not an "artistic value" but rather "historical value." The result of this is that the distinction between "art- and historical monuments" is inaccurate since the former are contained in and subsumed by the latter.

Is the historical value in fact the only aspect of these art works we appreciate? If this were indeed the case, then it would follow that all art works of earlier times and artistic periods must necessarily appear as having an identical value, variable by nothing other than its rarity or age. In reality, we appreciate more recent works more highly than older works – one by Tiepolo from the 18th century more highly than a 16th century Mannerist. Beyond its historical value, there must therefore also be another factor which arouses our interest in early art, residing in its specifically artistic qualities, that is to say the conception of form and color. Aside from the art historical value, which all older works of art (monuments) have for us, there is also a purely artistic value independent of its place in the chain of historical development. Can this artistic value be as objective a fact as the historical value? Does it provide an essential part of our conception of the monument, independent of the historical aspect, or is it perhaps a purely subjective aspect invented by the modern spectator, defined and shifting according to their whims with no relevance to the concept of monuments as works with a memorial value?

Today there are two parties with different opinions in this question, an older school that has not yet been completely surpassed, and a younger one emerging triumphant. From the period of the renaissance, when, as we shall see, the historical value was first recognized, and then on into the 19th century, it was held that an infallible canon and objective artistic ideals existed, and that all artists strived toward this without ever quite reaching it. Originally, this was considered to have been most closely achieved in antiquity, and that some of the ancient works might actually have realized the ideal. The 19th century finally eliminated this unique claim for antiquity and emancipated nearly all of the other periods of art as significant in their own right. It did not however abandon the faith in an objective artistic ideal. It was not until the beginning of the 20th century that the necessary conclusion was reached from the idea of historical development, that all previous art belonged irretrievably to the past and could not be upheld as a canonical ideal. When we go beyond the consideration of exclusively modern works and also evaluate those from earlier periods, then the reason is that certain earlier works to some degree coincide with the modern artistic will (Kunstwollen), and that the appearance of these aspects of the earlier works has an effect on us today which no modern work can match. By the current standards there cannot be an absolute, but only a relative artistic value for the modern period.

Depending on which opinion we endorse, this will entail differing conceptions of artistic value (Kunstwert). According to the traditional point of view, a work of art has an artistic value insofar as it corresponds to the presumed requirements of an objective aesthetic that has still never been adequately formulated. In the new view, the artistic value is measured in the extent to which the artifact fulfills the modern artistic volition. Yet the qualities of this volition are even less well defined and strictly speaking must even remain elusive since they vary from subject to subject and moment to moment.

It is important for us to make this distinction completely clear, because this has a decisive influence on the theoretical orientation of historic preservation (Denkmalpflege). If there were no immutable artistic value, but only one that is relative and modern, then the artistic value of a monument would no longer be one of memory, but only a contemporary judgment. Historical preservation will take account of this since it is necessary as a practical quotidian judgment to counterbalance historical memorial value, but it has no place in the concept of the monument. If we accept the idea of artistic value as it very recently emerged as a direct result of the overwhelming amount of 19th century research, then it will no longer be possible to speak of "art- and historical monuments" but only of "historical monuments," and this is the sense with which we shall be using the term in the following pages.

By contrast to the "intentional" monuments, historical monuments are "unintentional." It is nonetheless immediately clear that all intentional monuments might equally well be unintentional, but make up a very small part of the unintentional group. Since the original authors of these works which present themselves to us today as historical monuments, were generally pursuing little more than a practical or ideal need for themselves, their contemporaries or possibly their immediate heirs, and they had no reason to remark on their (own) artistic or cultural life and work, the term "monument" can only be applied in a subjective and not in an objective way. The meaning and significance of monuments is not inherent in the objects themselves by their original appointment, but is instead attributed to them by us, the modern subjects. Both the intentional and the unintentional monuments are centered around a memorial value, and for this reason, we speak of memorials (Denkmale). In both cases, we are interested in the work in its pristine and undisturbed form as left by its creator, and as we persist in viewing it in thoughts, words or images. In the case of the former, the memorial value is imposed upon us by the original authors from without, while in the latter we devise it ourselves.

Living in our own time, our interest is far from exhausted by the "historical value" of the works surviving from earlier generations and nations. The historical value can hardly be the reason that our interest is aroused today by the ruins of a castle with dilapidated walls and little in the way of form, technique, disposition of spaces, and no historical records. In dealing with an old church tower it is also necessary to distinguish between the various more or less local historical memories that it might evoke, and the general non-local conceptions of the times, which the tower has "lived through" and which reveal themselves directly in the traces of its age. The same distinction can be drawn among written monuments. A 15th century piece of parchment with the most insignificant possible content, such as the sale of a horse for instance, might evoke memories in a twofold way. These could be historical by the formal factors of the sheet, the letters etc., or also by the yellowing and "patina" of the parchment and pallor of the script – not merely like the ruins of the castle or the church tower – but also by the subject of what is written on it. Its historical aspects might include the conditions of the sale, an obsolete use of language, unfamiliar expressions, or concepts and judgments obviously not modern and belonging to the past. In these cases, our interest is indubitably rooted in a memorial value, which is to say that we consider the work to be a monument from this point of view, specifically one that is unintended. Yet the memorial aspect does indeed cling to this artifact in its original state of preservation although this is due to our imagination surrounding the time that has past, and is evoked by the traces of its age. If we designate the conception of "historical" monuments as subjective in relation to those which are "intentional" while still involving a solid object, an originally self contained individual work, then this third class of monuments, the object, seems to have devolved into a simple necessary evil. The monument survives as nothing more than an unavoidable and evident substratum, arousing atmospheric effects in the modern spectator and running through the regular cycle of growth, decay, the immersion of the individual, and its slow migration back to generalities. While historic preservation demands academic experience, this emotional effect is not contingent on any knowledge of history. It requires no more than an immediate perception through the senses and can presumably reach all people of all educational and intelligence levels. This memorial- (monument-) value, which we shall in the following pages call the "age-value," runs very deep, shares these qualities with the emotions of religion and for now we are unable to assess the significance of its influence.

These observations already demonstrate that the modern cult of monuments is not limited to the cultivation of "historical monuments" but also calls for pious attention to "age-monuments." Just as the intentional monuments are subsumed among the unintentional monuments, so do all historical monuments provide a sub-set of the age monuments. Outwardly, the three groups are distinguished by a steady expansion in the range of their accepted memorial value. The class of intentional monuments is limited to those which their creators intended to commemorate a certain moment in the past (or conglomeration thereof). The class of historical monuments extends itself to include those commemorating a given moment, the choice of which is however left to our subjective whims. The class of age monuments includes all those artifacts made by human hands, regardless of their original meaning or function, as they chance to have "survived" into the present. The three appear as successive stages of increasing generality in the conception of the monument. A brief survey of the previous history of historical conservation reveals how these three classes in fact developed in the same order.

In a period before an appreciation arose for the unintentional type, the intentional monuments were exposed to dissolution and decay as soon as those people disappeared for whom their preservation had meaning. The intentional type of monument was the only one known throughout antiquity and the medieval period. In the present pages, we cannot give a precise historical account over such a long period of time. It should be recalled that in ancient Asia Minor and Egypt, monuments were primarily devoted to individuals or families, while the Greeks and Romans discovered the patriotic monument which from its very inception served a larger circle of interests, guaranteeing a longer survival, but also bringing a greater latitude in the choice of more enduring materials. Further on, we shall have occasion to discuss the apparent discovery of age value during late antiquity. It is also only natural that a transition to the concept of unintentional monuments began to emerge particularly during the medieval period.

During the medieval period, when the old empire had expired, a monument such as Trajan's Column which celebrated its glory and impregnability, must have been something like a "moving target."

It was indeed subjected to much mutilation and never considered worthy of repair. Its survival is primarily due to a lingering feeling of ancient patriotism which never completely left the medieval Romans, and however contingently, allows us to classify it, as an intentional monument. Well into the 14th century, there was always still the danger that the column might have been replaced without misgivings for some merely practical reason. This danger was not provisionally allayed until the renaissance, to the present day and for the foreseeable future.

This change was the result of a new memorial value, which had emerged in Italy beginning in the 15th century. The monuments of antiquity came to be appreciated for their "art- and historical value" and not merely for the patriotic memories of power and grandeur of the ancient empire which they conveyed, which even the medieval Roman continued to feel consistently with only slight interruption, however fantastic and fictional this feeling might have been. Since even modest fragments of entablatures and capitals were considered as worthy of attention as monuments on the level of Trajan's Column, it is clear that ancient art was now being evaluated in and of itself. The newly awakening historical interest is further apparent from the fact that inscriptions of very minor interest were being collected and recorded simply as testimony of the period. This newly emergent artistic and historical interest was originally of course limited to the cultural artifacts of the ancient world, which was seen by Italians of the renaissance as their own patrimony and also explains their loathing attitude toward what they saw as the barbarian Gothic. Be it political, national, communal, family or egotistic, its essentially merely patriotic impulse provides the link to the previous conception of intentional monuments. This must not cause us to overlook what is fundamentally new here. For the first time, we see people viewing the artistic, cultural and political activities of a millennium previous to their own as direct precursors. With an entire large nation interpreting ancient history as the work of its own ancestors and a part of their own activities, the interest in intentional monuments, which formerly began to decline as the following generations vanished, was now perpetuated for an indefinite period. The past thus gained an immediate value to modern life and its creations. Even if it was originally limited to their own national past, both factual and imaginary, an interest in history arose among the Italians. At the time, this limitation seems to have been necessary. Attention to history could originate in the semi-egotistical aspect of patriotic and national manifestations. It would still require centuries for such an interest to slowly gain its modern aspect, as we see it particularly among the Germanic cultures. This is the interest in all nations, even in the most minor deeds and fortunes of the most obscure and by nature irreconcilably antagonistic cultures, and the interest in the history of humanity generally, recognizing a predecessor of ours in each and every individual.

It was distinctive that the period becoming the first to discover the "artistic and historical value" of at least ancient monuments also issued the earliest regulations for protecting monuments. The brief of Pope Paul III from November 28, 1534 was particularly important among its milestones. Since traditional law had no sense of unintentional monuments, there was a feeling of obligation to formulate particular protections for such newly discovered values.

We are completely justified to conclude that the Italian renaissance initiated a completely modern conception for the care and preservation of artistic monuments along with the conscious appreciation of ancient artifacts and the implementation of laws to protect them. We must bear in mind though that the notion of the memorial value among the Italians of the renaissance was still remote from ours at the beginning of the 20th century. As we have already remarked, the limitation of interest to the putative ancestral art had on the one hand led to a situation in which the genetic connection between the emerging cultivation of unintentional monuments and the earlier intentional type was still quite manifest. On the other hand, there was as yet no sense of age value. It only existed very nebulously by that time. The historical value attached to the ancient monuments by the Italians was still remote from the clarity achieved in the late 19th century. The distinction between the artistic and the historical value, between artistic and historical monuments only began to emerge during the renaissance. As we have seen, it persisted into the 19th century and has only recently been superseded. Ancient forms were revered in and of themselves. The art that produced them was held to have been uniquely true, objectively correct and valid for all time, while all else (until Italian renaissance art) was considered either a crude anticipation or a barbarian distortion. Since it does not recognize any sort of development, this point of view is still normative and authoritative, ancient-medieval, but not historical in the modern sense. The renaissance did have a historical aspect however in reverently interpreting antiquity as a precursor to the Italian renaissance itself. While Michelangelo for instance was occasionally considered to have surpassed antiquity in some of his work, and ancient monuments therefore obviously claimed no eternal but only a relative and therefore historical value, there was no broad conception of historical development. The idea that the Italians of the renaissance had found the way back to themselves after a period of barbarian invasions and simply continued ancient art, as it would otherwise have remained innate to them is itself an undeniably historical idea. When a natural innate compulsion was attributed to the renaissance Italians on the basis of their nationality, obliging them to continue ancient culture, it also included a theory of development.

However unacceptable it may be to the modern point of view, the Italian renaissance concept completely justified the distinction between those unintended monuments which were artistic and those which were historical. It is probably true that the artistic value was originally more crucial, and the historical value as unique and individual facts must have receded somewhat in relation to it. The development of the cult of monuments in the following period, including the 18th century, can be succinctly defined. As other primarily Germanic and partly Germanic nations participated more, these groups increasingly appreciated other artistic modes and the objective model of antiquity was not yet directly denied, but was continually reduced from the sense in which the Italian renaissance had upheld it. During those centuries, the remains of classical antiquity incrementally lost their canonical importance, the renaissance popes felt the need to shelter them, the non-ancient artistic modes of antiquity did not yet achieve sufficient authority to call for official protection, and actual laws to that effect did not arise.

The 19th century has justifiably been called the century of history. From what we can tell today, the 19th century took greater pleasure than any before or since in the detection and affectionate study of individual facts, meaning the individual human action in its pure and original state of becoming. Its favorite objective was to experience an individual historical fact with complete precision. The so-called auxiliary sciences devoted to these subjects were not then considered auxiliary, but more as the primary activities of historians who seemed instead to exhaust themselves in such activities. Even most inconspicuous anecdotes were read with pleasure and studied for their authenticity. The postulate that a subject must have some importance for the history of humanity, nationalities, states or religion was not directly denied, but it did in fact disappear. This led to the rise of cultural history, in which even the smallest, and particularly the smallest factors can assume immense importance. Such an emphasis follows from the conviction that the minutest detail within the development is irreplaceable. Even the least significant detail in terms of materials, craftsmanship or function possessed an objective value for the sake of history. When this tendency inevitably reduced the objective value of the monument, the development itself, which generates all values, inevitably gained significance in relation to the individual monuments. The historical value inseparably attached to these details then naturally transformed itself incrementally into a value associated with the historical development, and this in turn viewed the individual object as such with indifference. This value attached to development is nothing other than the age value as we have just learned to recognize it. It emanates directly from the historical value antedating it by four centuries. If there had been no historical value in the first place, an age-value could never have arisen. If the 19th century might be said to have devoted itself to the historical value, then the 20th appears likely to become that of the age-value. For the moment, we are still in a transitional phase which by its very nature must be one of conflict.

If I am not completely mistaken, the entire development as we have described it in general terms is nothing other than an aspect of the emancipation of the individual as it has predominated the entire modern period. Since the end of the 18th century, the process has advanced most dramatically and in some of the European cultures even replaced the classical basis of education. This change in the memorial value manifested itself most clearly in the distinct, continually intensified trend toward apprehending all physical and psychological experience not as it exists objectively, but rather according to its subjective appearance, according to the effect it exerts on the subject either through perception or intellectual consciousness. This is evident in the fact that the historical value is still geared and related to isolated incidents as it presents itself fairly objectively to the individual subject. The age value completely disregarded the individual localized phenomenon, and without exception placed a premium on nothing other than the subjective mood in every monument. Age value does not consider the specific objective aspects which reveal its original contained objective individuality, but instead only its traces of age – those qualities appearing in the monument before the public, its traces of age.

The 19th century did not merely escalate the historical value to the highest possible degree of prestige, but also sought to lay the legal basis for its protection. After faltering since the renaissance because antiquity failed to fulfill it, the faith in an objective artistic canon was applied to all periods of art during the course of the 19th century, and this also explains the unprecedented surge in art historical research during that time. According to the 19th century view, some fragment of the eternal canon is immanent in every mode of art. For this reason, all examples deserved to be preserved forever with a view to our aesthetic edification. They therefore required buttressing by law, all the while accounting for the numerous antagonistic judgments then current. All of the 19th century laws and regulations endorsed the view that nothing more than historical values resided in the unintentional monuments and the presumed objective artistic value. They became inadequate as soon as the age value began to emerge.

By way of an appendix to this brief review of the development of the cult of monuments, we would now like to mention a few phenomena that might at first glance appear incongruous with the above explanations.

Although we know that individual art works were piously preserved as early as in antiquity, this still does not mean that a cult of unintended monuments already existed. It reveals more of a cult of the living and particularly religious imagination possessing a very real value in the present, but not one as a memorial or monument. This form of piety was directed not toward the work of man, but rather to the deity who had temporarily resided in the ephemeral form. Such pretense of immutability in its value as a presence could even lead us to consider every single image of a god to be an intentional monument, yet this is explicitly contradicted in its immortalization as a given moment, be it an individual deed or historical action.

In the early imperial period of Rome by contrast, we can see evidence of an undeniable cult of art works from earlier periods in and of themselves. There are numerous analogies providing the most striking parallel to that of our own time. Pliny and Petronius have given us particularly many references to the interest in antiques as it flourished in their time. Another important aspect, the preference for older rather than more recent works, provides another parallel to our own time. Today, we still know too little about the circumstances surrounding early imperial Roman art to give a clear enough explanation for this surprising phenomenon. It is striking that the collectors were then exclusively interested in acquiring works of the famous sculptors from the fifth and fourth centuries BC. It can be no coincidence that according to the available source, the collectors were less lovers of art than collectors of antiquities. There seems to have been a sport among a number of immensely wealthy people in desiring to create new values by their acquisitions and thus to trump one another. The decline of the ancient Greek religion of the twelve gods might have provided an external impulse. From the comparatively quick and traceless passing of this phenomenon which seems to have completely disappeared by the third century, we can also see that it was not a profound trait of ancient culture. It is completely understandable that the state would not write laws to regulate such a market in antiquities. No historian will deny that this phenomenon must have related to the general artistic development at the beginning of the imperial period. We are reminded of the optical approach to the objects of the world then taking hold in a very broad way. In its pure form, the corresponding mode in the visual arts still determines the arts of our modern period. In fact, if it is studied more closely, this antiquarianism of the Romans during the first and second centuries AD might turn out to be an anachronistic predecessor of the modern sense of memorial value. In any case, it was never developed further since the migration period felt no piety whatsoever for the ancient pagan art melded to the faith in the gods in thousands of ways.

A specific study might also reveal that the age value already emerged in individual obscure and limited manifestations, long before the beginning of the 20th century, where it has now become an influential cultural force. On the other hand, we must be careful about interpreting phenomena in this way when their similarity to the cult of age value might only be superficial. This is especially true of the cult of ruins, which we have also already mentioned as an example of modern age value, certainly traceable back at least to the 17th century. In spite of an outward correspondence in the basic factors, the modern cult of ruins is completely different from that earlier phenomenon, but this does not preclude a connection in the development, indeed it suggests it. From the very fact that the 17th century ruin painters, and even the most national among them – the Dutch – almost exclusively painted ancient ruins, we can see that they were addressing a particular historical moment. At that time, all remains of Roman culture were considered to constitute symbols of the greatest earthly power and glory. The ruinous character was intended to simply make conscious the truly baroque contrast between former greatness and present abasement. These examples express sadness at the depth of the decline, and with this the wish that such monuments could have survived.

However much it is often undercut by the occasional addition of an innocent pastoral idyll, it also embodies a joyful reveling in pain, which constituted an aesthetic value to the baroque pathos. Its modern manifestation could not be more remote from such baroque sentiments. In our time, the traces of age have a soothing effect as manifestations of the laws of nature which control all of the works of man with certainty and without exception. To the modern viewer, the traces of violent destruction of a ruined castle are in fact comparatively less suitable to evoke the pure mood of age value. If we have nonetheless just used such an example to illustrate age value, this is simply because a ruin illustrates age value particularly clearly. Indeed, it does so too clearly to provide satisfaction to the modern viewer and their preoccupation with mood.

2. The Relationship of Memorial Value to the Cult of Monuments

We have distinguished three distinct memorial values among the monuments, and must now determine the demands which each of these by their nature make from the cult of monuments. After this, it will be necessary to consider the further values of a monument for the modern viewer; in their totality, these contrast with the values of the past and memorials as they thrive in the present (Vergangenheits- oder Erinnerungswerte als Gegenwartswerte).

In discussing memorial values, we must of course begin with age value, not merely because it has been the most recent historical development and makes the greatest claim to the future, but also because it includes the greatest number of monuments.

A. The Age Value

Age value of a monument reveals itself at first glance by its un-modern appearance. This un-modern appearance is less due to un-modern forms of style. Such qualities could always be imitated, and their proper recognition and judgment would be limited to the comparatively small group of art historians. Age value to the contrary is able to affect large masses of people. At the root of age value, the differences to the present reveal themselves in an imperfection, lack of unity, and a tendency to the dissolution of form and color as directly opposed to art created recently.

All human artistic activity ultimately consists of elements found dispersed or generally formless in nature and then unified into a coherent whole, limited by form and color. Such creation shows humanity acting exactly as nature. Both produce limited individual creations. Today, we still expect this quality of containment or coherence from each modern work of art. From the history of art we learn that the development of the human will to art increasingly involves the relation of the individual work of art to its environment, and our own period has naturally progressed the farthest in this regard. In spite of our capricious layout of residential districts, and in spite of paintings such *The Daughter of Jorio* by Francesco Paolo Michetti, where a figure otherwise completely visible is truncated at the head by the picture frame, even today the isolating mode of conception for the whole with regular contours remains the absolute postulate for all artistic creation. This quality of containment itself already includes an aesthetic factor, an elemental artistic value, which we shall have to consider later in the name of "novelty value" as it exists among the values of our time. In modern works, a lack of coherence would only cause displeasure. Other than forgeries, we do not construct any ruins, and since we expect a seamless closure in terms of form and polychromy, a newly built house with flaking plaster or soot can only seem annoying. Signs of decay in a recent construction do not evoke mood, but alienate it.

Both in natural and human creation, the destructive process of nature sets in as soon as the individual unit is complete. Mechanical and chemical forces at one with the amorphous nature around it begin transforming it back into its original elements. The traces of this process are the evidence that a monument is not a recent creation, and this clear recognition is the basis for recognizing its age value. As we have already noted, the most drastic example is the ruin as it comes about by the gradual dilapidation of its larger more physically tangible parts from the coherent whole of the castle. The far less forceful effect of age value presents itself in the more optic and less tangible effects of surface decay in weathering, patina, abraded corners, edges and such, revealing the slow but relentless, inexorable, regular and therefore compelling dissolution by nature.

The fundamental aesthetic law based on the age value of our time might be expressed as follows. We demand that human hands produce complete works in the form of symbolic images in a necessary and regular creative process. On the other hand, nature works within time to dissolve the completeness of the ideogram in an equally inexorable and regular process. Signs of decay in a newly completed work from human hands would bother us as premature deterioration, and we feel the same about signs of recent work on earlier such objects such as overt restorations. Humanity at the beginning of the 20th century finds pleasure in the unsullied perception of the regular cycle of natural becoming and decay. According to this, each human creation is conceived as a natural organism with a development that should not be tampered with whatsoever. The organism should live its normal life, and human hands should not intervene other than to save it from death perhaps. In this way, modern humanity sees a part of its own life as projected upon the monument and feels any intervention to be an interference much as into its own organism. Even in its destructive and annihilating aspects, which are conceived as a renewal of life, the workings of nature seem to be accorded the same rights as those of man.[79] What arouses displeasure on the other hand and must be avoided at all costs are any haphazard interruptions of that law. They present an intrusion of becoming into the process of decay, and conversely the perceived sacrilege of human hands encroaching on the processes of nature with a premature destruction of human works by nature. If age value views signs of decay through the dissolution of the coherent human work by natural mechanical and chemical processes as its aesthetically effective aspect, then it follows that the cult of age value is not merely disinterested in preserving the monument in its unchanged state, but even regards this as contrary to its interests. When the process of decay is constant and inexorable, and the cyclical law that pleases the modern viewer of earlier monuments calls for the consistent

---

79 Other typical features of modern cultural life, particularly among the Germanic cultures, which point to the same origin of age value, are the efforts to protect animal life and natural beauty ("der landschaftliche Sinn überhaupt"), as it has risen to include not merely the protection of individual plants, but entire forests, and demanding the legal protection of "natural monuments" encompassing even inorganic formations among the individual items to be preserved.

movement of change rather than the stasis of preservation, then the
monument itself should not even be spared from the destructive effects
of nature if human activities could impede it. From the point of view
of age value there is one thing alone to be avoided at all costs and this
is the whimsical intrusion of human hands into the emergent state of
the monument. It cannot sustain any addition or diminution to distort
its original complete state, neither the supplement of an element which
nature might have removed, nor the removal of such that might equally
have accrued to the monument. The pure redemptive impression
of natural and regular decay should not be sullied by the whimsical
admixture of incomplete growth. In this sense, the cult of age value
not merely condemns any forceful destruction of the monument as
a sacrilegious intrusion into the regular degenerative processes of
nature and advocates the preservation of the monument on the one
hand, but also considers any conservational activity or restoration as
a no less unjustified intrusion into the process of natural laws. In this
way it actually directly opposes the preservation of monuments. There
can be no doubt that the unrestrained forces of nature necessarily
and ultimately lead to the complete destruction of the monument. It
is probably correct that a ruin becomes increasingly picturesque the
more its parts succumb to the process of dissolution. As the destruction
continues however, its age value is supported by increasingly fewer
factors, and it becomes less extensive but instead all the more intense.
The remaining parts have an ever more evocative effect on the viewer.
This process also has its limitations. When the extensive aspect of the
effect is completely lost, no substratum then remains for the intensive
effect. A mere pile of formless rubble is no longer sufficient to evoke

age value in a viewer. It requires at least a clear trace of original form from the previous human artifact surviving from a former creative phase, while a pile of stones presents no more than a formless splinter of encompassing nature without a trace of living change.

We can see that the cult of age value is in this way works towards its own destruction.[80] Its more radical devotees will not protest this inference at all. First of all, the destructive process of nature is slow enough that even monuments thousands of years old will probably at least remain at our disposal for the foreseeable future and the foreseeable duration of this attitude. Then there is the fact that the changes of the world also continue constantly without interruption. Things that might seem modern for now, aligned with all laws of change, and including an individual perfection will eventually become monuments and fill a gap which the natural forces must at some point inevitably cause within our traditional roster of monuments. From the standpoint of age value, it is not necessary to expend human energies in catering to the eternal preservation of monuments from earlier times. Instead, the goal is to display the eternal cycle of growth and decay which can equally well continue completely unharmed when other monuments have replaced those in existence today.

As we have already reiterated, age value has the advantage above

---

80 Of course nothing could be more remote from the cult of age value than to hasten the destruction. It does not by any means view the ruin as an end in itself, as it might appear, but would prefer a well preserved medieval castle. If the memorial effect of the latter is less intense than that of the ruin, it is all the more extensive and makes up for that omission with the richness and variety of its traces of age, by revealing the work of human hands in a less decayed state but more of the human artifact in a state of decay.

all of the other ideal values of art in presuming to address each work with equal validity and without exception. It claims to transcend not merely the religious creeds, but also the differences of education and artistic inclination. In fact, the criteria for recognizing age value are so simple as to be discernible even to those whose existence is consumed by the quotidian needs of physical welfare and material production. A peasant with the most limited conceivable views will be able to distinguish an old from a new church tower. This advantage of age value is particularly apparent in relation to the historical value based in education and can only emerge through a rational reflection. Age value on the other hand is obvious to the most superficial sensation on the part of the viewer, to our immediate sense of sight, and therefore speaks directly to the emotions. Of course the original source of age value once had the same educated character as that of historical value. Age value appears as the final achievement of science. It presents itself as a discovery with a rational basis but available universally through the emotions to those masses who can never be convinced by rational argument. It appeals to the emotions and their requirements. If we view things purely historically in terms of human reason and put aside the just claims of divine revelation, the situation is similar to that of Christianity in late antiquity. For the salvation of the remainder of the population who lived with their emotions and could never be reached with rational argument, it was necessary then to clarify the resilient core of what Greek philosophy had discovered in its own right.

When the adherents of age value are so compulsive in asserting themselves competitively and without tolerance to others, they are animated by this claim to general validity. They are convinced that nothing can be aesthetically salutary without the medium of age value. After having been intuited by thousands of people over a long period of time and originally posited by no more than a small group of pugnacious artists and laymen, age value is now gaining additional adherents day by day. This is due not merely to a technically appealing propaganda, but primarily to its inherent potential to predominate much of the future. A modern policy of historical preservation must necessarily come to terms with this conception and with this one primarily. However, it should not and cannot omit to consider the other, the historical and the contemporary values of monuments when they are present. It must weigh the historical and contemporary values in relation to the age value and cultivate them proportionally when they are the more important.

B. Historical Value

The historical value of a monument lies in the fact that it embodies a very particular and individual phase from the development of a given field of human creativity. From this standpoint, one is less interested in the traces of the decaying natural influences affecting it since its inception, but rather its original creation as a work by human hands. Historical value reveals itself all the more potently when the original perfect state of the monument, as it stood immediately upon creation, is preserved in a condition as unadulterated as possible. The disfiguration and partial dissolution appear as an interference and unwelcome addition to the sense of historical value. This is equally true for the art historical as well as for any cultural-historical value, and particularly for that in terms of historical chronicles. Whether they consider it from the point of view of a step in the development of Greek temple construction, as an example of the technique in the art of stone masonry, or in terms of the religious cult and conceptions of the gods, the historian will in any case regret that the Parthenon is only preserved for us as a ruin. The profession of the historian involves filling the gaps which the processes of nature have caused in the original image during the course of time. In the view of historical value, the symptoms of dissolution, which play a central part to the age value, must be redressed at all costs. This cannot be performed on the monument itself, but rather with copies or only in words or thoughts. In the end, historical value also sees the original work as fundamentally inviolable, but for reasons differing completely from those of age value. While these figure as irritating or at the very least indifferent, historical value does not seek to preserve the signs of age against the influence of natural decay through time. It is more concerned to preserve a document in as undistorted a form as possible for future art historical research. It recognizes that all human calculation and supplementation is exposed to the mistakes of subjectivity. For this reason, as the only element firmly given, the document itself must be preserved in as perfect a state as possible so that later generations can verify and eventually correct our current attempts at restoration. As soon as the question is posed as to the appropriate treatment of a monument according to the principles of the historical value, the fundamental difference to the age value becomes immediately apparent. Previous decay from the forces of nature cannot be reversed, and for that reason should not be adjusted according to the principles of historical value. From the point of view of historical value, it would not merely be futile to inhibit the further decay which begins immediately and is accepted and even postulated by the proponents of age value, but any such efforts should be completely avoided since all continuing dissolution will further encumber the scholarly complementation of the original human work in its state of becoming. The cult of historical value must therefore concentrate on preserving the monuments in their present state and come to the conclusion that human intervention is an obstructive influence, deterring the natural processes of dissolution to the extent that human influence can do so. Although both the age value and historical value are themselves memorial values, we can see how their interests diverge on the essential question of historical preservation. How can this conflict be resolved? If this is not possible, then which of the two values should be sacrificed in favor of the other?

If we recall that the cult of age value is nothing other than the ripe product of the centuries-old cult of historical value, then we are initially tempted to view the latter as an obsolete phase that has been surpassed. In practical questions of historic preservation it would follow that in instances of a conflict between these two forms of memorial value, the historical value would have to be given up as the more antiquated of the two. Yet is it true that the validity of the historical value is so completely obsolete? Has its mission as a predecessor and battering ram for the age value in fact been achieved in even the most general terms?

Even the most radical adherents of the age value, who today are still mostly members of the educated class, will admit that the pleasure they take in the viewing of a monument is not due solely to its age value, but to a great extent also derives from their satisfaction in the fact that the monument corresponds to a conception of style which they already know, such as ancient, Gothic, baroque and so forth. Historical knowledge remains an aesthetic source for them, combined with and parallel to the feeling of age value. Since it presupposes art historical knowledge, this form of satisfaction is not direct or artistic, but is reflected through scholarship. Yet this proves beyond any doubt that our conception of the age value is still not so independent of the previous historical stage as to completely thrive without the interests of the historical value. If we today turn from the educated populace to those with average levels of education, who after all comprise the greatest mass of those interested in cultural values, we find that they generally see the monuments as falling into the categories of medieval (since antiquity is too rare in our parts of central Europe to be recognized and judged as a separate entity), early modern (meaning renaissance and baroque) and modern. However crude such categories might be, this again demonstrates that age value can still not be distinguished from the historical value as completely as some of the pioneers of recent developments have imagined. For example, this is evident from the fact that the ruinous state of a medieval castle conforms more to our yearning for mood than does a baroque palace apparently striking us as too recent to be seen in such a state of preservation. In doing so, we postulate a certain relationship between the state of decay in which a monument appears, and its age which presupposes a certain art historical knowledge.

While the memorial value is among the most important cultural factors of today, this demonstrates that it has not at all yet developed to the broad and ripe form of age value, and not completely superseded the historical value. Historical value is based on scholarship, and has no more potential in moving large segments of the population than do the doctrines of philosophy. Through four centuries of the modern period, we can see how the interest in history has continuously and increasingly embodied a redemptive meaning for the idea of development, similar perhaps to the role we have noted for philosophy in antiquity (p.252 above). Yet age value will also not provide its final and ultimate formula. This can account for the continuing interest in education which today involves the idea of historical development – although there is no lack of those who deny historical education to be either a goal or means toward human culture.

Today, we still have every reason to do all possible justice to the demands of historical research, and in those cases where it conflicts with the requirements of age value, not to treat it simply as unimportant or negligible. In prematurely putting aside and ignoring the historical value which itself generated the modern development, and with it the concept of age value itself, we would be doing harm to the more elevated interests which age value itself intends to serve.

In the practice of historical preservation, the external inducement to a conflict between age value and historical value is fortunately much less common than we might initially imagine. The two competing values normally have an inverted relationship to one another. The greater the historical value, the less the age value. The more familiar age value is repressed by the more sincere but also more objectively tangible and forceful historic value, and in cases of the intentional monuments this is further increased almost to the point of completely suppressing the age value. In such cases, the individual character of historical value assumes a greater importance than the development itself. Like all individual qualities, it has a strong effect of presence, and allows the past and transience to sustain the age value only peripherally though sufficiently. In standing before the Ingelheim columns at Heidelberg Castle, the viewer is so overwhelmingly reminded that these once stood at the palace of Charlemagne, that the emotional resonance of their absolute age is almost completely overcome. In such a case, there should be no misgivings in treating the monument according to the demands of the historical cult rather than that of age value. By the same token, the age value will emerge all the more one-sidedly and stronger when the historical ("documentary") value is weaker, and concomitantly be treated more exclusively according to the demands of age value.

It is far from rare that age value is forced to call for the very human intervention into the life of the monument that it otherwise eschews. Such an instance arises when a monument is in danger of a premature complete demise by the forces of nature, an abnormally quick dissolution as an organism. If the well preserved fresco on the outer wall of a church for example, were suddenly to be progressively damaged in each passing rain storm, and in danger of being completely lost, even the contemporary adherent of age value would condone a protective roof to prevent this in spite of his conviction that this would constitute an intrusion into the autonomous natural processes by contemporary human activity. Even when the source is natural rather than human, the premature demise of the monument as organism appears no less as a forceful, irregular, unnecessary intervention and therefore disruptive. However powerful we may be among its forces, humanity is after all itself a part of nature, and for this reason, even a forceful human intervention into the life of a monument can give the appearance of creating a mood that might appeal to the contemporary viewer, assuming that enough time has passed since it was done (as with the ruins of Heidelberg Castle). Human activity, which would seem intrusive and disruptive at closer quarters, can from a distance easily appear to be a part of regularity and necessity of nature.

In the first of these examples, the need for a protective roof over a fresco, we see the age value also calling for human intervention, something otherwise the prerogative of historical value – in compellingly preserving the documentary quality, and antagonistic to age value. In contrast to the forces of nature, we also have the more gentle human intervention that the cult of age views as the lesser of evils. At least superficially, the interests of both values work in tandem, although age value aims to merely slow the course of things while historical value wishes to completely subvert the process of dissolution. From the point of view of historical preservation, the central concern is to avoid the appearance of a conflict between the two values.

Although it is apparent that not every monument necessarily involves a conflict between age value and historical value, the potential for such a thing is frequently present, especially in those cases where the values bear an approximately equal weight in the eyes of the viewer. Then they face one another as a conservative and a radical principle. Since it strives to preserve everything, and in its current state, the historical value presents the conservative attitude. Age value has an advantage here by the fact that it is simpler in practice, and ultimately embodies the only principle possible to implement. Preservation for eternity is beyond us. In the final analysis, the forces of nature are more powerful than human craft, and as individuals, we ourselves face nature and are destroyed by it. In questions of applied measures for preservation, the two values can strike a balance, and the conflict never assumes so strident a character as in decisions about restorations involving changes of form and color. In such questions, age value is far more sensitive than historical value. If a few pieces of fragmented masonry are removed and replaced in an old tower, the historical value of the tower will not have suffered in any meaningful way. Its original form has been maintained, and enough of the original character preserved to satisfy any subsidiary historical questions. The few exchanged pieces of stone are unimportant. On the other hand, age value might even find such a minimal addition highly disruptive, especially if a "new" color glares out at us from the configuration. Especially so since our period in history is particularly sensitive to the relative and subjective factor within the objective total appearance of things.

In spite of the fact that it only considers a monument to possess documentary value in its original condition, we should also note in conclusion that the cult of historical value could in certain circumstances find a use for copies when the original (the "document") has been irretrievably lost. An intractable conflict with the age value will in such cases only come about when the copy is no longer seen as merely an aid to scholarship, but taken as a fully valid original work in historical and aesthetic terms. This is true of the tower of St. Mark's in Venice. As long as such cases persist, the historical value cannot be considered to have been superseded, and the age value cannot be considered as the sole authoritative aesthetic memorial value of humanity. On the other hand, we can be confident that relatively useful surrogates for original documents might be found, particularly when color photography is perfected and can be combined with facsimile reproductions. We might then satisfy at least that particular need of historical scholarship, which provides the only possible source of such conflict, and avoid any alteration or disfigurement in terms of age value.

C. The Intentional Memorial Value

Contrary to age value, the historical value had shown the tendency to isolate a certain moment of the development from the past and display it before us as if it belonged to the present. From the very beginning, that is to say from the moment in which a monument was erected, the intentional memorial value does not allow this to become a thing of the past, but seeks to preserve it as ever present and vivid in the consciousness. This third class of memorial values thus provides the apparent transition to those values attached to the present.

Age value is based exclusively on decay and historical value seeks to prevent the complete destruction beginning with the present day, justifying itself by the previous process of decay. The intentional memorial value then makes a claim to timelessness, an eternal present, an incessant state of becoming. For this reason, the destructive forces of nature that prevent this, are to be persistently combated and their effects continually neutralized. A memorial column with its inscription lost would cease to be an intentional monument. For this reason, restoration presents the fundamental postulate of intentional monuments.

As a value based on the present, the character of the intentional memorial value is further characterized by the fact that it has always been protected by law against human intervention. In this class of monuments, the conflict with age value is a natural and relentless fact. Without restoration, the monuments would soon lose their intentional character. Age value is therefore the natural archenemy of the intentional memorial value. As long as humanity does not renounce earthly immortality, the cult of age value will always face an insurmountable barrier in that of the intentional memorial. This irreconcilable conflict between age value and the intentional memorial value provides less difficulties for historical preservation than might at first be expected. This is because the number of "intentional" monuments is so comparatively small in comparison to the great mass of purely unintentional monuments.

3. The Relationship of Contemporary Values to the Cult of Monuments

Most monuments are capable of also satisfying those human sensual and spiritual needs. These are obviously not affected by its origin in the past or the memorial value springing from it, which could be accommodated equally well or better by more recent modern configurations. It is this potential which provides the basis for the "contemporary value" of a monument. This attitude could lead us from the very outset to view the monument less as a monument, more as a recent modern creation, and to expect from earlier monuments to sport the same outward appearance as a recent human product in a state of becoming. They might make the impression of a complete containment and physical integrity in face of the destructive forces of nature. According to the character of the individual quality in presence, symptoms of this latter attitude might gain acceptance. Eventually, this must necessarily reach an impassable limit beyond which the contemporary value becomes impossible and raises a challenge to the age value. Monuments treated according to the cult of age value are consistently and practically left to their completely natural state and this leads inevitably to a conflict with the contemporary value which can only be resolved by the entire or partial sacrifice of one or the other.

As we have remarked, the value based in the present can arise from the gratification of worldly and intellectual needs. In the former case, we refer to practical functional values or simply functional values. In the latter we speak of artistic values. Within the artistic value, it is necessary to further distinguish the elementary or novelty value as it exists within the enclosed totality of a newly created work, and then the relative artistic value based on a concurrence with the predominant artistic will. In this connection it should also be borne in mind that monuments serve both secular and sacred artistic purposes.

A. The Practical Value

Physical life is the prerequisite of all psychological life, and is more important than the latter in the sense that physical life can exist without a psychological superstructure, while the reverse is not possible. This is the reason that an old building still in use must be in such a condition as to still properly shelter people without danger to the security of their lives or their health. Any gap that might be broken into its walls or roof by the powers of nature must immediately be filled to stop the penetration of water as far as possible or at least to freeze the process, and so forth. We can generally conclude that the treatment of a monument is indifferent in terms of the practical value as long as its existence is not placed in danger. Yet beyond this, no concessions should be made to the age value. When the novelty value is intricately mingled with the practical value, the bounds within which age value is permitted to unfold must be drawn even more narrowly, and we shall have to speak of this later on.

We need not belabor the fact that innumerable secular and ecclesiastical monuments today survive in a functional state and are actually still in use. If their continued use were not permitted, replacements would have to be found in most cases. This requirement is so coercive that the counterclaims of age value, that a monument should be allowed to deteriorate according to the natural process, can only be countenanced in those cases where at the very least an alternative location of equal proficiency is available. Such a demand can only be satisfied in comparatively few exceptional cases. It is prevented by completely insurmountable difficulties.

Works that it has taken centuries to produce are proposed to be replaced at once or within a comparatively short term, and costs and labor which originally required centuries are substituted nearly instantly. Even when extended over a number of years, it is all too obvious that such a procedure is practically impossible and would require more time. In individual cases, this route can and will certainly be taken. However, it cannot become a common principle, and the functional value of most monuments can therefore not be ignored.

The negative demands of the functional value, calling for the destruction of a monument, can be equally pressing in terms of human physical needs. An example would be the case of a tower that is in danger of collapsing due to the normal influence of nature, with possible harm to life and limb. There is no question then that the considerations of human life take precedence over any regard for the ideal circumstances of age value.

Even if we assume that all monuments in a functional state could be duplicated by modern replacements, and the old originals allowed to live out their natural existence without any restoration or continued function or use, would this in fact satisfy the demands of the age value? The question is not merely justified, but it can only be flatly negated. If people stopped using the monument, there would be an irretrievable loss of an essential part of that living play of the natural forces allowing our perception of the age value. In gazing upon the basilica of St. Peter's in Rome, who would wish away the living staffage of the tourists or its religious functions? Even the most radical adherent of age value would not find a moody evocation in the sight of a residential structure, however old, damaged by lightning, or the ruins of a church on a busy street, but would see them more as an unwelcome distraction. We are used to seeing these works in full human use, and they make a more annoying impression when they are not fulfilling their customary functions, while providing an unacceptable example of forceful destruction to the cult of age value as well. On the other hand, there are remains of monuments that can no longer have any practical function where we no longer miss the effects of natural human activity. This would include the ruins of a medieval castle on a steep cliff within a forest or those of an ancient temple in the busy streets of Rome itself, exuding the complete and unadulterated appeal of age value. We have therefore not yet reached the stage in which we can apply the measure of age value in a completely equal way to all monuments without selection. Yet we continue to distinguish between older and more recent, between relatively functional and dysfunctional works, considering the historical value in the first case, and the functional value in the latter. It is only the works that have deteriorated beyond any use that we are able to treat and to enjoy completely and purely from the point of view of their age value. Those with some trace of functional potential bother us if they do not display something of the expected contemporary value. This is the same modern spirit which has led to the agitation against the "prisons of art." Despite the fact that it be spared the exposure to possible restoration within the confines of a museum, age value necessarily militates more vehemently than historical value against the alienation of a monument from its previous, relatively organic context.

If the continuing practical use of a monument also has a significant and often essential meaning for the age value, this considerably limits the possible conflict between the age value and the functional value, which had seemed so unavoidable just a moment ago. Since such artifacts are so comparatively rare in our area and with very few exceptions were removed from the practical sphere so long ago, this conflict cannot easily arise in the case of the ancient and early medieval antiquities. In the reverse case of monuments of a more recent origin, age value will have little difficulty in making concessions for the maintenance to allow these to also continue accommodating human circulation and manipulation as the age value wishes it. For these reasons, the monuments most likely to lead to a conflict between the functional value and the age value tend to lie on the border between use and disuse, between the medieval and the modern period, and the decision is most likely to be made in favor of the one with parallel requirements among the other values.

Since a conflict with age value is already given in such cases, it is not necessary to discuss the treatment of monuments caught between the functional and historical values. Since it is so much less brittle, the historical value will more easily cling to the requirements of the functional value.

B. The Artistic Value

According to modern conceptions (as discussed pp. 231-232 above) each monument only possesses an artistic value to the extent that it conforms to the modern artistic will. These requirements are of two kinds. Modern artistic value shares the first of these with earlier artistic periods in that each modern work of art presents a self contained whole with no sign of decay in either color or form (cf pp. 247-248 above). In other words: by the very fact that it is new, each new work possesses the elementary artistic value that we might call the novelty value. The other requirement refers specifically to the quality of decay in the conception, form and color of the monument, and provides the difference to the modern artistic volition. Since these requirements are in a state of continual change and do not possess an objective or lasting validity, we might use the term "relative artistic value." It is obvious from the outset that a monument cannot conform completely to the definition of either.

α) The Novelty Value

Since every monument will reveal the effects of natural forces according to its age and the comparative circumstantial favor or disfavor, the completeness of form and color contained in the definition of the novelty value remain a practical impossibility. This is the reason that the modern artistic will of each successive period and still today can only view strikingly old works of art as not completely pleasing. The implications of this are obvious: if a monument with traces of decay is to appeal to the modern will as thus defined, then it must be purified of all traces of age, its forms and color rounded out to reflect the character of something new or newly created. Novelty value can only be maintained in a way that directly contradicts the cult of age value.

This creates the possibility of a conflict far deeper and more irreconcilable than any of the others mentioned previously. The novelty value is indeed the greatest adversary of the age value.

The complete coherence of something new, recently created, presenting itself with the simplest criteria – unbroken forms and pure polychromy – is most easily recognizable to those with any level of education. This is the reason that novelty value has always been the predominant value of the masses of less or completely uneducated people, while the relative artistic value only became accessible to those with an aesthetic training in the most recent periods. The largest part of the population has always taken the greatest pleasure in that which was clearly the newest. Among the works of human artistry, it always preferred to see the creative victorious products of the human hands and not traces of the opposing natural forces. Only what is new and complete can be considered beautiful in the eyes of the majority. Anything old, fragmented or discolored is considered ugly. This view according to which youth has a clear advantage over age is thousands of years old and has taken root so profoundly that it cannot be displaced in a mere few decades. To the majority of our contemporaries it seems most natural to replace a damaged edge of furniture with a repaired piece or a darkened layer of plaster with a fresh one, and this perfectly explains the great resistance greeting the apostles of the age value. Furthermore, the entire trends of 19th century historical preservation were essentially based on this traditional view, or to be more precise, on the intimate union of the novelty value and the historical value. Every striking trace of decay from the forces of nature was to be removed. Gaps were to be filled and fragments completed to restore the impression of a unified whole. The open and eagerly propagated goal of all rational historical preservation during the 19th century was to introduce the document back into the process of becoming.

It was not until the emergence of the age value toward the end of the 19th century that we have been able to observe the contradictions and struggles that we have been witnessing in recent years wherever monuments call for protection. The conflict between novelty value and age value is definitely at the center of the controversy, and has been assuming a bitter pitch over the question of how to treat monuments. Novelty value presents the "happy possessor" which is being dislodged from the place it has held for a millennium. Age value is conscious of this and not inclined to sacrifice any possible means or weapon in the struggle to unseat the established opponent. In those instances where a monument no longer possess any functional value, age value has already widely succeeded in fortifying its principles about the treatment of monuments. It is a different story when the requirements of function also play a part. The great majority of humanity still desires anything in use to appear young, vital, and to contradict any traces of age, dissolution or diminishing energy.

Among the secular monuments (ecclesiastical monuments will occupy us further on) there are also those in which the dignity of the owner – what we tend to call decorum – demands the complete elimination of any sign of disrepair. Dignity refers to nothing other than self-assertion and encapsulation against the surroundings. Consider how badly the owner of a dilapidated palace of the highest nobility or a seat of government with flaking or discolored plaster would appear in the eyes of the population.

We seem to be facing a hopeless conflict. On the one hand we see age being esteemed in its own right and any restoration condemned without reservation. On the other we have an appreciation of everything new in and of itself, disdaining and attempting to obliterate any sign of age. Novelty value seems natural, traditional, almost eternal in the eyes of its adherents, and for the mass of the population today its effect of immediacy still far surpasses that conjured by age value (above pp. pp. 252-253), and gives it a nearly invulnerable status. This makes clear why the cult of age value still requires the battering ram of the historical value to forge its progress. A much larger segment of society will need to be converted to the cult of historical value before it can ripen to the cult of age value. When the age value meets the novelty value of a monument with a persistent functionality, it will for practical (the functional value as discussed above pp. 263-267) as well as ideal (elementary artistic) reasons always have to find the best possible compromise with the novelty value. Fortunately, this task has not yet become so very difficult as it might at first appear. In the first place, the cult of age value does not at all negate the existential right of novelty value. This is only denied to monuments with a certain memorial quality, but expressly admitted for the freshly made recent works and even claimed more passionately and unilaterally in recent decades. The modern view demands that the recent creations of human hands show a flawless perfection of form and color, extending also into the style, which is to say that the modern work should include a conception and treatment of details of form and color recalling earlier works as little as possible. This brings out the unmistakable tendency to separate the novelty value from the age value as strictly as can be done. In recognizing the novelty value as a highly potent aesthetic entity there is already the seed of a possible compromise as soon as the conditions for it become favorable. These circumstances are by no means lacking.

We have already alluded to the fact that human activity can be counted among the natural forces contributing vitally to the dissolution of categories of monuments which are not completely old and still in functional states. This human influence does not work randomly or forcefully, but rather with a certain regularity. By placing a work into service with human energy, a slow but constant and inexorable process of abrasion and dissolution is set into motion. This explains how a monument we are used to seeing in use, such as the residential palace on a busy street can convey to us an embarrassing impression of forceful destruction if it is not in use or abandoned: it will seem older than it otherwise would.[81] This was the reason that we saw the cult of age value forced to recognize at least those more recent and still functional monuments preserved in a state which would guarantee their continued use. Novelty value also conforms to the practical function value in its aesthetic aspect: because of this, the cult of age value is forced to admit the novelty value to a limited degree – at least in the case of post-medieval and functional works. If a baldacchino from a prominent spot in the upper tiers of a gothic city hall were to break off, the cult of age value would certainly be most pleased to leave this as a sign of the traces of time, but would hardly raise great objections today if the party of novelty value would rather fill the gap in the name of decorum, and complete that part of the building in its (reliably documented) original form. The violent controversies to have flared between the two groups are based on a further inference drawn during the 19th century from the novelty value in favor of the historical value.

This refers to monuments not completely preserved in their original condition, but have been subject to various stylistic changes by human intervention. Since historical value resides in the clear recognition of the original state, as long as the cult of historical value as an end in itself still predominated, there was an aim to eliminate all later additions (cleaning, uncovering) so as to restore the original forms that had been thus obscured, with no regard to proper documentation. The cult of historical value was more pleased with something merely

---

81 By contrast, there are some who feel awkward in the use of new items, such as clothing ("a new key does not fit well"), which is not exclusively due to a practical resistance at the beginning, but also to an aesthetic inhibition.

resembling the original than with one element that might actually have been original, yet stylistically different and added at an early date. The cult of novelty augmented this interest in history to the extent that the original state being reconstructed was also supposed to reveal a complete whole while each added alien element constituted an interruption of the whole and presented a symptom of dissolution. This led to the postulate of stylistic unity, and then to match the style of the original state it ultimately led to elements from a later stylistic period being changed to match. We might say that the 19th century treatment of monuments rested on twin postulates of original style (historical value) and unity of style (novelty value).

This system was bound to confront the most vehement objections when the cult of age value arose, with an interest neither in the originality nor in the coherence of style, but instead in the violation of both. In this case, the cult of age value was no longer seeking necessary concessions to the functional value and its aesthetically sympathetic novelty value in order to preserve a monument with a living function by such a compromise. It instead aspired to sacrifice almost every aspect of the monument contributing to its age value. This would have led to a capitulation of age value, and to avoid this, its adherents inaugurated the bitterest struggle against the earlier system. Such conflicts always arouse exaggerations from the opposing side and cause confusion in the objective state of affairs. In this case the overstatements of those arguing for the renewal have caused the neutral parties to doubt some of the justifiable elements of the existing system. Those elements can be retained in the revised conception and provide undeserved sustenance for the arguments against the old system. Some of the justifiable points in the cult of age value have by now already been accepted in the natural development of opinion. One example might stand for many others. Eight years ago, the decision was made to demolish the baroque choir of the parish church of Altmünster [on the Traunsee in Upper Austria] in spite of the fact that it was not at all in a state of disrepair, but in order to replace this with another in the gothic style so that it might match the existing nave. Four years ago, financial constraints prevented the construction of the gothic choir, which would have been dubious in terms of historical but acceptable to the novelty value. Today, all adherents of the old as well as the new system are unanimous that the removal of the original choir of Count Herberstorf was an indefensible sin not merely against the age value, but also against the historical value – Herberstorf was a remarkable figure in suppressing the Protestant peasants of Upper Austria and introducing the art of the Counter Reformation. This recent but generally accepted postulate of stylistic unity was abandoned, and the gulf separating the more reflective members of the old order and the more circumspect of the new was even bridged in this example of an ecclesiastical work. We shall see that the church and churches raise a special set of problems.

What we have said about the novelty value is generally true of the secular as well as ecclesiastical monuments. Novelty value possesses a particular importance for the Catholic Church, since the treatment of a monument is not the decision of an individual proprietor as would be the case in secular examples, but instead falls to the strictly hierarchical constitution of the Church and the novelty value allows a unified approach, however remote such questions are from its dogma.[82]

---

82 Since the views and constitutions of the other religions which are practiced

Religious and secular art are probably fundamentally the same, and until the early modern period no basic distinction was ever drawn between them. Since the Reformation, Catholicism has upheld their relative unity, while Protestantism gave it up completely. Among the Romance cultures, the division grew ever wider, and seems to have become irreconcilable since the 19th century. In the 20th century we have entered into a situation in which a painting with a religious subject and made according to the principles of modern art, by Fritz von Uhde for instance, could not possibly serve a Catholic religious function. Such paintings depict Christ as a modern person accomplishing His salvation of His own accord, while Church doctrine insists that the supernatural Christ and vicariously the mediation of the Church necessarily participate. It is equally inadmissible for the figures of the saints to be identified with us the spectators, but they are required to give the clear impression of an objective, independent and self-contained existence. Rembrandt sought the divine within humanity and depicted this rigorously, and even his conception is unacceptable to the church. The normative character stipulated by all ecclesiastical activity and ecclesiastical art seems to be completely irreconcilable with the random subjectivism of modern humanity and its preoccupation with mood. In spite of this, it would be completely incorrect to consider a confluence of Catholicism and modern art to be an impossibility, and its continued insistence on the necessity of ecclesiastical art provides an encouraging symptom. Solutions to the

---

in Austria do not allow these specific questions to come up, our remarks about ecclesiastical art and historical preservation can be limited to those arising in connection with Roman Catholicism.

large encompassing problems of the world have never been reached without struggles, conflicts, proposals tentative or not apt.

Things are similar with the Catholic Church in relation to novelty value and its opposite, the age value. For the time being at any rate, novelty value seems to represent an ineradicable aesthetic postulate of the great mass of people in the secular sphere, and apparently advanced in the religious realm by popular acclaim as well as basic practical views, and more difficult to circumvent due to the latter. Church buildings, statues of holy persons or of saints and images of the lives of saints relate to the divine redeemer and therefore represent the most dignified possible productions of human hands. Out of consideration of decorum, and as we have sufficiently stressed already, this calls for a clean perfection in form and color, more so than any other area of human creativity. At first glance, the conflict between age value and novelty value seems to be completely unbridgeable in the religious sphere, which involves the profoundest and most compelling emotions dominating the human spirit. Yet we should not abandon hope that a certain reconciliation might still become possible. First of all, the adherence to novelty value is nowhere dogmatically dictated by the basic values of the Catholic Church – however much the human image might reflect divinity and outshine nature. This is nothing more than a temporary policy, which the Church could easily change in the future if it seems necessary or might align its interests with the faithful. On the other hand, by its nature, Catholicism also includes a natural seed of memorial value. We have but to recall the cult of the saints and the numerous memorial feast days or the eager and burgeoning activity of church history (which is exemplified in every work of ecclesiastical art). Of course, these are primarily only historical values. Yet after having recognized them as the necessary predecessors of age value, we are not unjustified in hoping that the Catholic Church might again as so often in its two thousand-year history, find a compromise with the leading intellectual trends of the time. Age value after all includes a truly Christian principle at its core – that of pious conformity to the will of the Lord, which should not be blasphemously contradicted by a type of humanity with limited awareness.

A felicitous symptom for a possible reconciliation of this sort can be seen in the fact that the Church has already been taking account of the age value in the treatment of its urban monuments in order to accommodate the sensibilities of the predominantly educated circles among the faithful living in the cities. It is not felt to violate any of its vital interests. The most tenacious adherents of the novelty value as an end in itself are to be found among the priests working in rural areas, no doubt following the elementary artistic impulses of its largely less educated communities as well as the traditional conventions of ecclesiastical attitudes to art. For this reason, the next step will be to convince the country priests to rein in their exaggeration of the novelty value. On the other hand, the cult of age value will also be required to oblige the ecclesiastical demands for novelty value to the same extent as it has already done in relation to the functional value.

β) The Relative Artistic Value

Relative artistic value is based on our appreciating works of earlier generations as examples of creative human energies overcoming nature as well as for their specific and unique conception of form and color. The modern point of view holds that no objectively valid artistic canon is possible, considers it normal that a monument should not include any artistic value for the modern viewer, and the less so with increasing historical distance from the present. Yet experience teaches us that we often prize works of art from many centuries earlier as more valuable than those of our own time. Indeed, there are monuments appearing to our modern period as the greatest conceivable revelation in the arts, which were not approved of and even vigorously opposed in their own time. Dutch 17th century painting provides us with a number of particular good examples. A simple explanation for this was put forward as recently as thirty years ago. Many at that time believed in an absolute artistic value, however difficult it proved itself to define its criteria, and the greater appeal of earlier monuments was explained by the idea that the artistic activity of those times had approached the absolute artistic value more closely than modern artists have been able do in spite of all of their efforts. At the beginning of the 20th century, we have arrived at the view that such an absolute artistic value does not exist, and that it would be a complete presumption to believe that we can assume the role of more just judges and in some cases vindicate and "save" earlier masters who had been "misunderstood" by their contemporaries. A fictional absolute of aesthetic value cannot exist as such, and there must be another explanation for the fact that we often appreciate earlier art works more than modern examples. The modern artistic will can never share more than individual aspects with an earlier work. Presumably, the earlier artistic will can also never be completely identical with that of today, and this difference inevitably reveals itself in certain given qualities. The latter aspects which appear less interesting to us nonetheless do not spoil our total impression, and this can only be explained in that those aspects congenial to us make such an overwhelming impression as to overcome and to obliterate those which appear less so. Even in our times with the widespread acceptance of the slogan "each period its own art" ("Jeder Zeit ihre Kunst"), the presence of such formal and chromatic qualities of a monument at odds with the current artistic will can contribute to an intensified recognition of the remaining sympathetic aspects within the same monument, sympathetic qualities which might never be achieved by a modern artist limited to the elements of artistic will peculiar to our own time.[83] We cannot imagine a period seeking aesthetic redemption in the visual arts while escaping the influence of that from earlier periods. We have but to imagine ancient sculpture or 15th to 17th century painting as absent from our own cultural treasury to realize how much poorer our modern artistic needs would be satisfied. This is also independent of the fact that those qualities which we thus omit from earlier art are nevertheless art historically proper, since the earlier artists were animated by an artistic will completely different from our own.

Although it is necessary to recognize that the monument cannot contain a simple novelty value, that is to say an artistic value perfectly encompassed within in its developmental state (Geschlossenheit des Werdezustandes), we must admit its relative artistic value, that other possible mode of contemporary artistic quality. In regard to this question, it is appropriate to distinguish between a positive and a

---

83 ["Der Zeit ihre Kunst Der Kunst ihre Freiheit" had been the motto installed at the door of the Vienna Sezession, designed 1898 by Josef Maria Olbrich]

negative appraisal.

If the relative artistic value is positive, if some of the qualities of its formal and chromatic conception accord with our own artistic will, then we naturally wish to avoid seeing it decline in significance, as would occur if it were exposed to natural deterioration according to the dictates of age value. With enough reason to assume that it would appeal better to our own artistic will in an original un-aged condition than with its natural age, we might even feel moved further still to reverse the natural process of decay (as with the cleaning of paintings) and return the monument to its original state of becoming. In the positive category of relative artistic value, its present state of preservation generally calls for maintenance in the current condition or even for a restoration to its previous state, boldly contradicting the demands of age value.

Such a case becomes especially piquant since it exhibits a conflict between two of the most recent aesthetic views. Relative artistic value is identical with the modern artistic will and endorses the novelty value while opposing the age value (although naturally not in the elementary character discussed just above). It will be interesting to see which of the two will ultimately predominate in the future. If we imagine a painting by Botticelli with overpainting from the baroque period, doubtlessly added with the best artistic intentions in its own time to enliven such a dry quattrocento image, the added layers must for us possess an age value and even historical value (since older additions by human hands have the same appearance to us as the effects of nature). Today, nobody would hesitate to remove the pentimenti, uncover and reveal the pure work of Botticelli. Such a decision would be made not merely on an art historical basis, but also for essentially historical reasons. Since the drawing and coloration of Botticelli appeal more to the current artistic will than does that of the Italian Baroque, we today would tend to decide on the clearest possible evidence of an Italian artist important to the history of 15th century painting and his own personal artistic development. Those parts added more recently, the modern human addition to the older art work appears here as the more forceful in relation to the expressiveness of age, transience and the all powerful processes of nature.

Conflicts with age value are far less imminent when the judgment of relative artistic value is negative. The negative attitude represents worthlessness and indifference to the modern artistic will, but even acts as an irritant. A lack of value would represent nothing more than a lower level of the positive value and suggest that the monument be treated according to the predilections of the age value. When the quality of a monument is felt to be objectionable, its stylistic discordance and ugliness might directly arouse the modern artistic will to removal or intentional destruction. Although feelings have become more moderate over the last twenty years, it is still said today of many baroque monuments that we "cannot stand" them or would "prefer not to have to see them." Such a call to hasten the destructive process by human intervention contradicts the precepts of age value much as a restoration might do by artificially delaying the process of natural dissolution. It is probably rare in the present that a monument is destroyed for no other reason than its relative artistic value or lack of artistic value. As far as historical preservation is concerned, such a negative example of the relative artistic value should also not be omitted from consideration since in cases of the added conflict with another contemporary value in the same monument (such as functional or novelty value) it might lead to a decision against the age value.

When the modern element within the old constitutes the relative artistic value, then a problem arises as to what accounts for the relative artistic value of ecclesiastical monuments. Since the secular approach does not distinguish between sacred and secular monuments, this is limited to the ecclesiastical approach. It assumes that a clearly directed modern ecclesiastical art exists whose intentions can be partially identified in earlier art. Is there in fact such a modern form of ecclesiastical art? In one sense it does indeed exist, since a not negligible amount of architecture, sculpture and painting is being produced daily for those purposes. Modern religious art works generally show such a large number of elements from earlier stylistic periods as to completely overwhelm the modern core to the point of indistinguishability. Yet such a core is doubtlessly present. Modern church art is immediately recognizable as not dating from an earlier period. This is not merely due to its newness, which is most obvious in the colors, but also from the more subconscious feeling difficult to express in words which we sense for differences of conception and the formal relationships as distinct from the earlier models. It is necessary to immediately obviate a possible misunderstanding which might arise from the basic antiquarian tendency of modern church art as we have described it – namely the conclusion that such a preference for earlier styles is somehow congruent with the cult of age value. Quite to the contrary. Even to the present day, the Church generally shows no interest in the transient values. If there are a good many Catholic clerics who have devoted themselves to the cult of historical value with piety and commendable success, then this is proof that the Church does not feel any of its vital interests to be infringed by this cult. The cult of the transient things, the conscious and assiduous cultivation of transience itself has been seen as completely outside the interests of the Church. It looks favorably upon the style and conception of the earlier art, but not its forms and colors as such. For the sake of novelty value, it prefers to see an ecclesiastical artwork completely new, but with the incorporation of traditional stylistic expressions. It nonetheless chooses the more characteristic elements from among the existing historical styles.

Since the advent of Romanticism, that is to say when the historical value entered its last, greatest and decisive phase, it has been the medieval styles and particularly the Gothic that have predominated church art. There can be little doubt as to the reason for this. In recognizing the alienation that ultimately arose between ecclesiastical and secular art, the Church returned confidently to those styles flourishing at a time when the divorce of sacred from secular did not yet exist. This choice of the medieval and particularly the Gothic brought with it a phenomenon parallel at the very least if not actually identical to the relative value of the secular monuments. Even today, the relevant government offices are approached on an almost daily basis with proposals to eliminate the baroque additions from a gothic portal or tracery, alter a baroque onion roof into a gothic spire, or a baroque ceiling painting into a vaulting with painted stars. This phenomenon certainly quite decisively reflects the eagerness for restorations arising from the novelty value. It is no coincidence that it is most often gothic or even earlier works being sought to liberate from later additions or traces of age. The fact that individual priests have spent years agitating against many of these projects only serves to prove that there is no vital religious interest of the Church involved. A similar observation we have had occasion to mention in connection with novelty value (pp. 276-277 above) can also be made in connection with this: the tendency to re-Gothicize monuments has primarily been a preoccupation of the rural churchmen while those in the urban areas have shown themselves to be more restrained and in some cases even critical.

Among new works of art, we should allow this undoubtedly deep-seated preference for the medieval styles to run its course with no inhibitions. Even these gothicized works certainly include a kernel of independent and truly modern church art and even outwardly, the autonomy of the Church should never be infringed upon unless it conflicts with actual and vital cultural interests of the general public. As modern ecclesiastical works are being contemplated for the liberating aesthetic edification of groups extending far beyond the traditional borders of a parish and therefore of broad and deep public interest, representatives of the Church must be pressed to observe the conditions of age value in tandem with the Church gaining greater freedom to express its preference for medieval and other styles.

Lovers of Art Ancient and Modern[84]

Our organizations and clubs are among the most striking phenomena of modern life. What is the reason for this, and what is the nature of this compulsion? The answer is that there is a community of interest. Groups of people converge on the same activity and consider it profitable to pursue the same goal together. Yet something else is also involved. When a group of individuals unite in a purpose, they strive to improve not merely themselves, but also the whole, and by dividing the labor in one manner or another they fulfill a given need on behalf of the others. Bare egotism can never become a principle of society. It is true that there are some societies apparently espousing it in a superficial way, but they must also contain some inner necessity – otherwise they could never function properly. This would be intolerable to the totality, which they jeopardize and never promote.

It would seem at first glance that nothing could be more private and egotistic than the art lover, and it would appear particularly true when they also collect art – although in our own time the two no longer necessarily go together since we have public collections. They collect exclusively according to their own personal preferences and

---

84 Originally held as a lecture and only posthumously published as "Über antike und moderne Kunstfreunde Vortrag gehalten in der Gesellschaft der Wiener Kunstfreunde," *Kunstgeschichtliches Jahrbuch der K. K. Zentral-Kommission zur Erforschung und Erhaltung der kunst- und historischen Denkmale*, vol. 1, 1907, Beiblatt für Denkmalpflege, column 1-14.

for their own pleasure. As a social matter, they might allow a circle of friends to partake of their activity. Although there are some who make their collections available to larger segments of the public, they are the exception and such opportunities are rare. Such exhibitions are not among the defining characteristics of the art lover.

Now the art lovers have banded together, and this requires no further demonstration because otherwise I would not be honored to speak to this gathering today. Yet the very fact that the lovers of art join together in this way is itself a sign that they consider their activities to be profitable for all of society. The social functions must have a particular significance for them, and in the present cultural situation they must fulfill a certain mission. What is the nature of this mission? It strikes me that the time has now come to pose this question and to propose an answer. Whether I have been successful or not is for you to decide, but I nonetheless beg the indulgence normally reserved for such unprecedented forays.

First there is the preliminary question of what actually is a lover of art? This would literally refer to any of us with a favorable relation to the visual arts, yet this would be casting the net too broadly. There are for instance many factory workers who attend popular lectures about art and undoubtedly demonstrate a love of art, but they would not be counted among the art lovers. The general principle normally applied to questions surrounding the visual arts is that of supply and demand, production and consumption, the separation of productive artists from the consuming laymen. This principle also fails in regard to the art lover since the group present this evening includes both artists and laymen. It is not the production which interests the art lover since this would eliminate the laymen, but neither is it the consumption in the current sense of our modern art since there would then be no artists in our presence here any more than grocers would come to a food co-op. What is typical of the art lovers and draws them together into such organizations is therefore neither the production nor the consumption (that is to say the pleasure in modern art), but rather a third factor. When we peruse the list of previous lectures held before this society there can be no doubt as to the identity of this third factor.

These lectures have been exclusively devoted to what we call earlier art, art that is not modern. If we apply the phrase "art lover" as a strict technical term, then it can only refer to an admirer of the art of earlier periods. What thus defines the art lover is an aspect of consumption, a consideration of old masters and not of modern art, and this is also the reason that practicing artists, modern by definition, are also among us here today in their capacity as consumers of art.

The question immediately arises as to the relation of the art lover to modern art. To address this now would only complicate and confuse the development of our actual subject. This is unnecessary and I therefore content myself for the moment with observing that art lovers are in fact generally not at all averse to modern art. We can say this seeing that our present group also includes a number of modern artists who would certainly not compromise their own livelihood. This is a relationship we must return to later on.

It follows that the mission of art lovers is a consistent appreciation of older works as they have come down to us, and not of modern art. The question we must consider is the extent to which the art lovers are fulfilling a public interest in their mission.

As our thinking is organized today, it is only possible to arrive at a convincing answer on the basis of historical data. Have there not been other times in history when art lovers like those of the present also thrived, and what were their circumstances? These circumstances themselves might provide a key to clearly recognizing the imperatives followed by our current art lovers either consciously or not. Similar conditions produce similar effects.

From our place at the beginning of the 20th century we can observe a considerable number of art lovers extending back to the 15th century. If we go back in time and examine the phenomenon more closely, it becomes clear that the art lovers to varying degrees admired the work of their own as well as earlier times. In the 15th century, Lorenzo the Magnificent was familiar with only the art of the Florentine renaissance and antiquity. In Germany in the 16th century, the great collectors such as the Fugger were more patrons of contemporary art than admirers of earlier art. This had changed somewhat by the time of the Emperor Rudolph II, and in the 18th century, we already discover a much finer distinction. We can now recognize that a stricter differentiation arose toward the end of the 19th century, which honors the art of earlier periods as a temple constructed as an end in itself and no model for us, and then more or less accepts the art of its own time as an unavoidable craft being produced at the moment. The art lovers from the 15th to the 19th centuries appear as the mere predecessors of their modern descendants, with no difference in either quality or quantity. As interesting as it would be to study them, it would not help us in our question, since they are ultimately alike and would not provide the substance for a fruitful comparison. We must consider the patrons and collectors who have no direct connection to those of today, and also the distinct historical circumstances in which they arose. If it should turn out that they nonetheless bear comparison to those among our contemporaries, then this will confirm what we believe. Were there such art lovers further beyond the medieval period? Yes indeed, they did exist. For some time now we have been aware of them and of the characteristics they share with their descendants of today. They existed in the early period of Christianity and their activities reach an apogee in the first and second centuries of the Roman imperial period, between Augustus and the last of the Antonines. There were also others in the final centuries before the advent of Christianity. This is of interest to us both in terms of the origins as well as the decline of this phenomenon – although the decline can obviously not be studied in comparison to the art lovers among us today.

I must limit myself to just a few details from the lives and proclivities of these ancient lovers of art, which might serve to illustrate their similarities and differences to those of the present.

In the plan designed by Vitruvius for the house of a well-situated man of the period of Augustus, there is a room to be used as a picture gallery, while there are also sculpture galleries documented in other sources. Works in metal were particularly popular because they could be used as ceremonial dishes. Silver and bronze objects are mentioned with great frequency, particularly the so-called Corinthian bronzes. Yet never in all of this is there any reference to a contemporary piece. Most of these objects were associated with names from the archaic and classical period of Greek art. Among the sculptors, Polycleitus, Myron and Phidias are mentioned most often, while it is Polygnotus and Apelles among the painters. Quintilian [*Institutionis Oratoriae* XII, 10] was struck by the fact that some people considered the old fashioned work of Polygnotus to be more valuable than the paintings of Apelles, and declared this to be the result of a sort of coquetry among connoisseurs as we can also see it occurring today. Works in silver with rubbed and worn details were also valued more highly since they were considered to be older than objects in better condition, which made the impression of being more recent.

Of course an art market becomes the unavoidable ancillary phenomenon to such things. Most of these objects could only reach these Roman collectors through dealers from Greece and the Greek east. Their names are only preserved in very few instances, but Horace has left us with a vivid description. Aside from this there were also agents, two of whom were employed by Verres, Greeks who were referred to as his tracker hounds.

One of the inevitable consequences of the art market are forgeries, and there are many references to them. It is clear that copies were being made and sold without misgivings, yet the copies were often being associated with the names of the greatest earlier artists. Gaius Iulius Phaedrus, the author of fables, has recorded an interesting remark about such forgeries when he says, "In our own time, gnawing envy favors what is old rather than what is good" [Adeo fucatae plus vetustati favet/invidia mordax quam bonis presentibus, *Fables*, book 5, prologue, 8-9]. Specific tributes to the work of contemporaries are very rarely recorded in that period. It recalls many artists in our own time who also cannot understand why their own work is not appreciated and purchased at the same prices as older items, and who consider the same sort of envy to be the reason.

It is difficult to conceive of an art lover without a certain knowledge or connoisseurship of the older artifacts. Of course there are many references to such connoisseurship, and then as now, there were many degrees of such connoisseurship, ranging from the authentic and well founded to the completely spurious.

Dionysus of Halicarnassus [*Roman Antiquities*] defined the duties of connoisseurship very cleverly – it exists to determine the authorship and to reliably distinguish originals from copies. Most of the art lovers of that time were confident of their ability to do this. Their confidence often had very little justification and aroused the ridicule of poets and authors. These dubious connoisseurs were recognizable by the way in which they spoke mostly of the monetary value and technical aspects, with the material almost never being omitted from mention. They bandied catchwords about which are still recognizable today: a strong cast, mixed bronze, contours, application of color, shading, proportions and so forth. There were some who claimed to discern the compound of the bronze by smell, and I have still experienced such things myself. It was already remarked at that time, that there was so much said about the age, rarity, the material and previous owner with famous names – and nothing about the absolute aesthetic value. Collectors were attracted by the name of a famous artist and a high price. Petronius [*Satyricon*, pt. 2] has given us a delightful description of Trimalchio, a socialite with newly acquired wealth and presenting himself as a lover of art.

We should not overlook that these were particularly notable as examples of excessiveness, and that the authors were more inclined to record sensationalism and exaggeration. Beneath all of this there was nonetheless also a core of justifiable activity exemplifying a characteristic and earnest aspect of ancient cultural life. Historians have recognized this and proposed their own explanations. Key passages among the 1st century texts of Pliny and Petronius have been collected in this regard and include criticism of contemporary art and praise of older Greek examples. This has led some to conclude that the collectors of the time recognized the superiority of the early classical period over the later decline, and considered them to have therefore turned their attention exclusively to the earlier art. Yet this interpretation has been shown to be incorrect.

First of all, there was no less interest in art during the earlier Roman imperial period than at any other time. Among the remains of Pompeii we have evidence from that very time for the role of the visual arts in the daily life of the Romans and Greeks. It applies not merely to the official and cultural life, but also to the intimate private surroundings, independent of all artificial exaggerations and outward pomp. It is well known that that city excavated from the ash has revealed to us an aesthetic sense, which seems to have been unprecedented in any of the earlier periods of human history. Within the houses of Pompeii, from the decoration of the walls themselves down to the patterned perforations of the colander in the kitchen, every surface and object available to the wandering eye was required to bear a certain characteristic stamp of artistic treatment. Are we to seriously believe that this society immersed itself aesthetically as no other, but was indifferent or even rejected the art of its own time? This would be inconceivable.

We can imagine that the art lover would have recognized a great difference between the art of the classical period and all of these marvels of the Roman imperial age – much in the way that people from Winckelmann until recently considered Roman art to be nothing better than a series of copies after classical models, progressively duller and weaker as time wore on. A close study of the monuments from the time of Augustus into that of the Antonines has revealed that they relate to the classical period in approximately the same way as our contemporary painting does to the Renaissance. A development could be discerned which extended from Phidias and Polygnotus through the Alexandrian artists and the period of the Diadochs into the first two centuries of the Roman imperial period and beyond. The art of the Roman imperial period has been compared to that of our own time. Professor Wickhoff in Vienna, who has done pioneering work in illuminating this relationship, has even gone so far as to directly describe this art as Impressionism, not claiming of course that it could ever be confused with our modern variant. This does indeed offer us an enlightening parallel. There have been two periods in human history when the creation of art was governed by so-called impressionistic principles – at the beginning of the Roman Imperial period and in our own modern times. In both of these periods, we are confronted with the phenomenon of the art lovers, enthusiastic in their appreciation and admiration of the art of earlier periods. – Just as modern art continues to develop inexorably beside and in spite of all this excitement over older art, so too must it have occurred during the Roman imperial period. Those things to be seen every day were considered inevitable and not worth special reference. Yet the enthusiasm of a group of nobles or wealthy citizens was a new and unprecedented phenomenon (although an attentive examination of the artistic monuments in their content and extrinsic functions would show that these conditions emerged slowly over a long period during antiquity). This is the reason that it is referred to so often in the literary remains of the time.

And thus the emergence of what is called Impressionism in art has historically gone hand in hand with the appearance of art lovers as admirers of earlier art on the basis of its age alone. An obvious conclusion suggests itself: there must have been something about Impressionism that arouses an interest in earlier periods of art in a portion of society influential by its number and education. What is the essence of Impressionism?

I have already mentioned that Impressionism is considered a certain trend of modern art, which on not strictly solid grounds can be compared to a parallel in ancient art. For this reason I would like to pinpoint those qualities which modern Impressionism shares with the analogous stage of ancient art. This is a certain quality of optic subjectivism. – Fear not that I might assault you with some aesthetic hair splitting. On the contrary, I hope to be able to explain myself in very few words.

All of the objects of the world, as the arts of man depict them, share two common characteristics: 1. those which are properties of the object whether or not they are contemplated by a human being (these are the objective qualities), 2. those which a human subject at a given moment perceives about them (these are the subjective qualities). There will always be some, but not all, of the objective aspects among them, but then consistently those, such as the illumination, which can never be objective. – We describe an art as objective when its goal is to reproduce the objective qualities of things. On the other hand, we describe an art as subjective when it fundamentally seeks to reproduce the momentary image of things as it appears on the retina of the individual viewer.

The qualities of objects are defined by the stimuli with which it affects the individual perceiving them. These stimuli are of two kinds: 1. purely optical – qualities of color, which stimulate nothing other than the eye. 2. the so-called tactile stimuli, these are the bodily qualities of the objects and their limits in space, as they stimulate the sense of touch in the individual viewer, while remaining discernible to the eye at a distance. – An art depicting the objects purely in terms of color is described as optical, while that demonstrating the corporeal qualities above all is described as tactical.

It should be simple to understand what optical subjectivism is. It is an art depicting the objects as momentary stimuli of color, the stimuli experienced by a single viewer. Anybody with a knowledge of modern art will understand this without difficulty.

As we have said, this optical subjectivism is present in the art of the Roman imperial period as well as in modern art. There are however certain differences between the two, which at present I can do no more than to point out. Like the art of all of antiquity, that of the Roman Imperial period was fundamentally geared to objectivism. This art became relatively subjectivist only when it undertook to depict the optical qualities of things in place of the tactical, which had been preferred by the earlier arts of Asia Minor and classical Greece. This is due to the fact that the purely optical stimuli of color are by nature more fugitive and subjective than the extension and outlines of the sense of touch. In the dark, the objects lose their visibility but retain their tactile accessibility. Medieval art, which gave rise to that of the modern period, became far more subjectivist, but, since its goal was above all a clear delineation of things, it must still be seen as relatively objectivist. The actual common factor between the art of the Roman imperial period and modern art lies in the exclusive consideration and escalation of the optical, coloristic qualities of things.

We arrive at the final decisive question: how does optical subjectivism succeed in arousing interest in ancient art, indeed imperiously provoking it?

The quality of optical subjectivism is an extreme randomness in treating those objects that the artist wishes to depict. It is random to limit consideration to the optical qualities of color and to suppress physicality, by which we mean the contours of height and breadth, as well as the shadow suggesting extension into space. It is also random to shrewdly isolate the most momentary and fugitive visual aspects, such as coincidental foreshortening and illumination. Finally, and essentially, it is random to transfigure the appearance of objects, not merely physically, but also coloristically, reducing the material phenomenon to a simple means of arousing subjective moods.

The naïve joy in the appearance of things as such, and that desire which the use of our senses of touch and sight awakens in us – as it has been a fundamental aspect of artistic pleasure through millennia – is here forcefully suppressed, exterminated for no other reason than entertaining our faculty of thought and feeling.

The art lover's contemplation of earlier artistic – not modern

– periods relates to our modern randomness in a double way. First, this occurs positively and in agreement. When we contemplate an old picture, we see more than its appearance to the senses, but it also has an effect on our feelings and creates a mood by its mere age and this exclusively intellectual aspect. In and of itself, this would be nothing new: 16th century painters already began including ancient temples in their work in order to arouse memories in their viewers of a life that was long past. 17th century paintings of ruins were made with the same intention. These differ from our present modern times in that no particularly selected motif is any longer necessary, and that the image of a simple 18th century domestic house suffices to arouse a mood in the spectator, and all the more so if the painting has the outward signs of having been made in the 18th century.

In its effect of conjuring a mood, our contemporary art lovers' contemplation of earlier art coincides directly with the modern artistic goals of optical subjectivism.

There is another aspect however, in which the affectionate interest in earlier art directly contradicts the goals of modern art. The older art specifically displays those qualities being suppressed from modern art: tangible corporeality and local color (festhaftende Farbe). In this sense, the admiration of older art presents itself as a flight into the realm of relative constancy, fixity and quietude, and away from the randomness in which everything is shown as flowing up and down into infinity and intangibility. Whether it occurs consciously or not, this strikes me as the truly beneficial and fruitful mission of the art lover.

There can be no doubt that the universal development of history displays a trend toward the emancipation of intellectual functions from corporeality – this can be seen quite stringently in the development of the history of art, as well as in the history of religion with the development of ethics in politics and social life. This trend has always halted before the complete negation of corporeality, since the spiritual phenomena would themselves become inconceivable without a corporeal substratum. And thus two souls live within our breasts: the one exulting in the joys of our physical world and its appearance is in danger of being short-changed by the trends of modern art. Whoever takes pleasure in the physical appearances, definite forms and movements, full and composed color, and recognizable effects of light and shadow, they will necessarily desert the modern exhibitions and seek refuge in the older galleries or private houses of our great art collectors.

I beg not to be misunderstood. Far be it from me to cavil about the development of modern art. Art historians have long ago recognized that it is not their task to prescribe – as Winckelmann once did – what contemporary artists should be doing. I am also convinced that art will by itself develop away from such extremes, and symptoms of this are already revealing themselves. Can it be a coincidence that an artist such as Jan Toorop, who sees the object of his work most purely in terms of mood, lends outward forms to these things, whose models are derived from Egyptian art – that form of art standing in the strongest conceivable contrast to our modern optical-subjectivist with the starkest tactile objectivism. How else can we explain that the line, that basic tactile element, assumes such an important place precisely in modern decoration, other than by the instinctive aspiration of our artists to balance an extreme randomness on the one hand with an equally extreme severity on the other.

If this tendency can be recognized among modern artists to render objects with firmer contours and not allow them to dissolve, how much simpler can it be to understand the same attitude among laymen who for the same reason have immersed themselves in the contemplation of older art. The interest in earlier art is the same interest that wishes to preserve modern art and all of the visual arts generally.

Allow me to voice a single objection and consider its value. We often hear it said that collectors of modern art desire nothing more than to smugly flaunt their wealth. This need not even involve braggadocio – the idea is that it satisfies such people to be aware that they are surrounded by precious objects that have cost preposterously high prices. There can be no denying that such a feeling of satisfaction in possession is to some degree present in collectors, yet it always goes hand in hand with that refined ideal which I have found to be the actual mission of the art lover. This is like human ideals: none of them could thrive without at least a modicum of material defectiveness, selfishness or egotism. Some observers are only able to recognize these defects. Whoever studies the matter thoroughly will soon conclude that even a person confessing with cynical candor that they collect solely to satisfy their egotism also serve a higher ideal in the public interest whether intentionally or not – they are also fulfilling the ideal mission of the love of art.

APPENDIX OF IMAGES

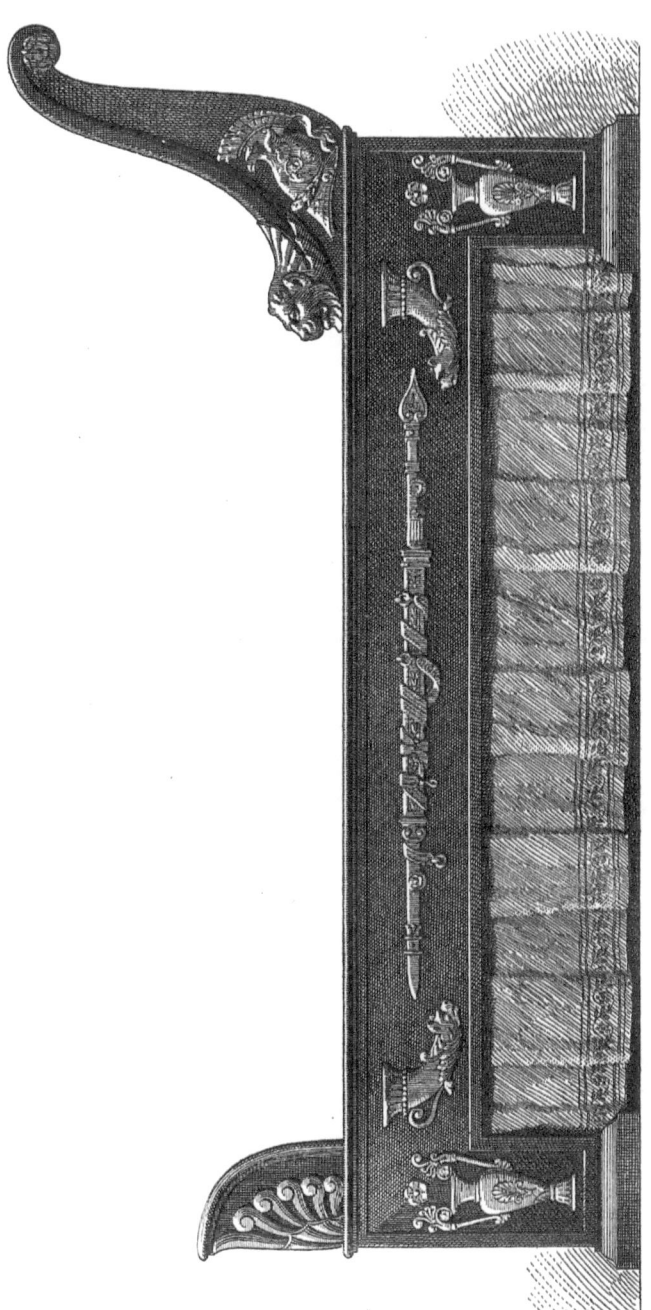

1. SOGENANNTES „BETT DES MARSCHALL BERTHIER"

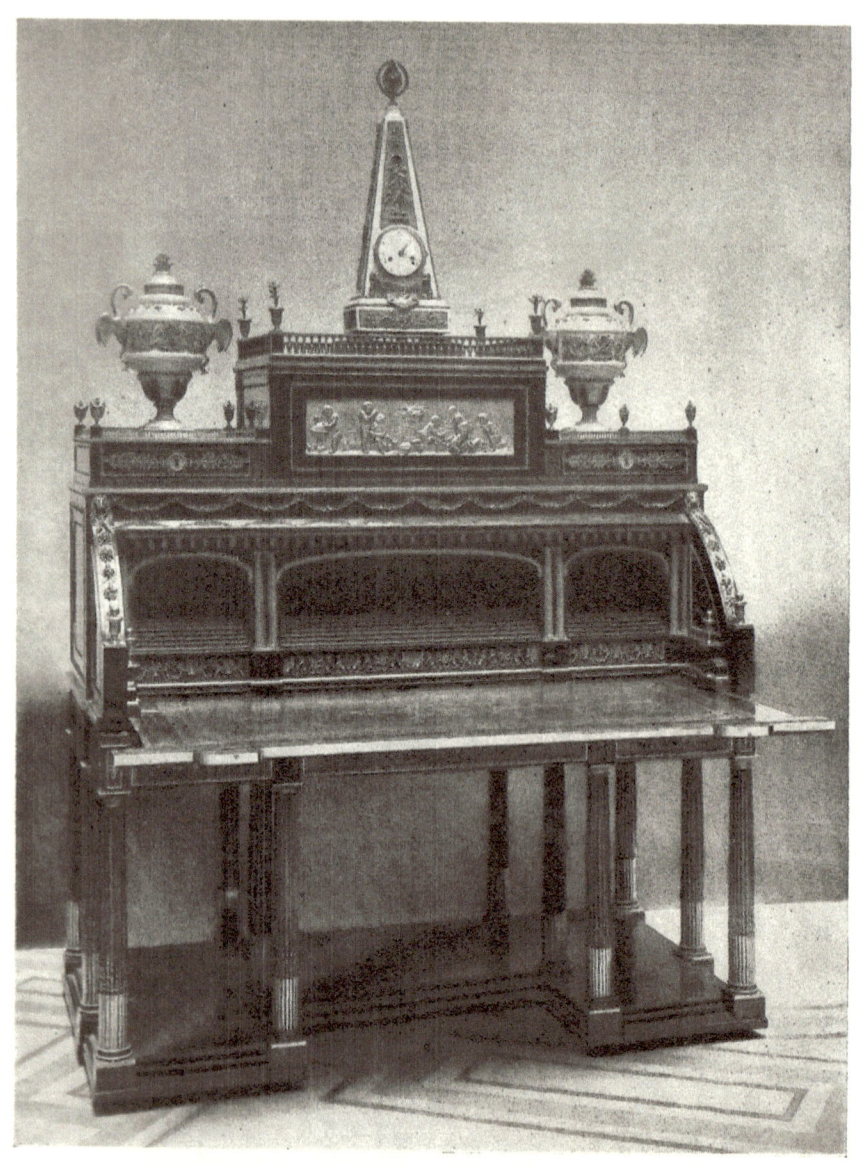

2. SCHREIBTISCH NAPOLEONS IN MALMAISON

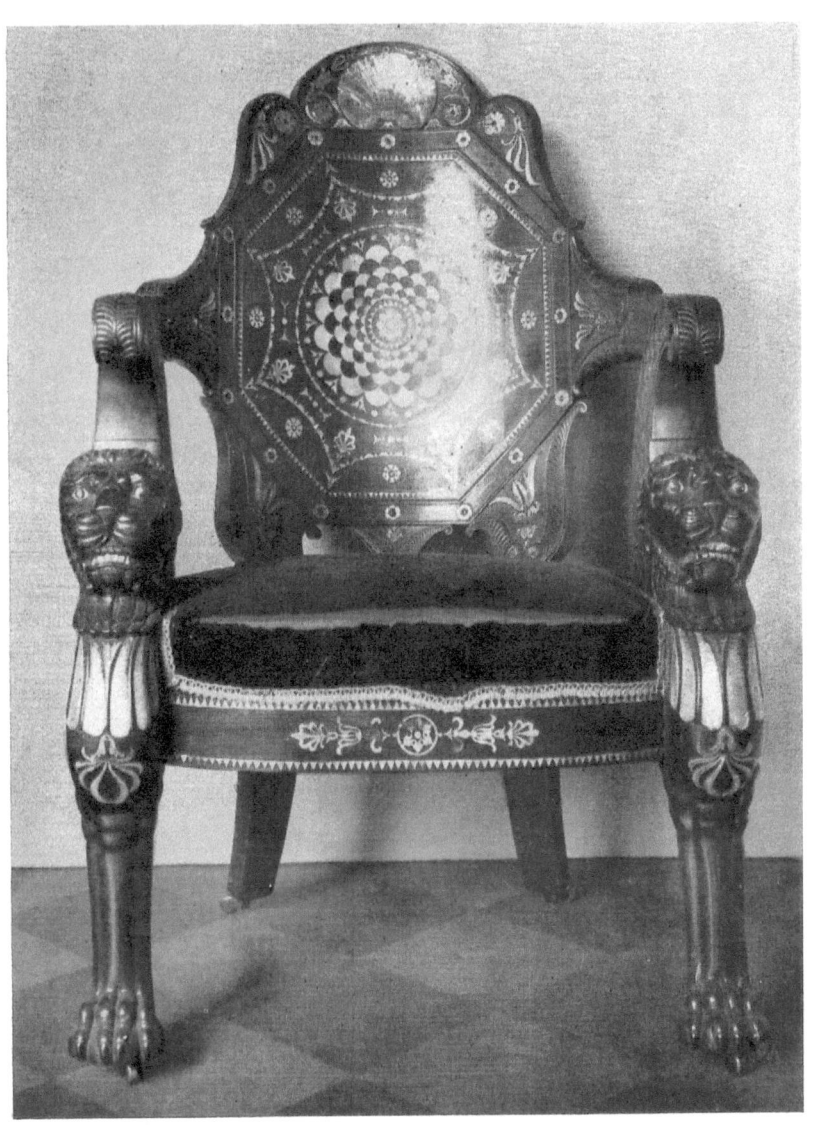

3. ARMSTUHL DES KÖNIGS VON HOLLAND

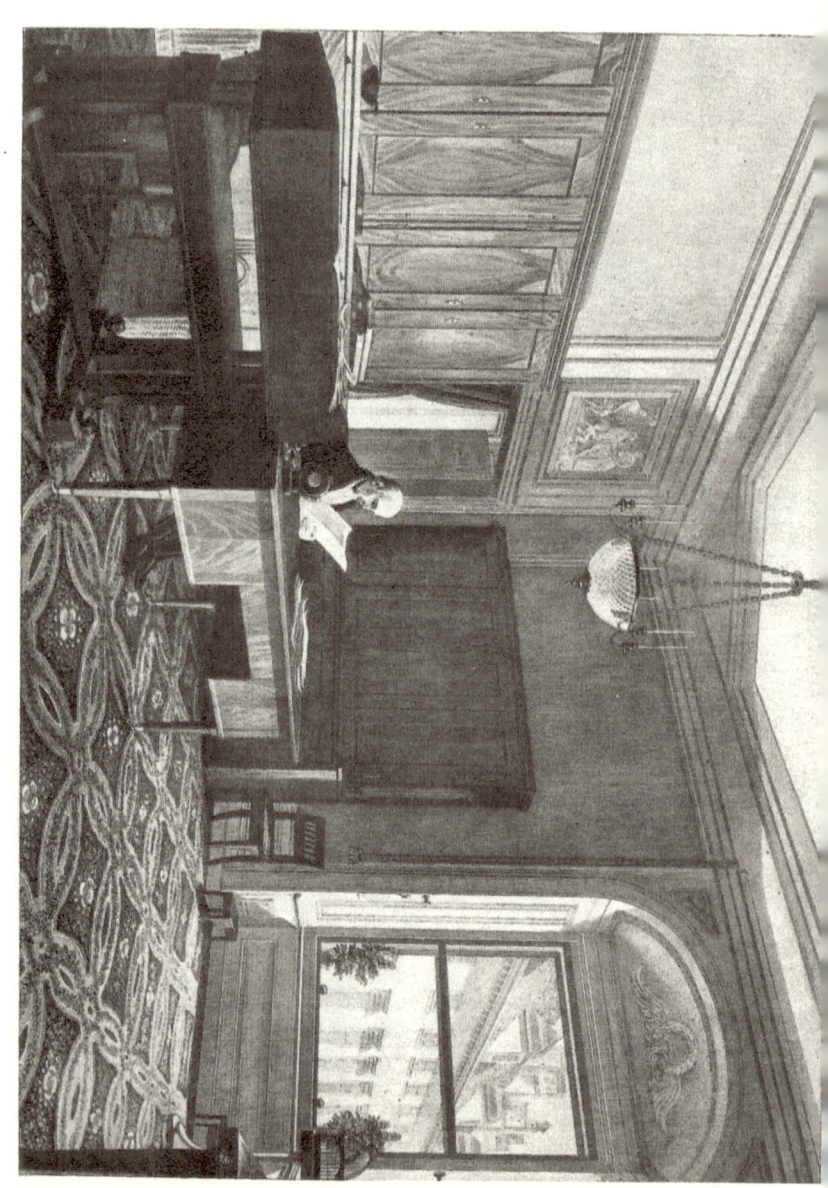

4. ARBEITSZIMMER DES KAISERS FRANZ II.
IN DER WIENER HOFBURG

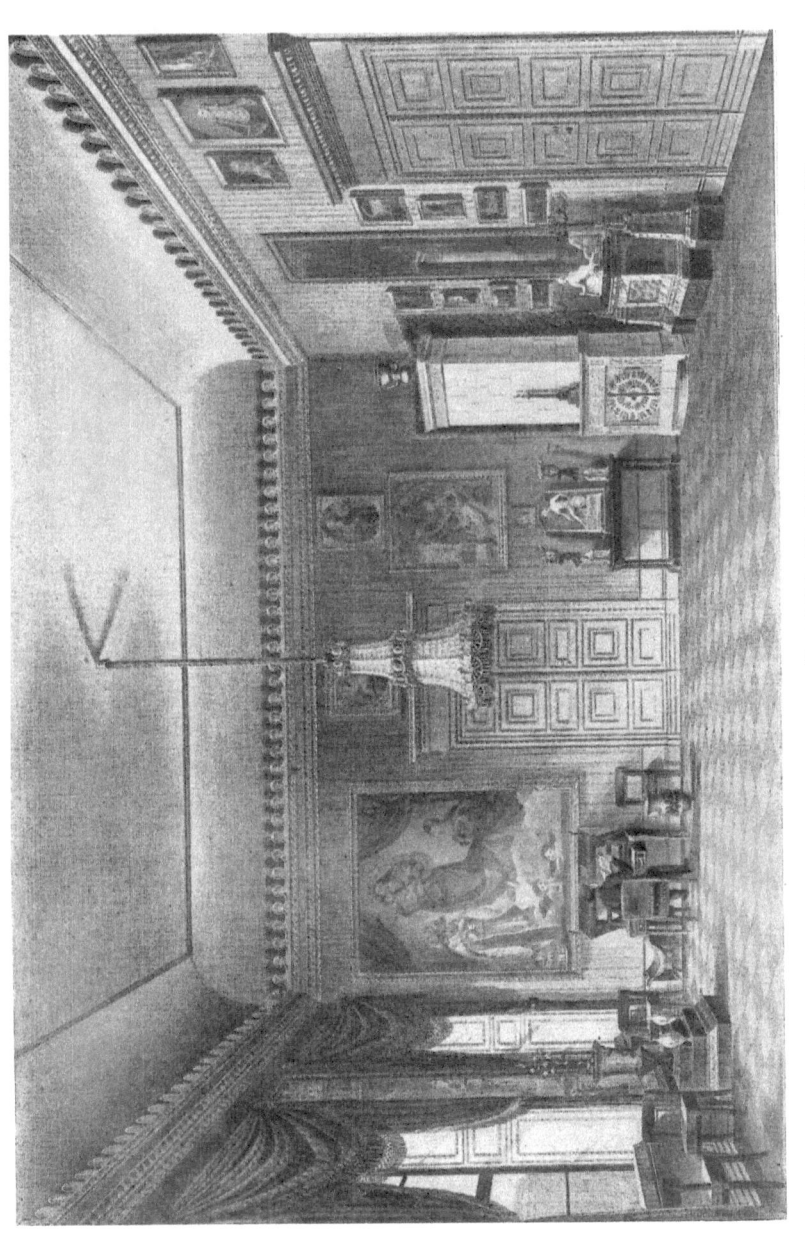

5. ARBEITSZIMMER DES KÖNIGS FRIEDRICH WILHELM III.
IM BERLINER SCHLOSS

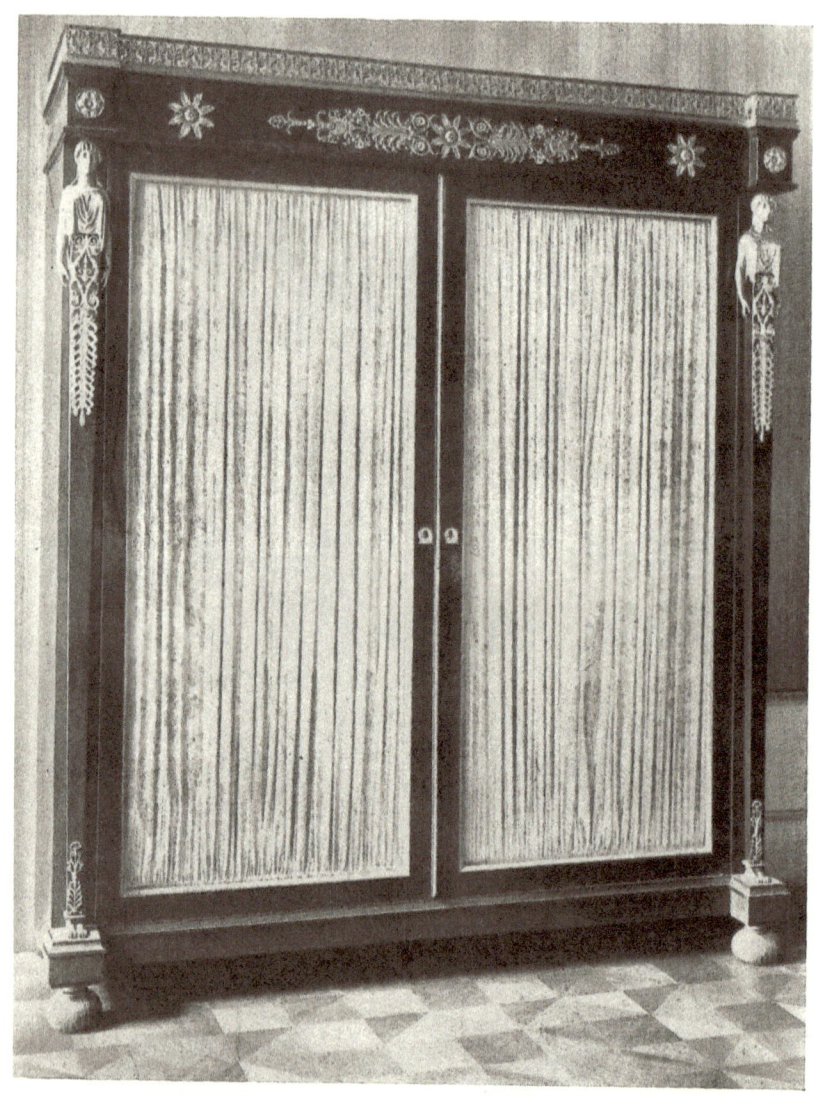

6. BEISPIEL EINES EMPIRESCHRANKS

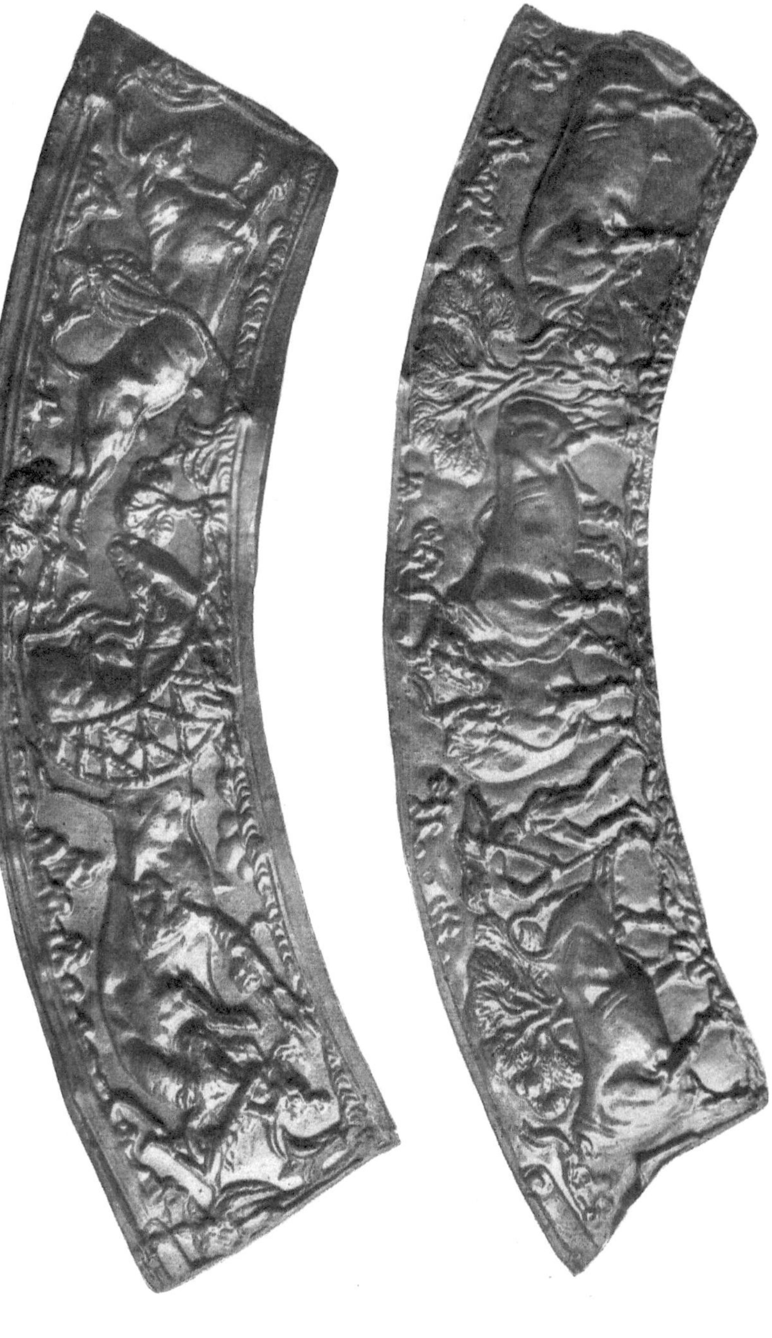

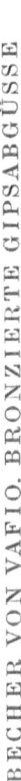

7. BECHER VON VAFIO. BRONZIERTE GIPSABGÜSSE

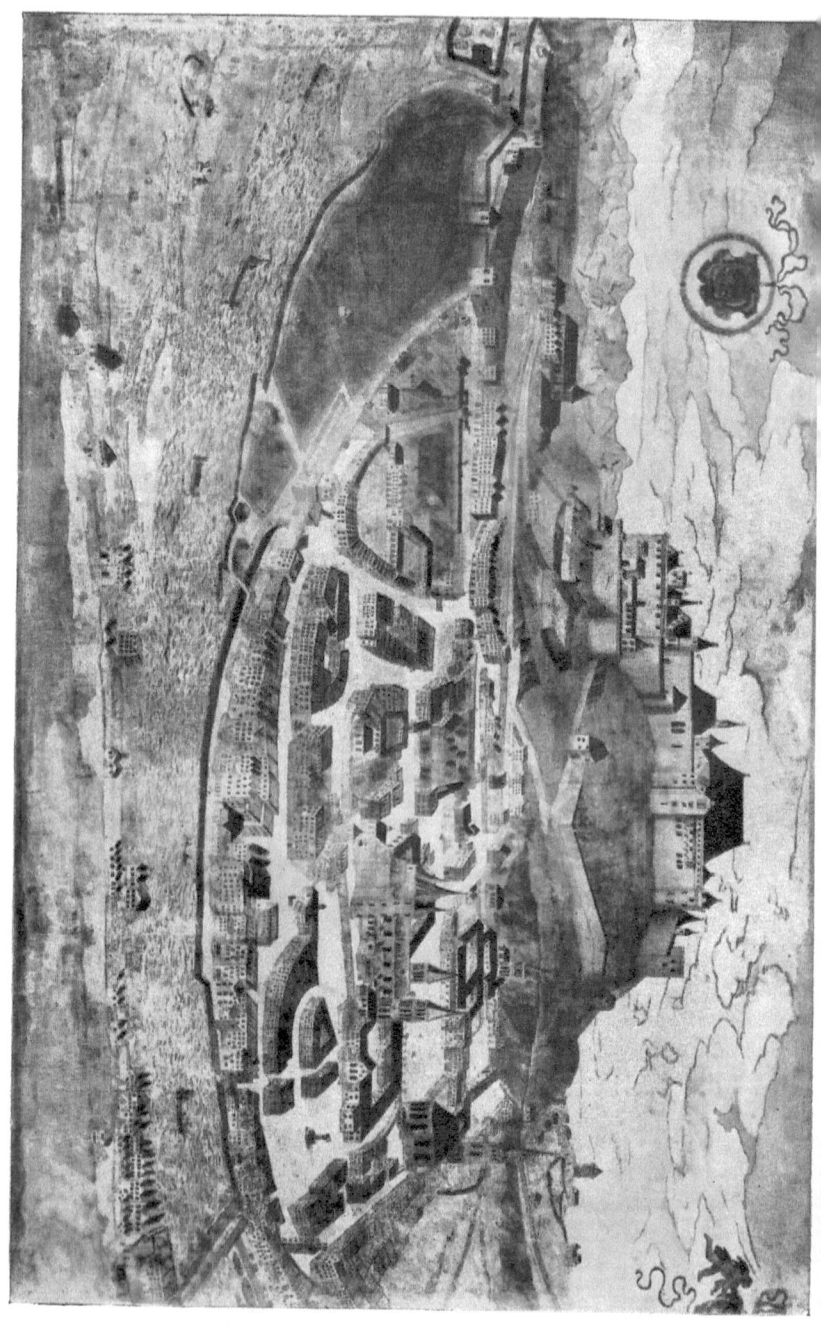

8. SALZBURG / ALTE STADTANSICHT VON 1553

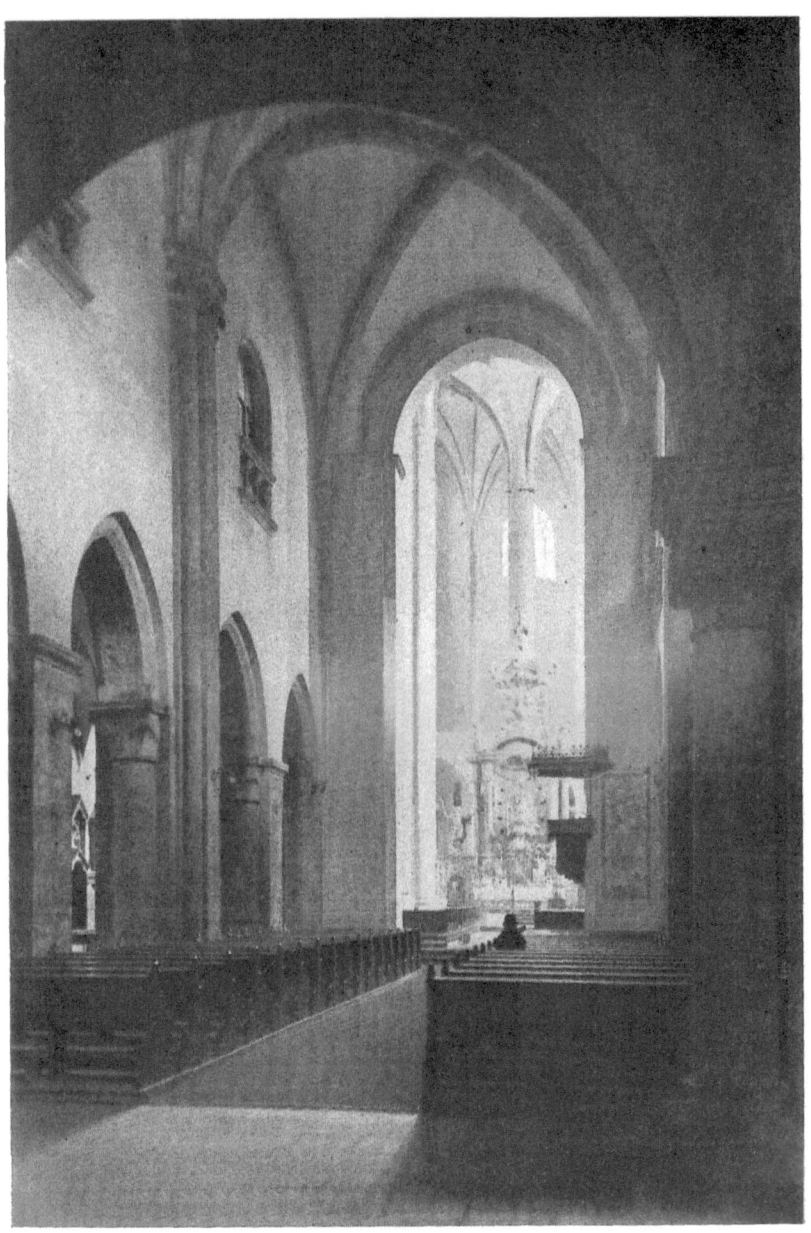

9. SALZBURG / FRANZISKANERKIRCHE

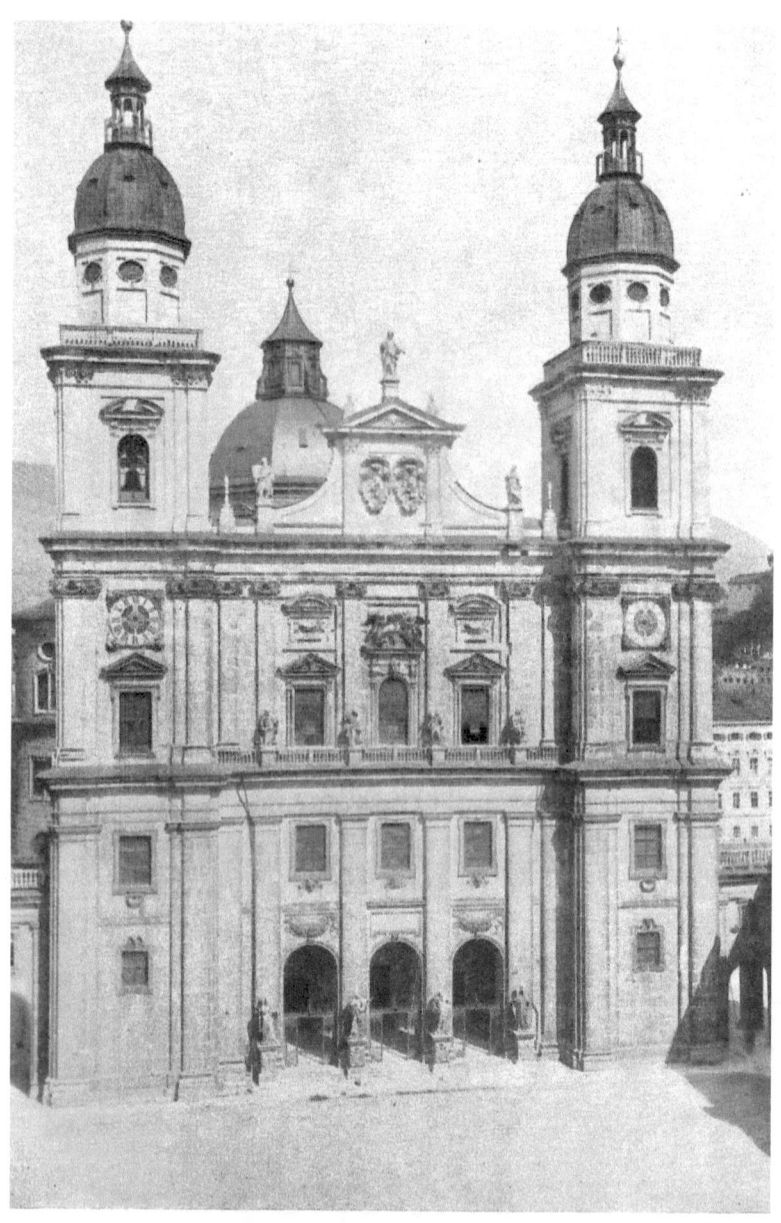

10. SALZBURG / DOM

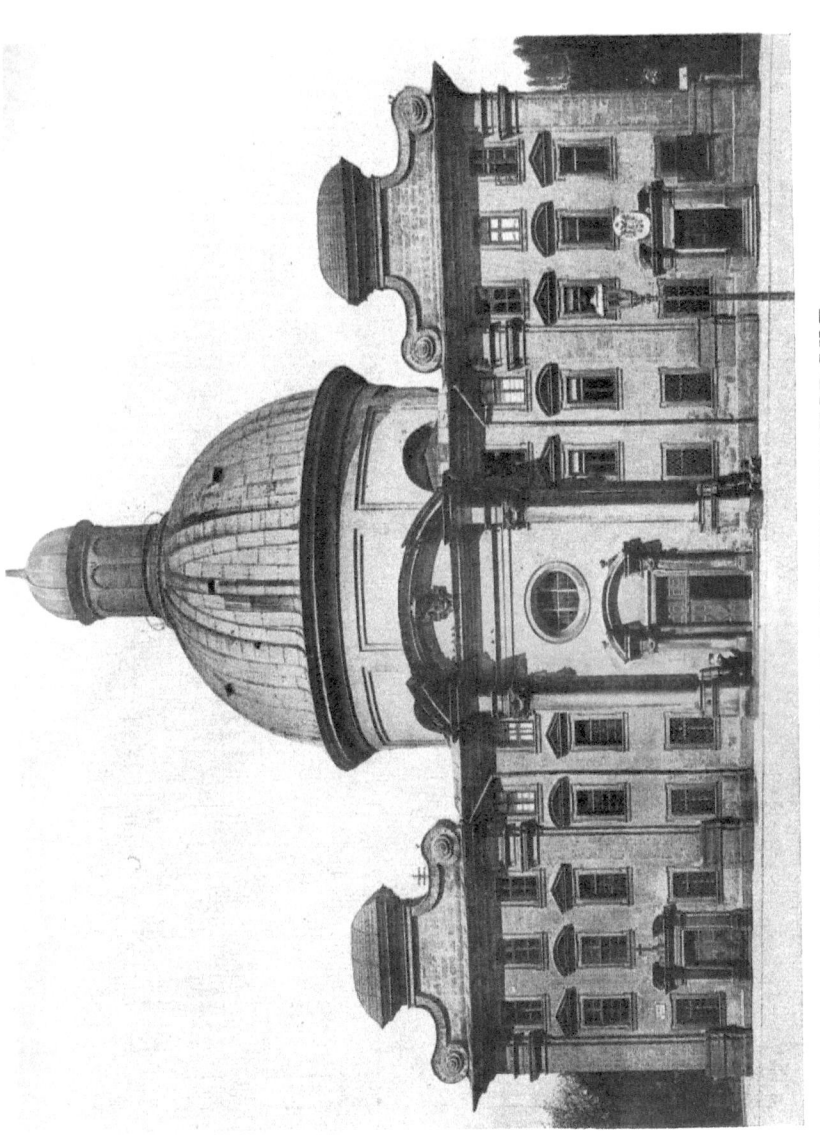

11. SALZBURG / KAJETANERKIRCHE
VON GASPARO ZUGALLI

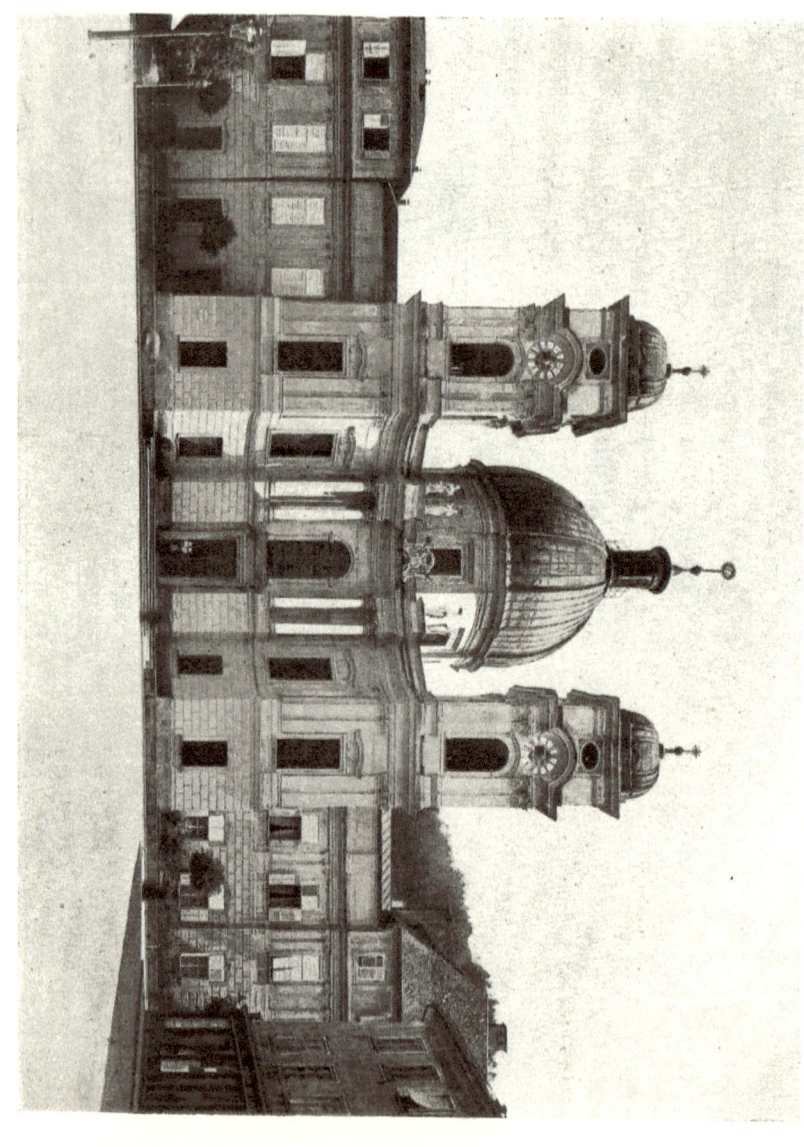

12. SALZBURG / DREIFALTIGKEITSKIRCHE IM PRIESTERHAUS
VON J. B. FISCHER VON ERLACH

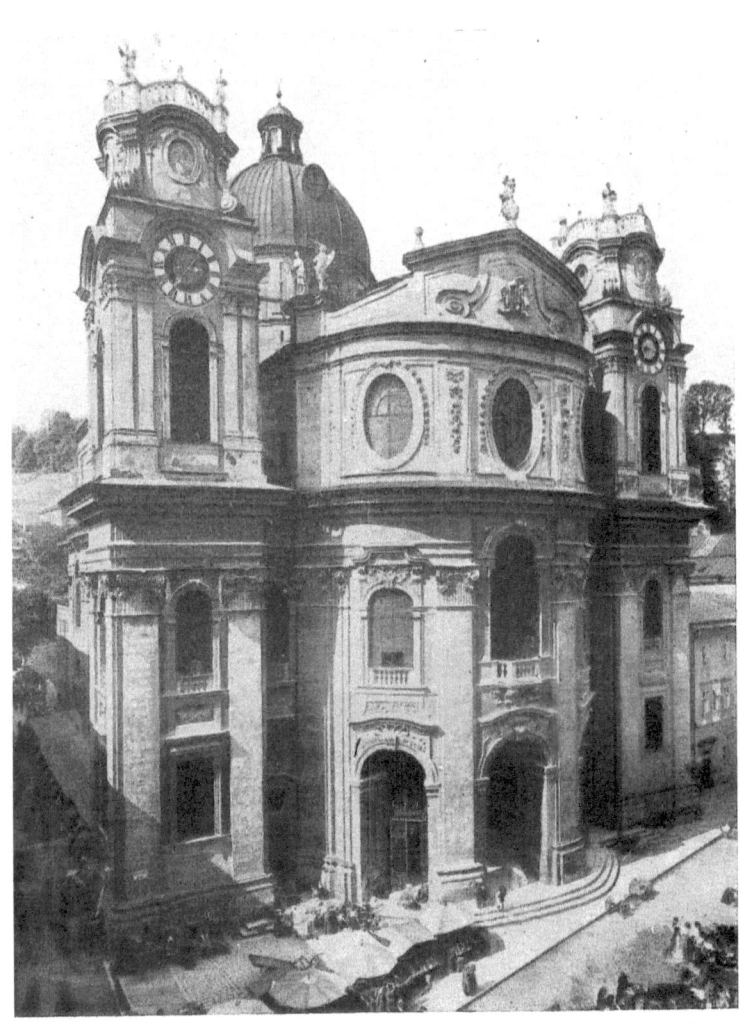

13. SALZBURG / KOLLEGIENKIRCHE
VON J. B. FISCHER VON ERLACH

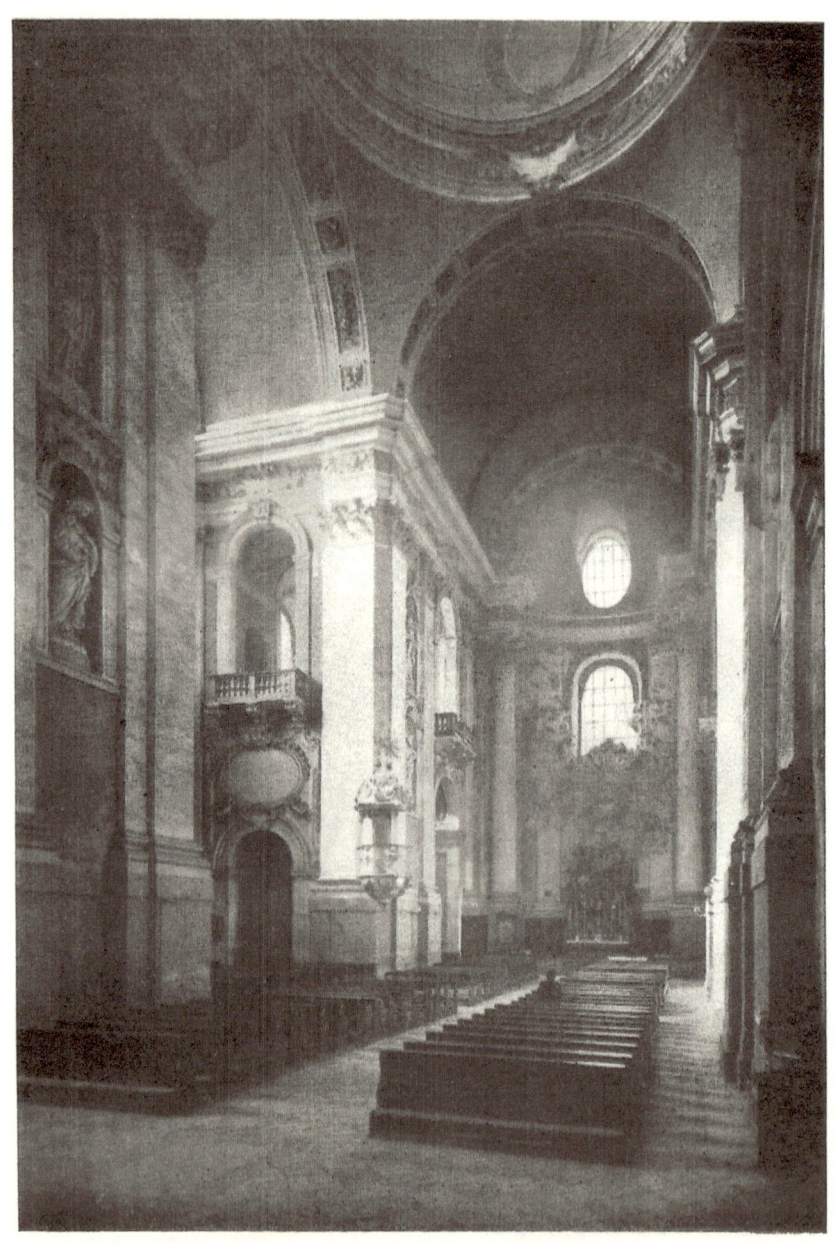

14. SALZBURG / KOLLEGIENKIRCHE
BLICK GEGEN DEN ALTAR

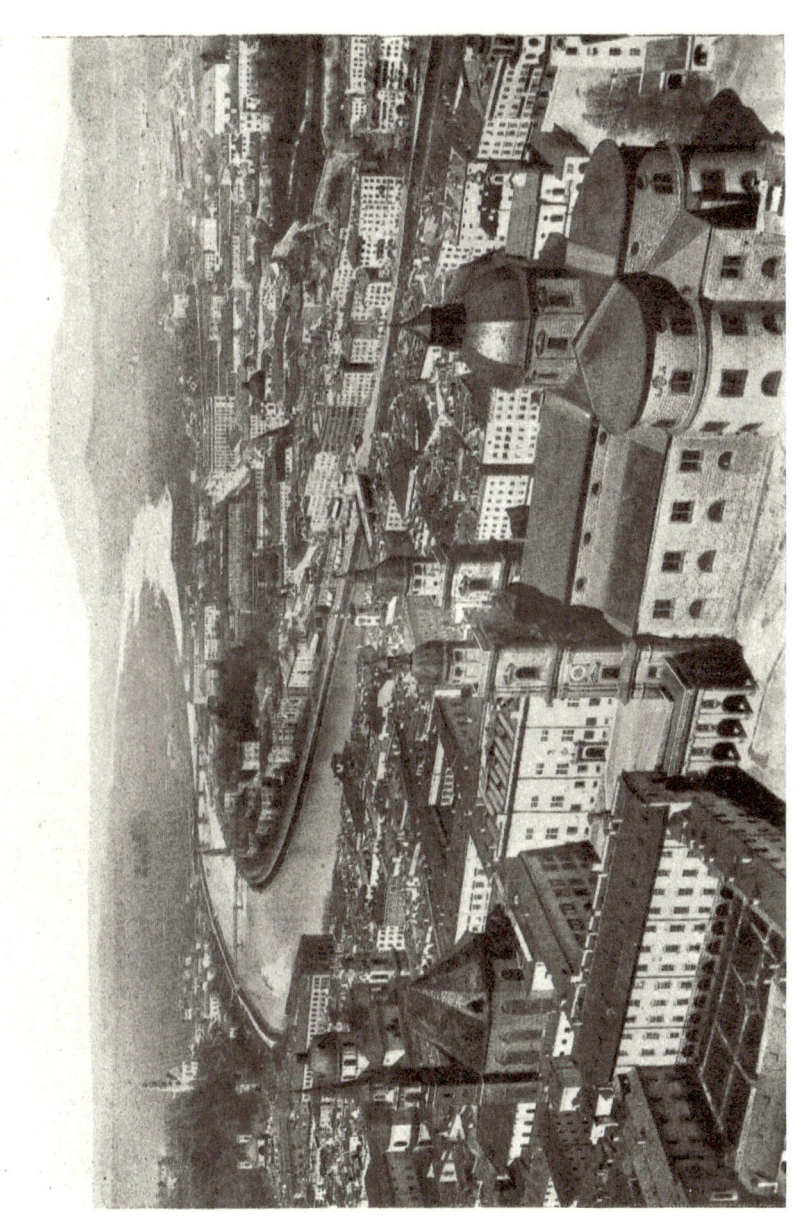

15. SALZBURG / BLICK VON DER FESTUNG

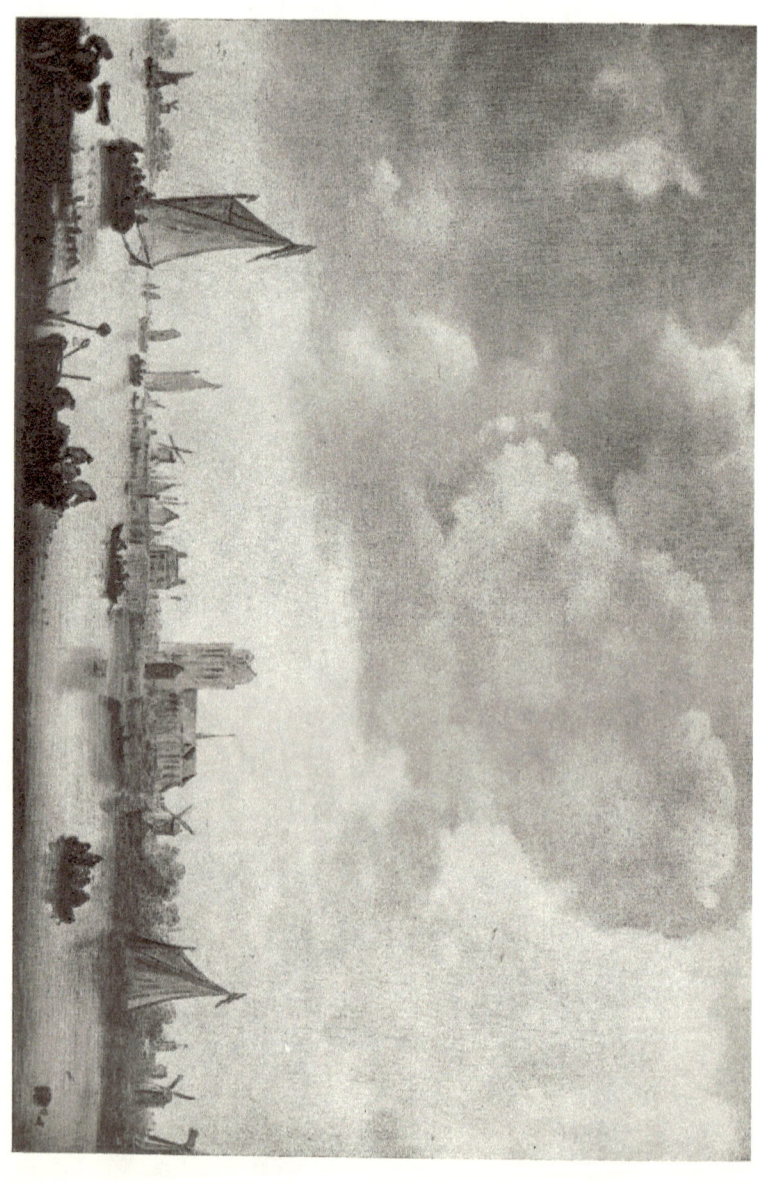

16. JAN VAN GOYEN / DIE MAAS BEI DORDRECHT

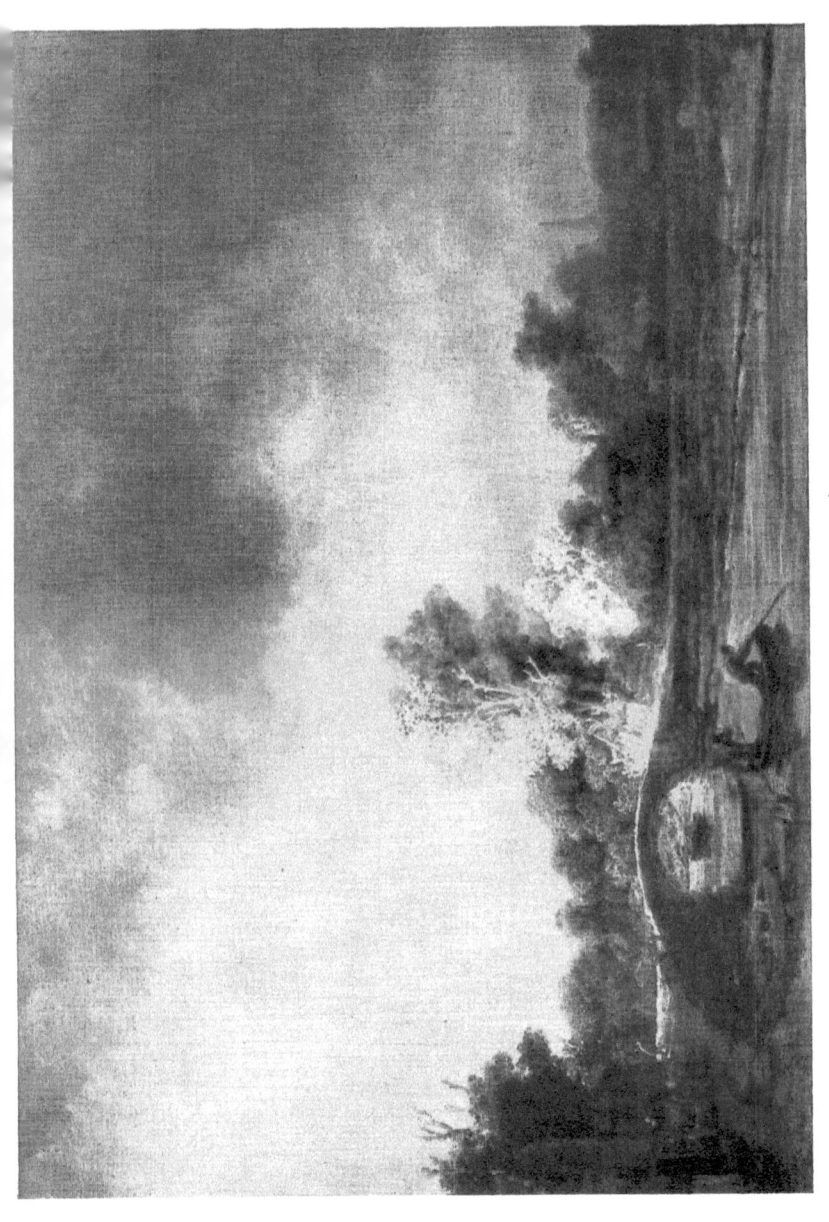

17. REMBRANDT / DIE STEINBRÜCKE

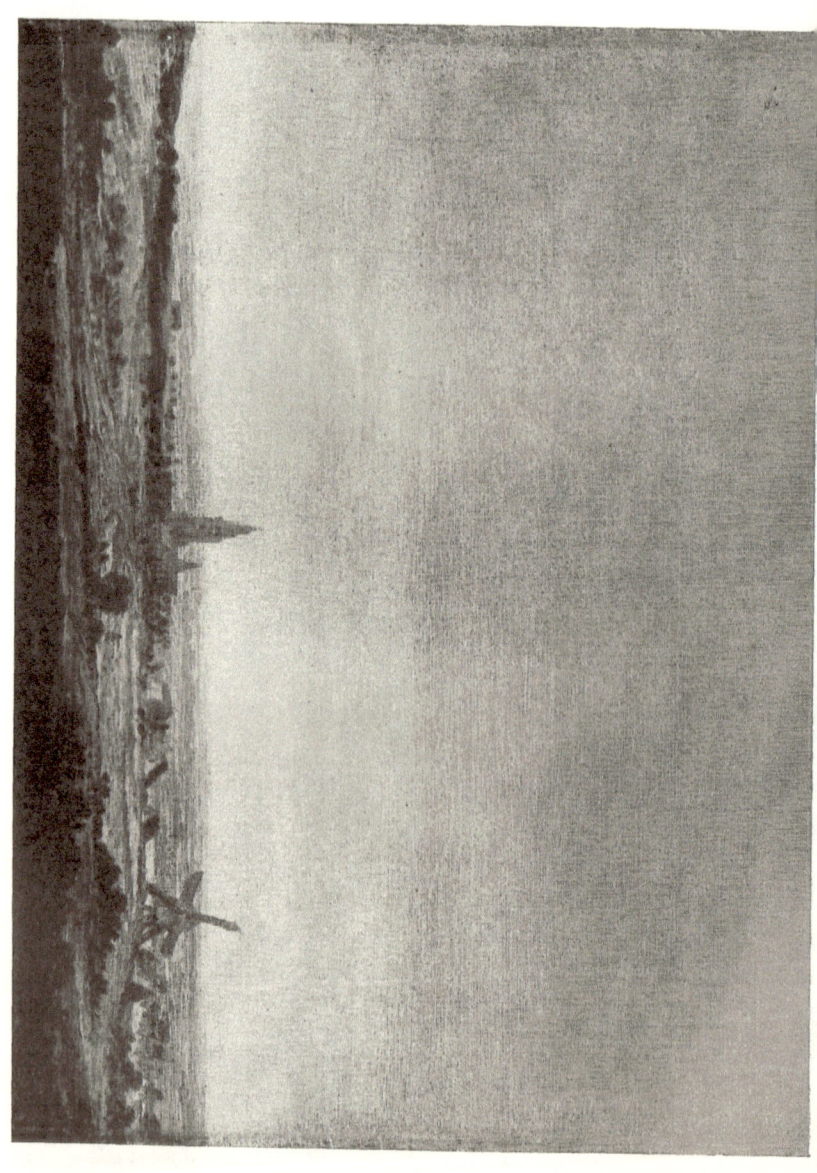

18. HERKULES SEGHERS / HOLLÄNDISCHE FLACHLANDSCHAFT

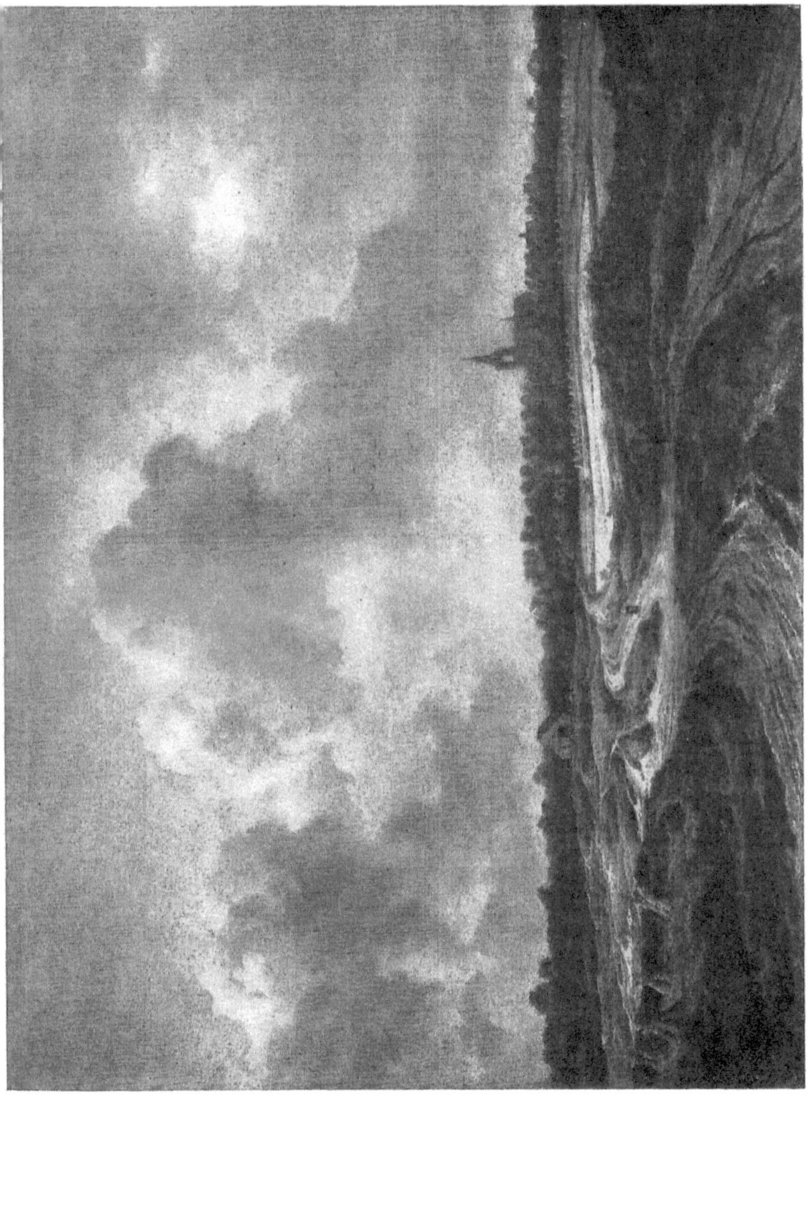

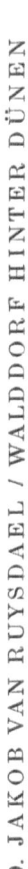

19. JAKOB VAN RUYSDAEL / WALDDORF HINTER DÜNEN

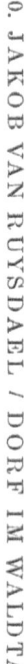

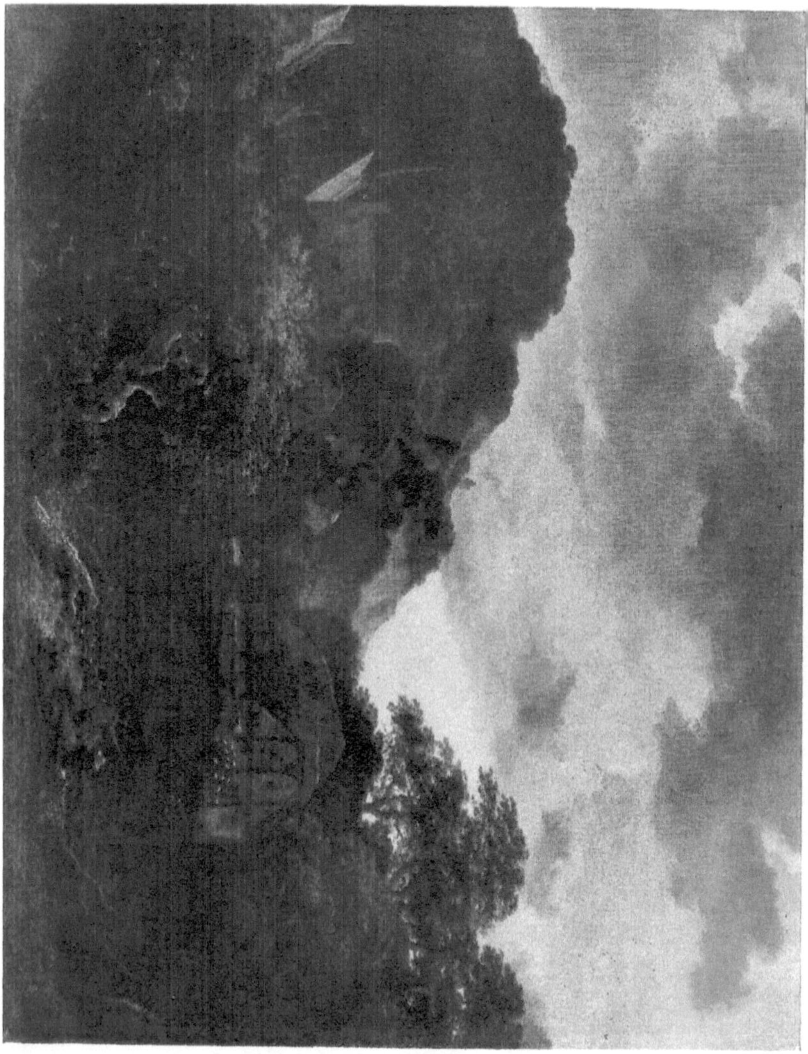

20. JAKOB VAN RUYSDAEL / DORF IM WALDTAL

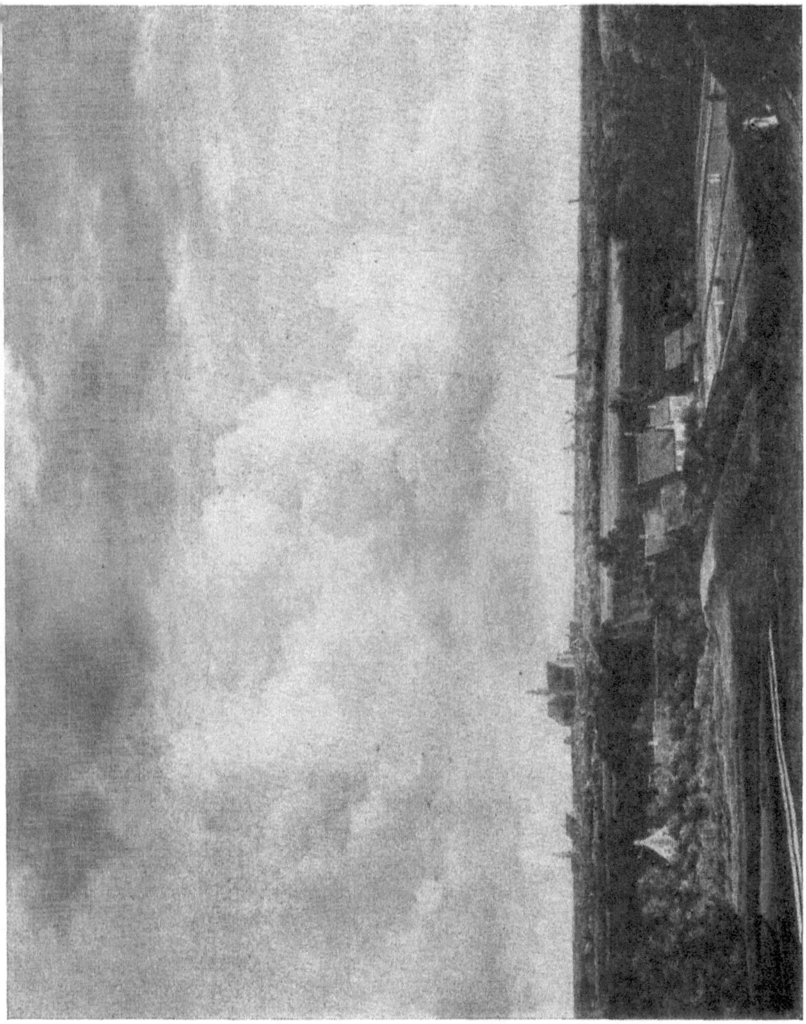

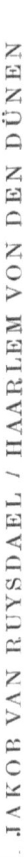

24. JAKOB VAN RUYSDAEL / HAARLEM VON DEN DÜNEN

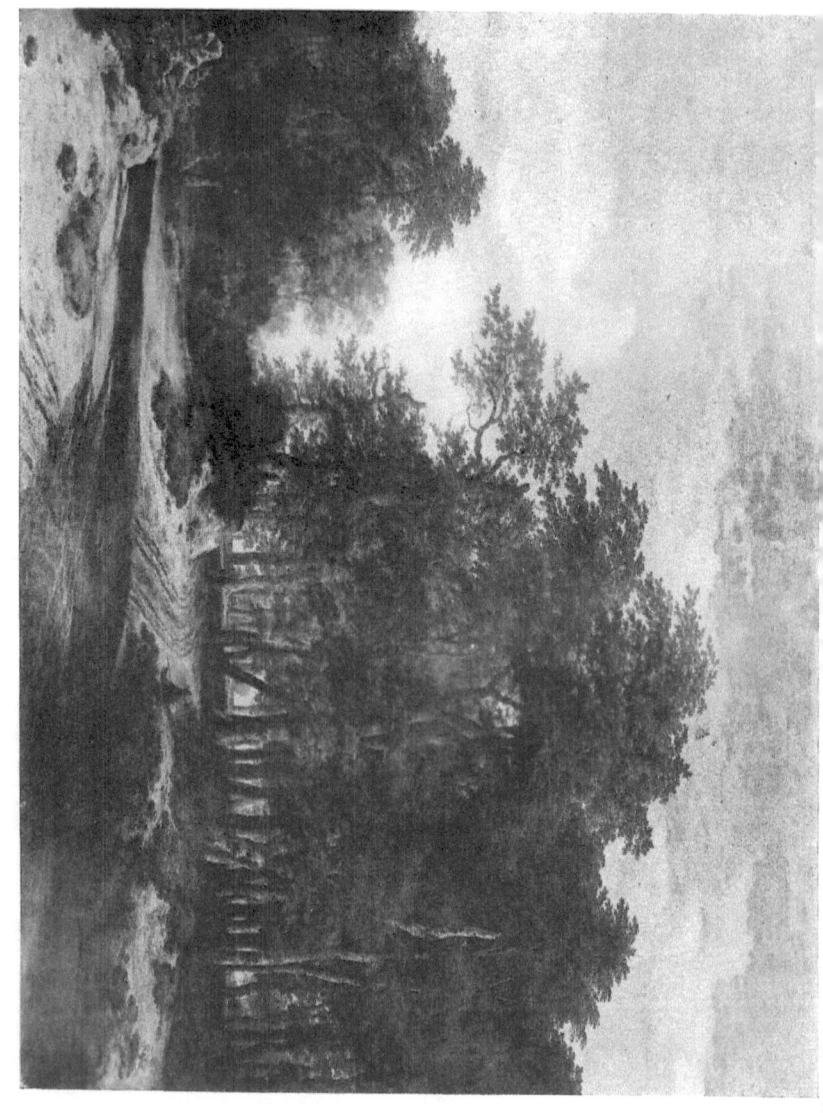

22. JAKOB VAN RUYSDAEL / DER „GROSSE BUCHENWALD"

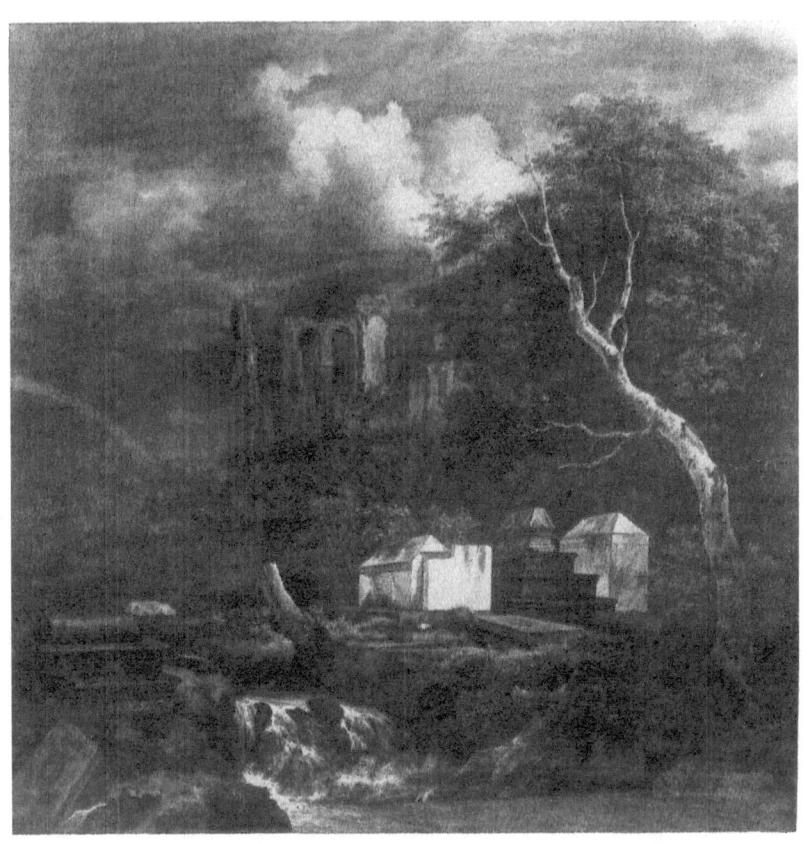

23. JAKOB VAN RUYSDAEL / DER JUDENKIRCHHOF

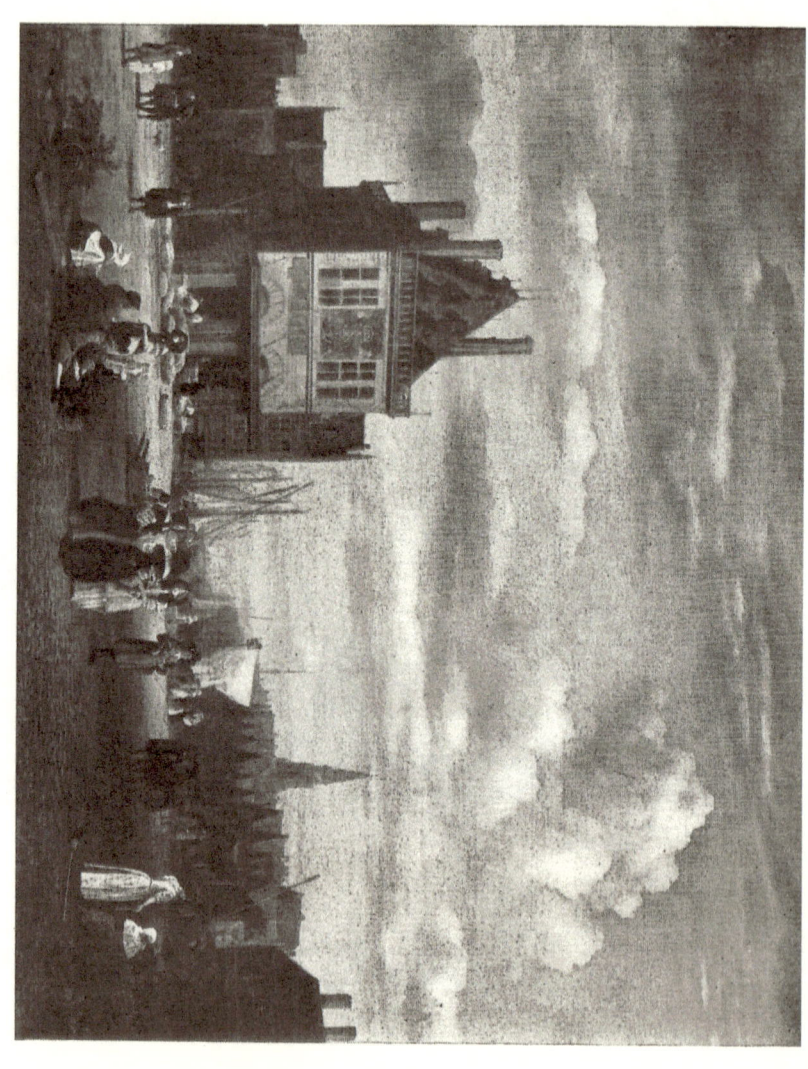

24. JAKOB VAN RUYSDAEL / DIE AMSTERDAMER STADTWAGE